PROBLEMS AND ISSUES IN
SOCIAL CASEWORK

Problems and Issues
in
SOCIAL CASEWORK

———◆◆———

SCOTT BRIAR AND HENRY MILLER

COLUMBIA UNIVERSITY PRESS

NEW YORK AND LONDON   1971

PREFACE

Work on this book began just before the Free Speech episode in Berkeley and the student movements that followed it, before the War on Poverty, and before the violence of Watts, Detroit, and Chicago. These events and their consequences, in one way and another, slowed the progress of this book. Far more important, they continuously altered, in both subtle and profound ways, our views on the social order, and therefore on social work as well. And social work also changed during those years.

Thus our views on social casework, the subject of this book, and casework itself were being transformed as we wrote about them. That is as it should be. We set out to review where casework has been, to analyze its current status, and to consider its future possibilities. While many of our ideas changed from then to now, one important theme persisted. When we began the book, we believed that casework was approaching an important crossroads, and subsequent events have reinforced that belief.

Social casework is a unique enterprise. No other profession has taken the individual person so seriously, nor has made the promotion of each person's particular aspirations and potentialities its primary function, nor has set as its cardinal principle the notion that each person deserves respect and dignity, no matter how offensive he may seem. Other professions and enterprises share some or all of these commitments, but none have made of them their central purpose. These are lofty and

therefore fragile and elusive objectives. So perhaps casework can be for-
given for the conspicuous discrepancies between goals and performance
that sometimes have appeared in casework practice.

For many decades now, casework practice has been largely occupied with one aspect of its commitments, namely the effort to treat or
help persons afflicted with certain kinds of psychosocial problems.
While treatment certainly is a legitimate activity for a profession that
seeks to enhance the welfare of individuals, this activity alone cannot
contain the broad objectives that casework set for itself. And yet the literature of casework and the education of caseworkers are largely preoccupied with treatment.

This restriction of function has opened casework to serious attack,
both from within and from outside the profession. On the one hand, it
is said that the narrow preoccupation with treatment has turned caseworkers away from many who have need of individual attention. And
on the other hand, research has accumulated suggesting that as therapists and problem solvers caseworkers have not been very effective.

There is enough truth to these criticisms to pose a crisis for casework. The question is how the profession will respond. If these criticisms are denied in favor of perpetuating casework practice only as it
has been, then there is the danger that casework will become an anachronism, for some of its critics seem to believe the society could well do
with less of it.

If that were to happen, the loss would be great indeed. Not so
much because of the past accomplishments of casework but because the
need has never been greater for an enterprise dedicated to the dignity of
the individual person and his particular needs and aspirations. Such an
enterprise is needed to humanize the inevitable and desirable development of ever larger programs designed not for individuals but for
groups and classes of people.

If caseworkers are to rise to the opportunities inherent in the crisis
confronting them, they will need to undertake a searching reexamina-
tion of their enterprise. It is to that task that this book is dedicated. We
offer no finished account of what casework practice is and should be,
but we have tried to indicate some of the directions it could follow to
better realize its commitments.

In writing this book, we have received help and inspiration from many sources. We would not know where to begin or where to end if we attempted to acknowledge all of them. Those who helped most immediately know of our gratitude. Others whose work contributed to ours are acknowledged in the text. We owe a special debt to our students whose ideas and questions stimulated and clarified our own. And the careful attention of John Moore, our editor, made the book more comprehensible and therefore, hopefully, more useful.

SCOTT BRIAR

HENRY MILLER

July, 1971

CONTENTS

PART I

Social Casework Theory

CHAPTER ONE

THE DEVELOPMENT OF CASEWORK TREATMENT

Looking to the past for the beginning of social casework we find no point at which it erupted suddenly. What we call social casework today seems to have evolved out of a slowly growing awareness of the necessity of treating individuals as unique in their differences from each other, rather than treating alike all instances of trouble of a certain sort.[1]

THE END OF AN ERA AND THE FIRST INDICATIONS OF A NEW AGE (1900–1917)

The human being as an individual has been the defining characteristic of that part of the social welfare enterprise called social casework. By the end of the nineteenth century casework had made a beginning toward viewing and treating people as individuals. The goals of the Charity Organization Society (COS) made such individualization inevitable. Moral reform was the objective of the COS, and it was the job of the "friendly visitor" to separate those people capable of moral reform from those who were not. To differentiate the unworthy from the worthy was the primary task of that pre-caseworker—the friendly visitor. That part of the Protestant ethic, Puritanism, that held poverty to be a badge of the unrighteous was vitiated somewhat by an evangelism that marched out to save the unworthy from themselves. The early friendly visitor tagged along on this march with his simple, two-category, diag-

nostic system of the "worthy" and the "unworthy." Early casework
theory was devoted to making the demarcation between these two entities ever more precise and refined.

By the turn of the century the moralistic tone of this diagnostic
classification became somewhat diluted. Reform Darwinists and the
pragmatists were making themselves heard. The unworthy poor were
not necessarily morally reprehensible people but the victims of an economically depraved social order. The frontier was closed; depressions
were coming a generation apart; the cities were congested, and more
immigrants were pouring in every day. Initiative, moral fiber, decency,
responsibility, and piety were no longer enough to feed the mouths of
hungry children. There was a spirit of reform in social work that did
not perish until the reaction that followed the First World War.

But the friendly visitor at the turn of the century—we can call him
caseworker [2] now *—still went out to the homes of the poor. And what
did he do? His task outline was simple: to gather facts about the life of
the family involved—facts concerning income and expenditures, health,
relatives, work history, dietary habits, etc. Once the facts were gathered
and clearance was given by the case committee to work with the family
considered "suited" for the attention of the agency, the caseworker
could proceed with the treatment plan. This plan was based on the particular facts gathered. If a mother had tuberculosis, the treatment was to
get her into a sanitarium. If a child had poor health, send him to a doctor. If a father had little income, a more solvent brother-in-law could be
reasoned with to help tide the family over. (It took the most meticulous
fact gathering to know that there was a brother-in-law available, let
alone a solvent one.)

By the early 1900s, however, there were more profound queries as
to the nature of the poor. The sociology and psychology of the day
could not provide answers that were any more satisfactory than those of
the clergymen who sat on the boards of the COS. Caseworkers noted an
inexplicable occurrence among their clients: The facts in a case would
be laboriously gathered, the cause of the problem found, and the self-
evident solution proposed to the family. And yet, so many families

* It is difficult to establish when the appellation "case worker" first came into
vogue. Bruno notes that the word was first seen in the 1887 Proceedings of the
National Conference in a paper by Devine. (See note 2.)

would persist in not going along with the treatment plan. Why? There could be no doubt as to the logic of the plan, and it came from a reputable agent of the community—indeed, the caseworker was an agent of the most dignified strata in American society. The intent was good. Yet many families went about their wretched way of life as though they had not heard the well-intended advice. The caseworker must have envied the "old days" when these recalcitrant families would have been classified as down-right unworthy and hence stricken from the rolls of the agency. If they were not unworthy, they were at least uncooperative.

Actually there was no basis of predictability for treatment of the individual and actually no prediction in treatment at that time. All things were possible to social case work which had so recently discovered the individual and his thrilling possibilities for regeneration. Since all individuals coming to a casework agency had been deprived, there was always room for the hope that under more satisfying conditions they might change their behavior. Treatment consisted therefore in supplying environmental opportunity, often in a stereotyped prescription, such as employment for men, recreation for children, standardized by scout and settlement movements, etc., and health exams and treatment for all. Obdurate and persistent refusal to respond to these efforts was the only sufficient reason for giving up treatment and in such cases the closing entry read: "Case closed. Family will not cooperate." [3]

It did not occur to the caseworker of the early twentieth century that the treatment method was faulty. After all, what better way to get another to do what is right than by advising? Oh, it was true that some of the old-time workers still used the archaic techniques of condemnation, blatant coercion, and high-handed, snobbish directive. But the more sophisticated caseworker did not resort to such outmoded techniques. The client was advised in the most benign and delicate manner; he was reasoned with as a man of dignity and intelligence. The crystal-clear logic of the plan was softly driven home until the client could only nod his head in agreement. No, the treatment method was not at fault.

Obviously the diagnosis was faulty—and this because the investigation (now called the "social study") was not thorough enough. And so the early years of the twentieth century saw the social caseworker gathering more and more facts . If only enough facts could be gathered, surely a remedy would be found.

But gathering the facts required the client's cooperation, required his willingness to give freely information about himself and his family. The beginning of the century saw a vital interest in the kind of association that grew between caseworker and client. Although it was not so named, a relationship had to be created in which facts could be gathered and, of course, in which the client would be more disposed to go along with the treatment plan. Thus, Professor Hollis could describe this relationship as follows:

The relationship between the worker and client was thought of as a friendly one, designed at first to encourage the client to give information freely about himself, his family, and his situation, and later to secure his confidence in the worker in order that he would cooperate in carrying out measures which the worker believed would help him to improve his situation.[4]

The fact-gathering process had become extremely complicated by 1910—so much so that the amateur could no longer be expected to do a thorough study. Schools of social work were being organized in various large cities. A summer session had been organized in New York as early as 1898, and by 1904 it offered a full eight-month program. New voices were being heard offering unique explanations of behavior. Krafft-Ebbing, Forel, Moll, and Ellis were talking about sexual behavior, and those caseworkers who dared were avidly reading these texts. Clifford Beers almost single-handedly organized a National Committee for Mental Hygiene. William Healy's *Individual Delinquent,* published in 1915, reemphasized the concept of individual behavior as the cause of deviance and spurred the enlightened caseworker to add more polish to his case study. In 1911 Dr. Adolph Meyer addressed the National Conference. At the conferences of 1914 and 1915 papers were read by no less than seven psychiatrists.[5] Individual differences were being stressed all right, but the differences were in terms of intellectual equipment and endowment. This seemed to be the new data that was missing in previous studies. Intelligence tests became a fundamental part of any really good social study. Eugenics was in the fore, and caseworkers gathered more and more facts about the remote ancestors of insolvent clients.

At that time it [casework] was concerned with those larger social problems in which psychiatry and social work were equally interested—the after-care of the mentally ill, the out patient mental clinic, the relation of mental defect to delinquency, and the allied problems of social hygiene, alcoholism, and syphilis. All the early activities centered about institutions, the psychopathic hospital, the hospital for the insane, the school for the feeble-minded, the prison, the reformatory, the court. This was the day of the eugenics field worker with her elaborate charts and her mass of unanalyzed, unassimilated facts, gathered in the hills and backwoods of Duchess County or some other spot where Jukes and Kallikaks abounded, at great risk of limb and loss of shoe leather. She was perhaps a prehistoric form of what we now call the psychiatric social worker, although she seems to us to have had very little understanding of psychiatry or social work.[6]

By 1909 the New York School of Social Work was offering courses on labor problems, race problems, penology, a whole host of courses on child care—even a cooking class for aspiring caseworkers. In that same year Professor Devine gave a lecture series on "Misery and its Causes." By 1911 courses were added in Medical Sociology and Hospital Social Service. (Medical social work was born in 1905 at the Massachusetts General Hospital and was already contributing to the mainstream of casework.) It was not until 1917, however, that a specific course in Social Case Work was offered at the New York School, although there were precursors in the form of courses in family work. The field was growing so rapidly that by 1912 the program at the New York School was expanded to encompass two full years.

The profession was racing along, not taking time to catch its breath and take stock. By 1915 Dr. Flexner addressed the National Conference and challenged the field on its hungry aspirations toward full professionalism. His address only served to spur the field on to a greater and more frantic search for a body of knowledge and a place to call its own.

In 1917 the indefatigable Mary Richmond published *Social Diagnosis,* which summed up the accumulated wisdom of the time and definitively outlined the thorough social study. The appeal of her book was so strong it threatened to turn all of social work into casework. *Social Diagnosis* was a "scientific and logical approach to social investigation";[7] it was to usher in a new era of casework. Grace Marcus, almost twenty years after the book's publication, had this to say about Mary Richmond and *Social Diagnosis:*

Hers was a vigorous scholarship, which applied itself to the labors of examining masses of detail which resisted tempting scholastic generalizations, and which ventured solidly into related fields and other disciplines at the bidding of a problem to be understood. In its firm stress on the deductive method her work established the individualizing principle of study and treatment as basic in the theory and practice of casework.[8]

The principles enunciated by Mary Richmond came mostly from family agencies, although casework was being nurtured by other sources as well. Ida Cannon initiated the first experiment in medical social work in 1905 at Massachusetts General Hospital; Bellevue Hospital followed with a Social Service Department in 1906; the New York State Hospital for Mental Diseases organized a similar department in 1910; and in 1913 the first formal hospital social service was created at the Boston Psychopathic Hospital under Mary Jarrett and Dr. Southard. During 1906–1907 visiting teachers were used in Hartford, Boston, and New York—all under the aegis of private agencies. By 1916 six states were using visiting teachers, and the deliberate use of social workers in the school system was on its way to becoming an important part of casework practice. Soon the case method of study would be found in the courts under the name of "probation and parole." The case method already had been long entrenched in the children's field, going back to the time of Charles Birtwell and his concept of differential treatment for different children. "Child experts at the turn of the century were preaching that a child's individuality must be considered, that a children's agency needed to make as thorough and discriminating an investigation as did a charity organization society." [9]

Social Diagnosis drew from all these fields and sounded the clarion call for a thorough, objective, and enlightened gathering of the facts. The following, then, were the principles that permeated casework when World War I engulfed the country:

1. The causes of human maladjustment could invariably be found in the economic and social order.

2. Nonetheless, individual differences existed, and people responded to these social forces in their own way with their own unique endowments—biological and intellectual.

3. People, no matter what their social condition, had an intrinsic worth and dignity—they deserved respect.

4. In order to correctly diagnose the particular problem an individual was suffering from, it was necessary to make a thorough investi-

gation of all the pertinent facts. These facts could be found in the social, economic, familial, eugenic, and intellectual history of the client.

5. In order to gather the facts, a friendly relationship must be established with the client.

6. After the diagnosis was made, a treatment plan was formulated by the caseworker, who then delivered it to the client for implementation. The more friendly and benign the relationship, the more prone was the client to go along with the treatment plan.

But no matter how many facts were gathered and no matter how friendly the relationship, many clients continued to live in squalor and misery and failed to respond to the earnest ministrations of the caseworker. *Social Diagnosis* was a beacon to guide one in gathering mountains of data and helped cleanse the caseworker of nontherapeutic beliefs and attitudes; but somehow it wasn't enough. Dr. Flexner had thrown out the challenge of professionalism, but in what direction was casework to go? Schools were growing and expanding their programs, but toward what end? Specialties were proliferating, but there was still no general answer to the question of why so many clients (in any setting) were remaining obdurate and recalcitrant.

With these discomforts plaguing casework, World War I came upon the scene—and with it came a revolution in casework.

THE PSYCHIATRIC DELUGE (1917–1929)

During World War I the Red Cross organized its Home Service Bureau, and casework found a place for itself "above the Poverty Line." [10] Helping families to live without their men was not charity, and Home Service Bureaus were found scattered throughout the country. The ministering of relief was not an intrinsic part of the service, and it was available to people regardless of economic need. Large segments of the population were exposed to casework services for the first time. Casework had gone democratic—and middle class.

World War I brought with it the mysterious "shell shock," and a few brave psychiatrists saw in the work of Freud what seemed to be an explanation for this puzzling disease. Social workers attached to the neuropsychiatric hospitals of the army were found to be a valuable adjunct to its treatment, and they were exposed first hand to the murmurings in psychiatric circles of new theories of behavior. Psychiatric social work was born as a result of these World War I experiences. All casework was soon to go psychiatric.

In 1919 psychiatry swept the National Conference. Not only were the concepts of the Home Service Bureau and the war neuroses buzzed about, but due to the impetus of the Mental Hygiene movement child guidance clinics were springing up all over the country. At that conference Mary Jarrett read a paper entitled, "The Psychiatric Thread Running Through all Social Case Work." [11] Caseworkers crowded in to hear her say that the great majority of social cases are in fact psychiatric problems. Fifty percent of the cases described in *Social Diagnosis* present psychological problems, claimed Miss Jarrett. Think of what the psychiatric orientation will do for us, she went on: clients of social agencies have mental disorders of various kinds; the psychiatric point of view will give casework an inroad into the vast mental hygiene movement; it will give casework a new objectivity; moreover, it will give the poor overworked caseworker an easier job! (For it explains much!)

The atmosphere of the 1919 conference is well captured by Jessie Taft:

Atlantic City in 1919 was a landslide for mental hygiene: the Conference was swept off its feet. In every section psychiatrists appeared on the program. The psychiatric social worker was present in person for the first time and violent indeed was the discussion which raged about her devoted head —what should be her training, what her personality, and what the limitations of her province? Should she remain forever different from other case workers or should every other case worker be reborn in her likeness? That was the meeting which burst its bounds and had to be transferred to a church a block away. Dignified psychiatrists and social workers climbed out of windows in order to make sure of a good seat. [12]

The bone of contention as to whether psychiatric social work was to be a specialty or was to permeate all of casework was raised for the first time. Robinson concluded that the consensus was for the latter: "The swing of opinion, then, as later, seemed to be in favor of accepting the psychiatric point of view as the basis of all social case work." [13] The psychiatric caseworkers at that memorable conference were looked upon with varied emotions by their fellow social workers—fear, admiration, but mostly envy; envy because they claimed to have the magic key that had so long eluded the field.

By 1918 Smith College had already opened a training school for psychiatric social workers. The faculty: Mary Jarrett of the Boston Psychopathic Hospital, Jessie Taft of New York, Anna King of the Boston Red Cross. Drs. Adolph Meyer and William Healy lectured in that year. And these were two of the new breed, Drs. Frink and A. A. Brill, practicing psychoanalysts. This was not to be a curriculum concentrating on eugenics and mental tests!

In the same year the New York School organized a Department of Mental Hygiene; 1919–1920 saw only one course offered in that department. In 1921, however, Dr. Marion Kenworthy joined the faculty, and the Bulletin of 1922 describes two new courses: "Human Behavior and its Disorders" and "Psychology of Individual Differences."

Within one year the department had grown incredibly: the 1923 Bulletin announced courses in Psychopathology, Human Behavior, Clinical Psychiatry, Mental Hygiene, and Criminal Psychology. The blurb accompanying the course in Psychopathology read as follows:

A lecture course designed to acquaint the student with the abnormalities in the functioning of the mind. The fundamentals of the psycho-analytic school of psychology are fully discussed, and their bearing upon the understanding of every day human relationships is particularly stressed.[14]

This was not the old psychiatry of Drs. Healy, Meyer, and White; it was something very new. The two psychologies of the 1920s—the behaviorism of Watson and the dynamic psychology of Freud—were engaged in a mammoth struggle. Only in casework was the struggle resolved so quickly in favor of Freud.

When one reads of those turbulent years, one would think that the impact of the new psychiatry was sudden and that it instantly pervaded the entire field of casework. If this were so, it was not reflected in the literature of the time. *The Family* was first published in 1920, the year the new ideas should have been in the fore. However, Volume I, encompassing the year 1920, offered only one paper that spoke of the new psychology: Jessie Taft's "Problems of Social Case Work with Children." Her position, at least, was clear: "In short, in the last analysis, real casework is nothing but the practical application of mental hygiene to individuals who need it, no matter where they may be found." [15] In 1921 Dr. Healy wrote on "The Application of Mental Tests in Family Case Work"—but this was the old psychology. In the same year there was a paper by Eleanor Johnson on "How Mental Hygiene May Help in the Solution of School Problems." The next appearance of a "psychological" paper was in October 1922, when Jessie Taft wrote on "The Social Worker's Opportunity"—the opportunity to treat people through psychological insight.

Gordon Hamilton's first contribution to that journal was a two-stanza poem entitled "A Social Worker," which appeared in December 1922. Speaking of the materials that may be found on a worker's desk, the final stanza says:

> Reference books are scattered far and wide;
> Medical journals piled up everywhere.
> Forel and Santayana almost hide
> Osler, and with Janet, Healy, Roscoe Thayer—
> Yet friends have noticed, lying to one side,
> Well rubbed and bent, the Book of Common Prayer.[16]

If this poem had been written five years later, Miss Hamilton could not have failed to mention Freud.

In 1923 there were two papers with a psychiatric focus. In 1924 Helen Myrick wrote on "The Mental Hygiene Movement in Social Case Work" and said: "Practically all the caseworkers in the United Charities (Chicago) have had courses in psychiatry and psychology." [17] But this was not the psychiatry of Jessie Taft who in 1924 submitted the first truly technical paper, "The Use of the Transfer Within the Limits of the Office Interview."

In the early years of the 1920s, then, the papers dealing with the new psychology could be counted on one's hands. But things began to pick up. There were more papers by Jessie Taft, who was like a voice in the wilderness. In November 1926, Dr. Marion Kenworthy published a most influential paper, "Psychoanalytic Concepts in Mental Hygiene," and Freud was discussed for the first time in the most important casework journal of the time. By the late 1920s many more papers were permeated with the Viennese psychology.

What was the effect of these new ideas on the casework of the time? The child guidance clinics were bringing a new clientele to caseworkers—voluntary clients from the emerging middle class whose problems could not be associated with poverty. Casework became something besides relief giving.

The sweet coercion of the first decade was a failure; now it became clear why this coercion failed. The client had to be enlisted in the struggle against his difficulties—caseworker and client were to be allies against the enemy within. The client became the primary source of data; since he was the only one who knew his problem, what was the use of scurrying about collecting information from scores of collateral sources? Besides, that smacked of investigation and relief giving. Data gathering persisted, but now the emphasis was on psychological development and history; the answer to the client's difficulty lay in the tale of his psychological development. The social study became even more elaborate. The new theory gave casework its first glimpse of the possibility of treatment in terms other than economic.

The precepts of Mary Richmond were ready to be overthrown by the zealots who had found a new master. Claimed Grace Marcus:

It was inevitable that casework, once it began to apprehend the role of the irrational, should seem at times to discount the values of her [Richmond's] rational procedures, that it should appear to ignore the eternal realities on which its efforts had formerly concentrated, and that it should be marked by reactions against the past in its struggle to free itself from the preconceptions of blinding habit.[18]

Freudian psychology brought with it two important principles that changed the face of casework: (1) behavior is purposeful and determined, and (2) some of the determinants are unconscious and unrecognized by the client himself. No act could be considered capricious and without cause; all problems could be answered. If ranging far and wide over the client's external life would not provide the answers, then plunging deep into his inner world would provide the key to treatment. Caseworkers, modeling themselves after their psychoanalyst consultants and some, at least, after their own personal analysts, entered a passive phase. The id was the thing; sexual conflicts were to be uprooted, infantile memories restored to consciousness, defenses to be punctured and done away with. This was the new method of a hardy few; the fifty-minute interview was born.

All of America was turning inward. It was an age of cynicism and disillusionment. Prohibition had failed; social reform seemed futile. The Palmer raids were fresh in memory, and "studies of individual behavior may well have seemed safer than a search for the causes of sickness in society." [19] The great age of reform in social work was practically over, and casework withdrew into itself to become more and more individual and "one-to-one."

The trend toward smaller and smaller units of study was also reflected in a drift toward fragmentation and specialization within casework. Family casework, psychiatric social work, probation and parole —all were organized as specific entities of casework. The Family Service Association of America (FSAA) had been organized back in 1911. The American Association of Medical Social Workers was organized in 1918, the National Association of School Social Workers was formed in 1919, the Child Welfare League of America in 1920, the American Association of Social Workers in 1921, and the American Association of Psychiatric Social Workers in 1926. This trend toward specialization was met with a counter trend toward unification and the appreciation of the common basis of all good casework. In 1929 the report of the Milford Conference was thought to have finally resolved and buried the issue. This conference was a milestone in casework—officially the profession as a whole had recognized the generic nature of all casework. Casework became a definite entity: ". . . the problems of social casework and the equipment of the social caseworker are fundamentally the same for all fields . . . [and] generic social casework is the common field to which the specific forms of social casework are merely incidental." [20]

With the Milford Conference casework entered a new decade with fresh ideas and a supposedly common field. Building on the concepts and principles that were already present, the profession could add these:

1. All behavior is purposeful and determined.

2. Many of the determinants are unconscious.

3. It is not the social order so much that determines behavior, but how the specific individual reacts to the social order.

4. Casework's job is the treatment of these individual reactions.

5. Such reactions are a function of the early life experiences of the client—specifically his sexual instincts and infantile experiences.

6. Casework will ultimately expose these early conflicts.

7. The formula of study, diagnosis, and treatment remains: a laborious study and fact-gathering related to the psychic history of the client; a diagnosis built on these events; and a treatment that would. . . .

And here is the rub. Just as in the previous decade, when the treatment plan was formulated and imposed from above, so now a treatment was proposed and imposed—this time in terms of a psychological solution rather than an economic one. If only the client would abreact or catharsize—if only his early conflicts could be brought into the open, then surely his problems would cease. But strangely enough clients weren't interested in catharsizing, and their infantile memories wouldn't come back. Moreover, clients didn't care too much about their past—it was their present that concerned them. And so again, the profession was faced with that old problem, the uncooperative client who just wouldn't respond to what caseworkers knew was best for him.

The relationship was as friendly as ever, and caseworkers could not be accused of too much overactivity—remember, this was the age of passivity. Something was still very, very wrong. (We have tried to indicate something very contradictory in the reports of what occurred during the 1920s. Hamilton,[21] Hollis,[22] Reynolds,[23] Taft,[24] Marcus,[25] Robinson,[26] and Klein[27] mention the tremendous impact of psychoanalytic theory during this decade and speak of the changes in casework reiterated above.) *

* One searches in vain for the age of "passivity" as it was reflected in the literature of the twenties. Physiological psychiatry was still dominant, and much of the psychiatric influence of the time was of this sort. What has been described above, then, is probably a reflection of a very small, yet very influential group within social casework. Much of the work of the decade is hardly different from that outlined by Mary Richmond. In spite of prosperous times and in spite of the changes indicated, most of the work in the twenties was with economically deprived clients.

The principles and events enunciated above are those of a small body of caseworkers, and their work blends with the thirties and forties. If passivity was existent in the 1920s, it certainly was existent in the 1930s and perhaps even to this day.

PSYCHIATRY, SCHISM, DEPRESSION, AND THE
RECENT PAST (1929–POST-WORLD WAR II)

By the early thirties social work had grown considerably. In 1930 there were 31,000 paid social workers in the labor force, half of whom were caseworkers.

The New York COS had adopted the psychoanalytic point of view in the giving of relief—the relationship between money and emotional dependency was a watchword of that society. The Smith College School of Social Work began to publish its journal, *Smith College Studies in Social Work*. Its credo was that successful casework depended upon an understanding of the mental and emotional life of the client. *Social Service Review,* first published in 1927, had a few articles on psychoanalytic subjects. By 1932 books on psychoanalysis were being reviewed in *The Family,* and there were many more technical papers on the application of Freudian theory to casework.

But all was not well. Casework was still ineffective with an uncomfortably large number of clients. And suddenly a catastrophic depression rocked the country.

Clients swarmed into relief agencies—a new type of financial need was manifest. Poverty had transcended class lines, and case loads grew, and grew, and grew still more. The caseworker looked a little more carefully at the economic world of his client. All could not be well with the social order. Mammoth case loads demanded the provision of a short-term service, and skills had to be developed to meet this need. No longer could workers luxuriate in an interminable treatment that resembled in duration the method of psychoanalysts. "Everywhere arose the need to clarify and limit practice." [28] The depression remade the face of social agency organization; a wider range of clients presented themselves for service.

The Social Security Act of 1935 brought rapid expansion of the public agencies. Caseworkers who had been wary of government participation in relief and social services saw no alternative to such an inevitable massive intervention. They became caught up in the spirit of the New Deal, and within a short time there was a large exodus of family caseworkers to the public assistance agencies. At the same time, many of the child guidance clinics that had sprung up due to the impetus of the mental hygiene movement were forced to close their doors, and psychiatric social workers moved into the vacuum of the family agencies to assume positions of leadership.

Two contradictory forces were operating. Family workers were moving into the public agencies, somewhat disillusioned with individual psychology and seeing in the public agencies a true arena for social casework; yet the newer family workers, fresh from the child guidance clinic and its Freudian psychology, welcomed the new opportunity to render their services to clients without the onerous complication of relief giving.

Casework was moving in two directions at once: toward a renewed interest in the social order, and a casework geared to that order; and toward a more intensive search into the inner world. Inner and outer—the two poles of the casework enterprise.

Another direction, however, was made available to casework during these years. In 1930 Virginia Robinson published the book that was to usher in the first real schism of the field. *A Changing Psychology in Social Case Work* decried the emulation of the psychoanalyst: people were not just organisms who drifted with the tides of their instincts or who were buffeted about by the vagaries of an economic system. They were creative people aspiring to become even more creative. Caseworkers could offer themselves as a medium through which this creative force could be unleashed. All the world might be in chaos, but the agency and worker would remain stable. The client could grasp this stability—this functional rock—and push on to greater accomplishment. Caseworkers had something uniquely their own to give—something dignified and noble. They could offer a relationship, geared to the present, and within which the never-ending process of separation-reunion could be worked through.

This reaction against the psychoanalytic caseworker, with his interminable dwelling on the past, and the reaction to the ominous forces of the social order had great appeal to the caseworkers of these eventful times. Here at last was something that belonged uniquely to casework, and one never had to worry about the "uncooperative" client, for wasn't it within the right of everyone to reject the service offered without stigma and without blame? Here was a new respect for the client in an age when the dignity of the individual and the common man had great meaning. Robinson, proclaiming the dignity of casework, could say: "As long as caseworkers feel, as some do, that they would never want to enter a casework relationship as a client 'to have casework done on me,' there is something fundamentally unethical in that relationship." [29]

And Jessie Taft had this to say about the reaction to psychoanalysis:

Perhaps the lay origin of social work, its original lack of professional freedom, of professional training, and of professional responsibility, all of which persist to some extent into the present, account for its readiness to see in psychiatry and psychoanalysis a way of helping that is better defined, more scientific, and therefore more desirable than anything social work can hope to offer of its own. The resulting tendency of social workers to rest upon the authority, even to utilize the supervision of this more firmly grounded, better trained, legally sanctioned profession, in order to fill what seems to be a void in their own, has been the source of much confusion as to what, if anything, is indigenous to social casework. It has also blinded both agencies and workers to the nature and potential values of their own task.[30]

The controversy deepened. The gap between the Functional school, clustered around Taft and Robinson in Pennsylvania, and the Diagnostic school, with headquarters in New York, was widening.

But all was not quiet in the Diagnostic school. The depression was demonstrating daily the fantastic resiliency of human beings. Casework was continuing to cut across the lines of the so-called dependent group. At first it seemed as though psychiatry was to be thrown out altogether.

I have the feeling that we overstress psychiatry as the one thing that has happened in the last ten years to affect casework practice. A caseworker remarked several years ago that she thought the depression would have at least one good result if it "whacked this psychiatry business" out of casework. At that time it did seem as if the enthusiasm for psychiatric casework might be a kind of whistling in the dark because the caseworker's reality was too unpleasant to bear. There was a healthy turn-about-face, not to a new but to a renewed study of economics, budgets, environmental resources, legislation—a concern for the real and present world of the client.[31]

Moreover, there was increasing questioning about the ethics of using the giving of relief as a wedge into the emotional life of the client.

Somewhere there would have to be a balance between the two groups within the Diagnostic school of thought, the one crying for a complete reliance on the psychological determinants of behavior, the other emphasizing social determinants. But even within the group that saw psychoanalysis as the better approach there were new things happening. In 1936 Anna Freud published her *Ego and Mechanisms of Defense,* and the world of ego psychology was opened to casework. It was not the id and infantile conflicts that were important but the adaptive apparatus of the client. Ego meant, in part, consciousness and reality—and reality meant social order and economics. One did not puncture defenses, one worked with them. Ego strength, defense mechanisms, adaptation, resistance, were the watchwords. By the late 1930s papers were being written on resistance and supporting ego strengths. The unconscious was not pursued relentlessly, but the everyday derivatives of the unconscious were dealt with.

Here at last was that happy synthesis between the social order and the psychological depths—the ego, which bridged these two worlds. Relationship took on a new dimension, and the long sought-after treatment method was here. Now adaptive mechanisms could be supported or modified. Resistance was not something to be brushed aside in the plunge toward the depths; it was to be respected and worked with and used. Study and diagnosis took on a new form. The ego was in the limelight, and diagnoses could be framed in terms of its strengths and weaknesses. A plan could not be formulated in isolation from the client—be it a plan based on economic procedures or on psychological insight. The client had to participate actively; his motivation must be nurtured, and his transference handled. "Now it finally became clear that the client's own conception of his difficulty, his own plans for himself, and his own wish for any change, were the keynote of both diagnosis and treatment." [32]

And yet, as the decade ended, with World War II on the way, the old problems returned to haunt the profession. What about the caseworker's function in terms of social reform? What really was casework's function and method?

World War II temporarily seemed to solve the problems of poverty and pauperism. Within a few years after its end, however, economic security again became a significant social problem—although it was well camouflaged by the affluence of a preponderance of the nation. The poor were with us, but through a complex of forces, they became invisi-

ble. It was not until the revolution in civil rights and the muckraking of
Harrington that the magnitude of American poverty became evident to
the country and to the profession.[33]

But even prior to the war on poverty, the social caseworkers of
post-World War II were aware of serious inadequacies in the profession's ameliorative armamentarium. The passivity of the psychoanalytic
era and the functionalist influence precluded, as a domain of activity,
whole populations of potential clients. The involuntary client was always a source of discomfort to a profession saddled with an ethic of
self-determination. The criminal, the delinquent, the psychopath, the
multiproblem family—these were clients who did not, of their own ac-
cord, come for help. Even when they were confronted with the presence
of a social caseworker, they often showed neither the capacity nor the
motivation for treatment. The significant change in the post-World
War II years was that the profession began to see work with these recalcitrant and involuntary clients as a legitimate endeavor. No longer were
they to be written off as outside the scope of a primary social work
effort. "Reaching the unreached," "aggressive casework," and "authoritative casework," became rubrics under which the involuntary client became a target of social work services. The meaning of such concepts
resides in the notion that the involuntary client is *not* to be seen as a troublesome parenthesis to casework; rather he is to be seen as a central
focus for the profession. And with a new focus, of course, comes a demand for new theoretical conceptions and techniques: family treatment,
group methods, and the renewed dignity inherent in "environmental manipulation."

SEARCHES AND BLIND ALLEYS

The search for the Holy Grail. Beginning with the Milford Conference of 1929, social casework was obsessed with a chronic search for
the unitary method that was to be called social casework. It was assumed that casework was something specific in method and that this
specified treatment endeavor was applicable to a wide variety of client
situations. It is difficult to appreciate why such a quest became so important and relentless. In part, it may have developed as a concomitant
to a desire for professional status. Flexner's challenge in this regard became a profound irritant to those who strove for the professionalization

of social work.[34] Professionalism imples—nay, it demands—a body of theory; it demands expertise; and it demands a claim of uniqueness or of preemption. Social casework as it evolved originally had a field of endeavor that it could call its own—serving the poor—but with the advent of psychoanalytic preoccupation it could no longer claim to have a field to itself. Indeed, caseworkers became interlopers on the preexistent domain of psychiatry. Appreciation of this encouraged a search for a unique and unified method. What was the point of being a caseworker if one did nothing more than the identical work of psychoanalytically oriented psychiatrists? No, there must be something distinctive about the method of social casework.

Unfortunately, the emphasis on the quest had the effect of obliterating differences among caseworkers that tended to arise quite naturally. In order to preserve the premise of a single method, theoretical and *methodological* differences had to be dismissed. An intolerance of diversity thus became characteristic in casework, in spite of some differences—namely, functionalism—that deserved a more careful airing and that were too great to be properly glossed over.

There is no compelling reason that social casework must be defined in terms of its *procedures*. The techniques of social casework may encompass an extremely wide variety of procedures, all of which may require extraordinary expertise. Nor does social casework have to serve a uniform clientele; the clients may come from a variety of sources.

What is left as distinctive in social casework are its values, goals, and philosophy—as a gestalt. The search for a unitary method was futile and erroneous; what was needed was a unitary purpose. Given this, social casework could employ a very wide array of procedures to accomplish its purpose—all of which are rightfully *casework* procedures.

THE CONUNDRUM OF CASEWORK VS. PSYCHOTHERAPY

Closely related to the search for a unitary method of casework was an attempt to differentiate its procedures from those subsumed under psychotherapeutic operations. Social caseworkers practice in mental hospitals and psychiatric clinics, in family agencies and in private practice. In the former two settings they are part of the traditional team of psychiatrist, psychologist, and social worker. All members of the team treat clients—and careful scrutiny of their activities reveal that they all do pretty much the same thing. Yet some would maintain that while the psychiatrists and psychologists do psychotherapy, the social worker does casework.

Differentiating the method of casework from the method of psychotherapy seems largely an exercise in semantics when one considers the aspects of each. A description of psychotherapy would typically specify that it includes the attempt to modify individual behavior; to that extent, caseworkers by definition are psychotherapists. Psychotherapy is a multifaceted endeavor that subsumes many kinds of therapeutic activities. On some sort of "depth" continuum, psychoanalysis would be at one extreme, followed by psychoanalytic psychotherapy, and extending all the way to vocational and pastoral counseling. Casework would cover a substantial segment of the "depth" band.

The psychotherapy vs. casework controversy cannot, then, be entertained on grounds of either clinical practice or definition. The controversy can be seen as an expression of other issues; namely, professional identity and legitimization. The professional identity issue is very much like that which prompted a search for a unitary method—how can social casework be differentiated from other, related professions? The legitimization issue is probably the more potent—who is authorized to treat psychological distress? American psychiatry has been uncompromising in its attempt to define behavioral disorder as *illness* and therefore place it in the domain of the physician-healer. Psychology is the one discipline that consistently attempts to challenge this preemption and has been seen, by the medical profession, as the "enemy" to be contended with in this struggle. For a variety of reasons, social work has aligned itself with the psychiatric profession, but the alignment necessarily involves casework being acknowledged as different from psychotherapy. Psychiatrists may do psychotherapy, but caseworkers do casework. If the legitimization and professional motives were not operant, however, there would be no need to change the name of the rose.

CURRENT THEORIES OF INDIVIDUAL TREATMENT IN CASEWORK

One can distinguish important aspects of casework. There are, first, *values* governing the treatment situation that, in spite of some internal contradictions, are shared by all casework theories. These values follow from a fundamental belief in the worth and dignity of the individual human being.

Second, there are prerequisites to the conduct of the treatment situation that are again common to all theories save the functionalist. These prerequisites include the *establishment of rapport* and a means of communication with the client.

Finally, there are specific strategies and tactics of intervention and assumptions that underlie these strategies and tactics, that is to say, *theories of treatment per se.* What do caseworkers currently rely on in their treatment of clients?

The diagnostic school of thought. The approach probably now used by more caseworkers than any other is that of the *diagnostic* school, for which Hamilton, Hollis, and Austin have been articulate spokesmen.[35] The reader is urged to examine the writings of these people for a detailed knowledge of the diagnostic system. By and large, two main treatment strategies are posited in it: the *development of psychological insight and psychological support.* A third strategy is sometimes put forth, namely *environmental manipulation,* but this can often be subsumed under support. Strategies intermediate between insight and support have been suggested—but not too explicitly. Thus, Austin posits an experiential treatment, something more than support but less than insight; Hollis originally saw an intermediate strategy, which she called clarification; and Hamilton suggested counseling for the same purpose. But the two basic modalities of insight and support continue to recur, in one guise or another, as the most clearcut distinctions in diagnostic treatment methods.[36]

Insight Development: In harmony with its Freudian assumptions, the diagnostic school sees development of insight in the client as the preferred strategy. The ideal basis of human functioning is thought to be reason, unfettered by the vagaries of unconscious conflict and impulse. To the extent that the client can recognize and understand his difficulties, he has been optimally helped. Diagnostic caseworkers would admit that the most potent insight therapy is psychoanalysis, which attempts a more or less total self-knowledge. Since psychoanalytic treatment is not appropriate for caseworkers, something less than total insight is aimed for. That goal is defined within a two-dimensional system. One dimension is an unconscious-conscious continuum. The consideration here is the *accessibility* of memory and of conflict. Using the analogy of a mineshaft, psychoanalysis may plumb the ultimate depths of the unconscious, whereas casework contents itself with reaching intermediate levels. The preconscious is a vast realm and cannot be easily demarcated from either the unconscious or the conscious. Casework certainly deals with the conscious and the more accessible strata of the preconscious; it may even proceed to mine the deeper levels of such material.

The other dimension is historical. It may be seen as a past vs. contemporary continuum or a "genetic" vs. "dynamic" one. Casework may operate primarily within the contemporary life of the client, although with occasional selected excursions into developmental—hence etiological—aspects of the client's life.

The assumptions of psychoanalytic theory presume that the most potent insight is that which reaches into both the ultimate depths of the unconscious and the developmental aspects. This assumption creates a serious dilemma for the diagnostic practitioner. Since the ultimate in insight therapy is denied him by his own definition of his work, he must be content with a strategy of treatment the results of which fall short of what could be achieved by a more skilled and longer-trained clinician. The self-deprecatory and dependent position, vis á vis the psychoanalyst, occupied by the diagnostic caseworker would seem to be an inevitable by-product of a strategy that both holds insight to be the greatest therapeutic good and denies itself the use of the most powerful insight-generating techniques.

A more heartening and perhaps more realistic point of view is developing within the diagnostic school of thought, maintaining that a little bit of insight is better than none—and that some clients only *need* a little bit anyway. That is to say, there is no such thing as an absolute amount of insight that is beneficial for all clients in all situations. Rather, the quantity and quality of insight needed varies from individual to individual. But even this more flexible conception does not afford a guide to treating two groups of clients. The largest of these consists of persons too disturbed emotionally to profit by the development of insight. The psychotic, the infantile character, the borderline schizophrenic, the psychopath, and other diagnostic entities are seen as people so fundamentally fragile that synthetic rather than analytic techniques are called for. This again is consonant with the psychoanalytic position than an intact and coherent personality is the most amenable to psychoanalytic treatment.

But the intact personality—indeed, the insightful personality—may also be subject to stress, and diagnostic casework provides a non-insight service to such a client. This second group of people is confronted with one of a number of realistic calamities for which they need help: death, divorce, illness, poverty, and the like. For these two groups of clients, then, there remain the non-insight techniques that fall under the name of supportive treatment.

Supportive Treatment: Whereas the tour de force of insight is the interpretation—be it pointed or connective discourse—the essence of support is reassurance. Within the diagnostic school of thought, support means emphasis on the preexistent strengths of the client, that is to say, bolstering existent ego capacities. A variety of rubrics have been conjured up to characterize different aspects of supportive treatment: encouragement, warmth, universalizing, benign advice giving, or ego-lending—to name just a few.

Supportive treatment, at heart, consists of procedures that selectively encourage some and discourage other client behaviors. In the treatment of an ambulatory schizophrenic, for example, the delusional system of the client would be ignored, or at least played down. Whatever normal interests the client exhibits would be encouraged, whether it be to find or hold a job, or secure a living accommodation, or to take recreation in some constructive and not too threatening manner. The worker thereby places emphasis on reality, not fantasy or delusion, on the current and immediate need, not the ruminating past. In the same way, a passive-aggressive and dependent mother might be instructed in specific child-care problems or in budgeting. The narcissistic needs of motherhood would be emphasized and nurtured; vengeful and destructive behaviors toward her children would be discouraged.

Supportive treatment by intent is essentially palliative. It attempts to return the client to a state of functioning that was present prior to the eruptive stress that brought him to the caseworker—with perhaps a few new strengths and resistive capacities. But, like insight treatment, support is ambiguously and unsystematically defined. It is exhortative rather than prescriptive; it is defined by intent rather than by procedure. And it relies primarily on subtle interactions between worker and client.

Manipulation Within the Relationship: The diagnostic techniques that have received the most attention within the casework literature have to do with the "use" of the worker-client relationship, and these techniques cut across both insight and supportive modalities. The techniques have focused about two main considerations, the affective climate of the relationship and the inevitable transference phenomena. The "climate" of the therapeutic relationship is prescribed as accepting or permissive or nurturant—but, depending upon the particular client, it should not be too accepting or permissive or nurturant. If the major thrust of treatment is supportive, these more sustaining relationship elements are heightened. The insight emphasis requires more distance within the relationship.

These issues are directly related to the transference phenomena. The development of positive transference is a *sine qua non* of supportive treatment. Negative elements within this transference are ignored or discouraged. Positive transference is also essential for the insight approach, but there negative components can be "dealt with" and, at certain brave moments, encouraged. Diagnostic theorists draw an important distinction between psychoanalysis and casework when they stipulate that transference by the casework client is not to be analyzed or resolved or made the fulcrum of treatment. Transference, even with a goal of insight, is primarily incidental to treatment. It is there, it is inevitable, it can be used constructively, but it is not central.

Evaluation: The theoretical superstructure of the diagnostic school is based on the assumption that insight is a necessary prerequisite for behavioral change. Allowance of another type of treatment, support, limits this assumption, but supportive procedures do not have the same therapeutic status as does insight. Support, despite efforts by some diagnostic theoreticians, appears anomalous.

The claim that insight is a prerequisite for changing behavior has been challenged repeatedly over the last several decades, but especially in recent years. Hans Eysenck, the psychologist, and others have charged that therapeutic procedures predicated on insight, namely psychoanalysis, have not demonstrated their effectiveness.[37] Eysenck's arguments will be presented in more detail when we discuss evaluation of casework. It is enough to note here that the insight assumption has not been empirically demonstrated.

A more serious criticism of the diagnostic school, however, is that made by Cloward.[38] Essentially, Cloward maintains that many prospective clients are turned away because they do not fit into a particular mold. To the extent that insight is the favored and preferred treatment, certain clients come to be viewed as untreatable. That is to say, caseworkers have a model of treatment and decide which clients can be helped on the basis of the degree to which they meet requirements of the objectives and techniques of the model. Within this context a motivated client is to the diagnostic caseworker one who desires self-knowledge; a cooperative client is one who responds eagerly to interpretative procedures; an ideal client is one who is both motivated and cooperative according to these criteria. Clients who do not possess these requirements of the insight approach tend either to be screened out of diagnostic social agencies as "unable to use the service," or tend to drop out after the intake interview. Many social agencies are explicit—and not at all apologetic—about this. They claim that they have a specific service to render, namely casework within the diagnostic frame of reference; there are many clients able to use and profit from this specific service; staff time is limited; hence: "We will serve only those clients we know how to help and who can receive benefit from our efforts."

But perhaps the most important criticism of the diagnostic school of thought is that it does not specify its techniques clearly enough or adequately indicate when to use them. Insight is not a technique; it is an objective. *How* does a clinician impart insight? Support is characteristic of the relationship in process; it is not a technique. By what means is a supportive relationship established and maintained? As most casework teachers and supervisors know all too well, it is next to impossible to explicate the specifics assumed to accompany the main treatment modalities of insight and support.

In sum, the problems of the diagnostic school have to do with: (1) the applicability of the insight model to social work clients, (2) the effectiveness of the model even to those for whom it is assumed to be applicable, and (3) the ambiguity of the procedures themselves.

But it would not be fair to leave this critique on so negative a note. The diagnostic school of thought in social casework represents several decades of sincere dedication to people in need, and it represents an attempt to place the casework enterprise on a rational and scientific footing. More importantly, perhaps, it stands for an extraordinary courage and foresight. It is easy to forget the antipathy with which psychoanalysis was greeted by a frightened world. Freud's revolutionary ideas were anathema to the bulk of the intellectual community. But the brave souls of the diagnostic school of thought saw quite clearly the power of Freud's metaphor, and—in spite of their initial unpopularity —these ideas were incorporated into the body of social casework. It took courage and it took integrity for the diagnosticians to accept psychoanalytic theory at a time when it had few adherents. At a time when casework is being sorely criticized for a lack of independence and courage, it would do well for us to remember this heritage of bold experimentation with unpopular notions.

The problem-solving school. This point of view within social casework, so well advanced by Helen Harris Perlman, does not claim for itself a unique doctrine or method.[39] Indeed, Mrs. Perlman sees her ideas as well contained within the theoretical conceptions of the diagnostic school. But many would say it is a departure and an attempt to meld the best of the diagnostic school with the best of the functionalist.

The basic assumption of the problem-solving school is that although clients come to social workers with specific concerns, their fundamental difficulty is in their manner of solving problems. That is to say, life is pervaded by conflict—decisions are always being made and problems are a constant characteristic of daily living. Most people at most times are able to respond and adapt to these inevitable problems, because they have developed adequate techniques for arriving at solutions and resolutions. But from time to time their problem-solving methods become ineffective, and it is at that point that therapeutic measures may be called for. The therapeutic goal is to restore the client's problem-solving capacities. The focus is *not* on the substantive problem that the client says has brought him to the caseworker, but rather on the processes of problem solving. The substantive concern is only a case in which to teach successful conflict-solving techniques.

The Perlman school is, at heart, educative. It attempts, quite directly, to teach or reteach the means by which conflicts can be treated.

But it is not the education of the classroom; it is more like the dynamic and intimate education of the tutorial. And herein the functionalist influence becomes quite evident. The casework relationship becomes both means and end: it is a medium of instruction and, by itself, an experience in living. The educative process is one of demonstration and repeated practice in problem solving. The model is exquisitely rational. Alternatives are proposed and evaluated; the different possible consequences of various actions are appraised—and all this with the presence of a teacher (the worker) who exhibits warmth and caring and a dedication to the ultimate fulfillment of client capacities.

The Perlman position's reliance on rational conceptions is both its greatest strength and greatest weakness. It is applicable to clients who have or have had a considerable capacity for problem solving. But what is to be done with those clients who have serious learning problems? The problem-solving dialectic requires an ability to weigh and measure alternative courses of action, to be free to choose. In essence, it requires a large dosage of rationality. But the clients of social agencies do not always possess these prerequisites. In a very real sense, problem solving requires the ability to solve problems—and the cure must precede the treatment. It is, therefore, primarily appropriate for the relatively healthy and stable client and less so as a treatment model for the damaged or infantile or psychotic client. The diagnostician's criticism that "problem solving" neglects the more irrational and even instinctive characteristics of man seems justifiable.

Indeed, a fundamental difference between the diagnosticians and the problem solvers can be seen in their different assumptions as to the inherent capacities of man. The diagnosticians see man as propelled by passion and instincts that tend to overwhelm the rational aspect of his ego; the problem solvers are much more optimistic as to the ultimate victory of reason over instinct. And the problem solvers' trust in man's reason is inherited from and shared with the functionalists and their other heirs—the existentialists.

The functional and existential schools. Functionalism and the Rankian psychology that fathered it are premised on radical subjectivism; man's perception and experience of reality is the only reality. Such a phenomenological position leads to a very noble and saintlike conception of man and his capabilities, and these derivatives serve to make the position extremely attractive. The therapeutic relationship becomes the main aspect of treatment; subjective experience, unconditional acceptance, and "becoming" are the holy trinity of functional and existential concern. Rank's psychology of will, Kierkegaard's existentialism, and Roger's nondirectional psychotherapy are kindred doctrines—if not identical triplets. Choice, dignity, potential, and, above all, the beneficent character of all experience are the hallmarks of a therapeutic position that knows no limits to man's ultimate capability. Conceptions of illness—in the psychoanalytic sense—do not exist. There may be inhibitions, a stultifying existence, a search for meaning, feelings of guilt, or despair—are all conditions of the human being—but they are not disease entities. To live, to become, to commune and relate with other humans—to become master of one's destiny—to exercise choice, to be oneself, to be free and creative and artistic—these make up the ultimate nature of man. Therapy is an enabling process that adds a little impetus to this.

But the functionalists and existentialists pay insufficient attention to the social requirements of existence. People function in a world of others—and the others have *their* needs and requirements; some of these are incompatible. There is a social order, and some conformity to that system is essential. Freud's tyranny of the instincts is replaced by a tyranny of the will; but there is a further tyranny—that of the community. A morality based on individual taste—as the existentialists would have it—results in anarchy. Freud saw the conflict between instinct and society as insoluble; Rank denies the struggle altogether.

The great contribution of this school of thought, however, consists of two basic conceptions: (1) the nobility of man and (2) the power of the therapeutic relationship. And these ideas are of sufficient magnetism—and of sufficient plausibility—to have a permanent effect on all schools of psychotherapy. The problem-solving school is, perhaps, an inevitable synthesis of functionalism with the diagnostic position.

CONCLUSION

In this historical overview of casework theory one significant theme dominates: casework has been a search, an incessant and chronic search for ways to help troubled people. The search has been frantic at times, and at other times it has been barely noticeable. It has been silly and brilliant; courageous and fearful. Dogmas have been generated and stubbornly defended; heresies proclaimed; dissent squelched. But, in a larger perspective, the search for theory and method has been inexorable. It is to the great credit of social casework that there was a quest for a holy grail—that there was a *Social Diagnosis,* an Atlantic City of 1919, a Milford Conference, a functional school of thought, and a problem-solving approach. There are people in trouble; social casework is called upon to help these people; it can do no less than try.

CHAPTER TWO

THE VALUES IN SOCIAL CASEWORK

The social work profession has always operated within the confines and context of a morality or value system unlike those of purely academic disciplines. Although other professional and scholarly disciplines seek as their ultimate end the perfection of mankind and the good life, social work has preconceived ideas as to what these ends entail. Everybody wants the good life; many strive for it in various ways; but social work as an institution sets itself the task of obtaining it for all.[1]

Preconceptions as to the place of man in the universe, the nature of man's relationship to his fellow man, and the good society provide a matrix of values within which the social caseworker goes about his daily business. Social work clinicians do not constantly ruminate about these value premises simply because they are shared by the wider society. That is to say, the value system of social work is embedded in the moral fabric of the larger culture and resides there in relative harmony and compatibility. It is when there is a clash between the values of the profession and the values of the society at large, or when contradictions within the values of the profession itself appear, that the social worker begins to look more carefully at his beliefs.

With the passage of time changes occur in the beliefs of a profession as well as of a society. Whereas at some points in history there has been harmony between the beliefs of social work and the major pattern of beliefs in American society, at other times there have been conflicts. And likewise within the profession value strains appear, resolve themselves, and reappear in another guise. Social workers may become isolated from what is going on in the moral climate of their clientele—which is society-at-large—or, through sloth or ignorance, lose touch with what is going on among their professional brethren.

If the values of a social work clinician were irrelevant to his practice, such strains and incompatibilities would have little consequence. But they are not at all irrelevant; many technical procedures in social work rest upon value-laden assumptions, and the entire therapeutic enterprise of the social caseworker is essentially meaningless apart from goals that are consequent upon beliefs. Further, in spite of a good deal of consensus within social work there is also disagreement; there are points of issue between what social work sees as its end and what society wants from it; and within the profession itself there are contradictions that create serious problems for the clinician.

THE FUNDAMENTAL TENET OF SOCIAL CASEWORK

One premise can be said to transcend all others in social work, and from it many secondary values can be derived: *the individual human being has an intrinsic worth, dignity, and importance.* There is nothing astounding or unique about this formulation; it is the operating principle of contemporary Western civilization and, as a homily, is shared by most people in our society. The principle holds that man is the most valuable of beings; that he is worthy of infinite respect and care; that he has a dignity and the inalienable rights that follow from this dignity; and all this simply by virtue of the fact that he is a man. No further justification is needed. This principle flows from concepts elaborated out of a Judeo-Christian ethic and a humanistic tradition. It is embodied in Walt Whitman as well as in *Genesis* and the United States Constitution. But it is a troublesome principle, and its validity as a *truth* has been questioned through the ages; the existential nihilism of a Camus or a Sartre was anticipated five thousand years earlier by Job.

Adherence to this fundamental belief provides a rationale for the very existence of social work—it argues that man is worth a good deal of time and money; hence we can construct elaborate and expensive social services to minister to his ailments. This is energy well spent, indeed it is energy that must be spent. But we shall see that such adherence places rather severe constraints upon the practice of social casework and, when resources are limited, upon the allocation of services. These constraints basically are of two types: those that emanate from clashes with the larger society and those that preclude certain technical procedures.

CONSTRAINTS IMPOSED BY THE POLITICAL AND
ETHICAL CLIMATE OF THE WIDER SOCIETY

The type of constraint we have in mind here can best be illustrated by an extreme and even macabre example: the hypothetical role of the social caseworker in the extermination camps of Nazi Germany. Obviously the caseworker would have no function in such a setting. It is theoretically possible that he might be put there by the state with a mandate to "keep those people quiet until we can dispose of them"— but he simply could not function in this context. What would he do? It is inconceivable that he would advertise his service as one that would allow the inmates "to make the best of a bad situation," or to adjust to an unpleasant reality. The contradiction inherent in a therapeutic service located within an extermination camp staggers the imagination.

This example illustrates a central point: social casework as we know it can operate only within a society that shares with it the basic value of the worth, dignity, and importance of the human being. The larger society must say, in effect, "yes, we share with you a profound concern for the individual—go and help him become what he can become." The apparatus of the larger society that orders political life— the state—thus must see itself as functioning for the benefit of the individual citizen.

In essence, then, social casework can exist only within the fabric of an equalitarian and democratic society, that is, a society that allows—indeed, encourages—its citizenry to find their unique way of fulfilling their potential. Further, the state must be prepared to expend considerable energy in facilitating this objective. The example of Hitler's Germany highlights the absurdity of a caseworker functioning in a society predicated on a different value structure.

Alas, all is not clear-cut. Germany of the thirties and early forties was a perverse extreme, and the democracy embodied in the Declaration of Independence has never been achieved. Most societies are somewhat equivocal about the democratic ideal, and those that are not have great trouble living up to it.

What about a society that claims to cherish the dignity of the human being and then proceeds to electrocute its murderers, or discriminate against its Black citizens, or starve its out-of-wedlock children? We are, of course, referring to the present-day United States. Does a caseworker have a function to perform on Death Row in Sing Sing, or in the Harlem ghetto, or in the Welfare Department of Louisiana? Let us be more specific and cite a not atypical example. The Alameda County Welfare Department in 1962 ordered its public assistance social workers to make night calls on welfare recipients in order to see if unauthorized males were living in their households. Now the ethic of the social work profession is more or less clear on this point—a professional caseworker does not barge in on his client, uninvited, in the middle of the night to see if he is having sexual intercourse without the sanction of marriage. The intrinsic *dignity* of the client prohibits such blatant intrusion.

This illustration is extreme and should not generate any meaningful paradox for the caseworker. However, the rationale for the night raids does, in less dramatic situations, present difficulties. The Alameda Supervisors did not issue their order without a reason, and we could paraphrase their logic as follows: Yes, people are entitled to be treated with dignity and respect, but such interest must be compromised when the individual's behavior conflicts with those of the community. Thus, we cannot let citizens do *whatever* they desire—we must constrain people from infringing on the rights of others. These welfare recipients do exactly this when they fraudulently claim to be husbandless; they bleed respectable citizens of tax dollars, and we must apprehend them in their destructive behavior even if it means infringing upon their dignity and privacy.

Although we may give the political fathers of Alameda County too much credit by providing this rationale, it is a fact that individual behaviors often do conflict with the rights of others. And what is to be done in such situations? Obviously, this is the great question confronting democratic societies—how are the rights of individuals to be weighted in juxtaposition with the rights of the community? In many cases, the paradox is more or less easily resolved: an individual's right to commit murder is overruled by society's duty to protect its citizens against murderous acts. But is an individual's right to courtesy and privacy in his home more or less fundamental than a community's right to protect itself against alleged fraud? Alameda County claims the latter right is more fundamental; the social work community, for the most part, argues the contrary.

Thus, even a democratic society wrestles with the problem of relations between individual rights and community rights; and whatever harmony may obtain at one period of time is found to be disharmonious at another. Indeed, American society once thought it a gross disservice to the individual's rights to provide him with any welfare at all. Now we sometimes argue that it is a disservice not to provide him with all possible welfare services. Advocates of the first position claim that we stultify a citizen's growing potential and individualism by making him dependent upon us; advocates of the second hold that we do not yet provide him with the physical and psychological accoutrements that could truly release his potential.

This last consideration raises a most significant question: what means are permissible to achieve valued ends? Shall we, for example, insist that a citizen live in poverty or deprivation toward the end that he be free of what may be a stultifying dependency on a paternalistic welfare state? Shall we make someone live up to his potential—even though he doesn't want to? We will return to these questions.

Social work's commitment to a basic belief in an individual's worth, dignity, and importance requires that the profession be embedded in a larger social fabric that essentially shares the same view. Even then, important conflicts arise when another significant value is involved: the rights of others. On the one hand the profession formulates principles and concepts such as "self-realization," "self-actualization," and "fulfillment of potential." On the other hand it invokes concepts such as "social responsibility," "the interdependence of man and society," and "the rights of others." Very often these parallel sets of concepts can exist in reasonable accommodation. Not infrequently, however, they clash; the caseworker is then placed in a paradoxical situation.

CONSTRAINTS UPON THE DAY-TO-DAY PRACTICE OF CASEWORK IMPOSED BY THE FUNDAMENTAL VALUE

These constraints can, with some difficulty, be subdivided into two gross types: (1) problems, defined as such by the society and the profession, that could be solved "efficiently" and "economically" by means that directly conflict with the fundamental value and (2) technical procedures in casework practice that appear questionable, or at least troublesome, when confronted with the fundamental value.

The first category of constraint can easily be disposed of because of its bizarre implications. Let us take as an example the dilemma of unwed mothers. This is a problem in our society for a variety of reasons, most of which center about established conceptions of the family and its societal functions—namely the socialization of children and the necessity of legitimizing offspring.[2] It would be very simple to "resolve" this problem—not in the sense of eliminating illegitimacy but in the sense of eliminating its consequences. One solution would be to kill all unmarried mothers and their offspring. Such a solution is, of course, inconceivable to social work simply because we don't kill people. But we must note that other societies *have* used this efficient "therapy" for the problem of illegitimacy—without much ado.[3]

The problems of the dependent aged or the seriously mentally deficient could be "solved" in a similar manner. And again, we should note, some societies of the past and the present have employed such remedies. Patricide and infanticide have had a long and persistent history on this planet.

And yet we may still be illustrating the paradox in too simple a manner. We may not kill but we can isolate, confine, sterilize; in some states we can flog; at another level we can impoverish, investigate, immunize, and evict. Thus, although we cannot kill our mentally retarded we may institutionalize them under conditions that are no less than brutal, and we may sterilize them; our elderly may be placed in geriatric hospitals or nursing homes that are almost beyond description in terms of their deterioration and sadistic administration. We claim that people should not starve and yet we allow them a maximum assistance budget that in many welfare jurisdictions ensures a starvation diet.*

But these may be merely aberrations of what is essentially an enlightened and benign system. Our institutions for the retarded and the elderly are old and decrepit through sloth and not through intent (although the inmate cares little about this distinction). A subminimum diet may be a function of public ignorance rather than of public policy, although this is not always clear and, again, it is rather irrelevant to the recipient.

By and large, however, we do not kill pople in order to eliminate social problems even though such a solution may be most efficient, nor do we remain comfortable with brutal welfare programs. Social work can go only so far within a range of permissible means as it seeks to cope with welfare programs. And the spectrum of available alternatives precludes murder, brutality, and discourtesy.

Given the preclusion of these more dramatic "rehabilitative techniques," what does the ethic of the profession have to say about the second category of restraints, about such things as coercion, manipulation, influence, persuasion, etc? These concepts almost immediately cause the professional to recoil; they connote activities that are seen as improper or unethical and beyond the acceptable range of techniques in the repertoire of casework. If the above methods were to be given other labels, however, they may be seen as much more acceptable. That is to say, it is the name that evokes the distaste rather than the actual procedures. Clients may be helped, treated, freed, released; they may be given insight and understanding; but they may not be coerced, brain washed, manipulated, or have their faith exploited. The latter conceptions are troublesome because of their implicit clash with the fundamental value —these are not acceptable ways to deal with human beings. If we look more carefully at the technical procedures of social casework, however, we find perplexing questions.

The diagnostic school of thought, for example, holds that the

---

* Compulsory sterilization laws existed in approximately twenty-seven states as late as the mid-sixties and over fifty thousand sterilizations of the mentally incompetent had taken place since the first law was enacted in 1907. At the present writing, flogging is still a possible sentence under the criminal code of Delaware. The miserliness of public assistance grants hardly needs documentation.

course of treatment is determined by the clinician; that is, after careful observation and study a diagnostic formulation is reached that calls for certain treatment measures. The client has no more to say about these measures than would a physician's patient. Within this context the caseworker becomes a manipulator of treatment wherein he leads, persuades, molds, and generally directs his client through paths along which the client may or may not choose to go. When these pathways are cognitive, we may not be too concerned; when they involve such things as educational and occupational goals, however, they become very different matters. Thus, Soyer poses the question of whether a social caseworker should interrupt a client's line of aspiration when he is convinced that the client would inevitably fail in it.[4] That is, the client claims to want A when the caseworker believes that A is beyond his reach, and that in the process of being thwarted in obtaining A he will be damaged. Should the caseworker allow the client to fail or should he "manipulate" things so that the aspiration for A is made to disappear?

Let us take another example. We will show in later chapters that the "faith" or expectation that a client has for relief is a powerful prerequisite for beneficial change. To what extent is the clinician allowed to exploit this faith? Mr. Jones may look upon his caseworker as someone who can help him; the caseworker may have serious doubts as to his own abilities in the particular situation. To what extent should these doubts be shared with the client?

Similarly, the client may look upon his caseworker as a man with almost magical powers: he is seen as a concerned expert; the client expects to be helped and is ready to respond to the influence of his therapist. How free should the caseworker be to exercise this influence?

Thus a series of antagonistic propositions can be generated that pose problems: on the one hand we have conceptions that, on the surface, conflict with the fundamental values; on the other hand we have techniques, procedures, and events that in themselves seem harmless enough. The hopeful and even desperate expectations of a client may lead to what is tantamount to "faith healing"; the construction of a case strategy and the setting of goals may be the most blatant kind of manipulation; the phenomena of transference and client identification may lead to "magic"; and the expertise, authority, and knowledge of the caseworker may eventuate in raw coercion if not actual brain-washing.[5]

These issues may be more clearly grasped in a discussion of the secondary values of social casework—and we turn now to one of these, self-determination.

The concept of self-determination has been of tremendous importance to the social work profession. It follows directly from the fundamental value and the ethic of a democratic society: people should be permitted to determine the course of their own lives. As an abstract concept, the principle of self-determination has much to offer—as an operating principle it generates considerable difficulty. Consider the following case:

Miss Jones is an eighteen-year-old unmarried woman in her ninth month of pregnancy. After a series of interviews, the caseworker concludes that Miss Jones is an infantile girl who has had rather profound deprivations throughout her life and who functions rather marginally at this point. There is reason to believe that she may be psychotic. The worker further believes that if Miss Jones were to keep the child the probabilities are great that she would not be able to offer it adequate mothering, nor even proper physical care. The caseworker relationship between Miss Jones and her worker is very good; she sees the worker as someone who cares for her, who is strong and capable, and whose advice is sound. During the course of several interviews it becomes clear that Miss Jones will respond positively to suggestions offered by the worker. Throughout a series of interviews, when the question of making plans for the expected baby comes up, the client responds with: "What do you think I should do?" The worker has avoided a direct answer to this for several weeks and has attempted to help Miss Jones see the advantages and disadvantages of the several alternatives. More recently, the client persists in soliciting a direct reply: "Please, tell me what to do. I know your advice will be the best thing for me."

The worker, faced with an important problem, is aware of several basic dimensions of the case:

1. The client will respond to the advice; the client's question is no longer rhetorical.

2. The client is aware of the alternatives; they have been thoroughly explored.

3. The client would keep the child only at great cost to herself and at probable risk to the child.

4. The persistent request on the part of the client for the worker to make the decision reflects a basic part of Miss Jones' character structure and cannot be dealt with in the brief time available to the caseworker.

The problem that confronts the caseworker is, at this point, a value problem, not a technical one. That is, the worker can no longer avoid responding to the question for reasons that have to do with closing off areas of therapeutic exploration, yet the caseworker knows that his response to the question will have an immediate consequence on the life of this client. His response implies choice between two alternative value decisions: (1) Shall he insist that the client make the decision herself, and hence do no violence to the principle of self-determination? (2) If he decides to influence the decision, in which direction shall he exercise such influence—toward keeping the child or relinquishing it for adoption?

The first decision calls upon the caseworker to ascertain how viable is the concept of self-determination. Does it transcend all other social work values? Can it be compromised in the face of certain extenuating circumstances? If the caseworker decides explicitly to direct the course of his client's life, he then confronts the rather staggering question of what direction such a course should take. Is motherhood or mother-rights more important than childhood and child-rights? The preponderance of law and tradition in Western society argues the former: parents have the right to raise their children. A more recent movement of welfare thought argues the latter: children have the right to a sound and healthy upbringing.

The facts of this case may make the issue appear too simple, for it is clear in this instance that the mother cannot provide adequately for her child. Alas, in most instances the prediction cannot be made with such certainty. Now, in those instances, the caseworker can resolve his dilemma by means of the following logic: Since I don't know how good a mother she can or cannot be, I might as well insist that she decide for herself. In that case, I spare myself the possibility of making an erroneous prediction and I keep the principle of self-determination intact.

This line of argument suggests that the notion of self-determination is a handy device for avoiding decisions in the light of ignorance about human behavior. That is, the knowledge of the profession is such that it cannot yet enable a clinician to make predictions about the outcome of certain decisions. Thus, he might as well allow the client to make these choices. Self-determination then becomes an expedient rather than a value. One can hope there will come a time when the professional can make better predictions. At that point what will he do?

Self-determination may be seen more as a therapeutic technique than as a professional value. That is to say, the experience of the profession suggests that people do not respond kindly to direct or even indirect advice—"you can't tell people what to do"—hence they might as well decide for themselves because no one can decide for them. But even more directly, the concept of self-determination, as a technical principle, may be employed to encourage a sense of responsibility and competence on the part of the client. It is as though the caseworker would say to his client: "Let us assume that you are capable of self-determination—your successful treatment will then depend in part upon your ability to act upon this assumption."

Thus, the secondary social work value of self-determination may be seen as a principle that (1) is used as an expedient in the light of a lack of predictive knowledge, and (2) is used as a therapeutic technique rather than as a value *per se*. But there are further considerations in regard to self-determination.

One such consideration revolves around the theoretical viability of the concept. Self-determination as a meaningful concept demands an assumption that people can in fact make choices from among an array of alternatives. Here we directly confront the philosophical morass of the "free-will determinism" controversy—a controversy with which all are more or less familiar. To enter the debate at this point would take us far afield; however, the following suggest certain limits on client choice.

1. Self-determination implies the availability of alternatives and, for many clients, some alternatives simply do not exist. Thus, an illiterate and "culturally disadvantaged" Negro male has no real choice among occupational alternatives. Likewise, to argue that a middle class woman, illegitimately pregnant, subjected to a host of overt and covert pressures, could "decide" to keep her baby would be simply a sophomoric exercise. The reader may supply his own further examples of sit-

uations where there are in fact limited or even no alternative courses of action.

2. Self-determination implies the ability to choose. This ability is presumed, by law, to be absent in children, mental defectives, and the mentally ill. Rightly or wrongly the society rules that only some people are in fact capable of making significant choices. But such determinations are rather arbitrary and generate many borderline situations. At what age does a child become able to determine the course of his own life—twenty-one, eighteen, thirteen, seven? And how mentally retarded must an individual be before he becomes unable to make choices—I.Q. of 75, 50, 45? Are all psychotics mentally incompetent (which is one way of saying that the notion of self-determination is no longer applicable)? Apart from legal definitions of mental incompetence, which are fuzzy enough, there are many situations not embraced by legal guidelines wherein the clinician would argue that the ability to make certain choices is not present. Obviously, the obsessive-compulsive client cannot choose to rid himself of his ritualistic behaviors. More importantly, he cannot choose certain occupation lines because of his illness. Extending this line of thought still further, it is suggested that most major life decisions are, in fact, not freely arrived at but are forced. One of Freud's major contributions to psychological thought was his tenacious reliance on a notion of "psychic determinism"—nothing in the psychic life is a function of chance or capriciousness (read: "free-will") but rather all psychic behaviors follow lawful and determined processes. If one pushes this consideration beyond a certain point, the concept of self-determination becomes trivial.

It is possible to argue that the heart and soul of casework revolves around the above considerations. That is, the social caseworker operates on the premise that the self-determining individual is the "ideal" individual. To the extent that someone is seen as constrained in his abilities to make choices and is confronted with few alternative courses of action, he is in need of aid. The business of social welfare becomes that of providing society's members with meaningful and viable alternatives; the business of social casework becomes that of enabling people to exercise choices among these alternatives. Both dimensions are necessary—one without the other is not sufficient. Obviously, this model rests on the principle that self-propelled, self-determining, self-actualizing peo-

ple are the kinds of people society wants—or at least that social work
wants. Such a model of health is perfectly consistent with the fundamental value. But, we must note it is not necessarily the *only* model that remains compatible with the fundamental value.[6]

This discussion of self-determination would not be complete without noting again two considerations referred to earlier. First, how is the
notion of self-determination to be reconciled with values concerning the
rights of others? Certainly there are individual behaviors that are
intolerable because they infringe upon the activities and rights of other
members of the community. In a world of increasing technical and social complexity, in a world of mushrooming population, indeed, in a
world of increasing knowledge that serves to highlight the subtle interdependence of mankind, the problematic areas of the individual versus
others dimension become much broader. It is probably reasonable to
conclude that there will *never* be clear-cut resolutions within these twi-
light areas; the areas themselves may shift along the spectrum, but there
will always be difficult and paradoxical situations facing the social caseworker in this regard. Indeed, such a reality becomes one of the chronic
burdens and uncertainties for the social work clinician and part of his
everyday professional life.

Second, the contradiction between self-determination and the case
planning inherent in a diagnostic approach becomes a perpetual concern
for the practitioner. The fundamental question of to what extent a client
should determine the course and nature of his treatment may never be
entirely resolved. This is an important concern within the context of a
psychodynamic or "insight" approach; the problem is even more evident within the context of the emerging and ever more popular behav-
ioristic or "action" approaches. In these approaches the client may not
be informed as to the rationale behind the therapeutic techniques, nor
even as to the goals implicit in the treatment.

It is one thing to hold to a "medical" conception of casework when
the problem is a neat, encapsulated symptom. In this instance the client
says, in effect: "I have a pain in my psychic or social life—please help
me—and I don't care how you help me." But when the problem concerns, more generally, the moral life of the client and has to do with attitudes or styles of living, or when the modality of treatment in itself
has an effect on the outcome, the client may not at all be indifferent to

the therapeutic regimen. To what extent can he choose not to be insightful into the cause of his difficulties, or choose not to be morally neutral about his behavior? Again, we hold that issues of this order will remain with the individual practitioner.

Thus, the goal of self-determination holds many pitfalls for the social caseworker. It is a value with implications for technique. As a technique it may be temporally bound by the state of existing predictive knowledge; as a value it is harassed by competing values and theoretical considerations as to man's ultimate ability to make choices. But self-determination is no worse a difficulty than other secondary values of social work.[7]

CONFIDENTIALITY

Again, following the standards of medical practice, the social work profession has been preoccupied with a notion of confidentiality. If social casework practice were in fact analogous to medical practice there would be no dilemma in this area; the issue would simply be one of convincing the community that the value be sanctioned by appropriate legislation. To the extent that the social caseworker functions similarly to the psychiatrist or priest, the analogy holds. In these instances clients are expected to share the most intimate and detailed aspects of their psychic and moral life. And such sharing can be reasonably expected only if the client is assured that these intimacies will not be broadcast to the world at large. A wife may be most reluctant to have her past or present peccadilloes revealed to her husband; a husband may not want his children to know about his early delinquencies. These instances serve to illustrate one of the central themes of the confidentiality value: people have a right to private behaviors and thoughts; if these are to be revealed toward the end of a therapeutic endeavor, they are to be treated with care.

Unfortunately, not all of social casework is practiced in the psychiatric modality or setting. Caseworkers often practice in agencies that are both public and authoritative. That is, they practice in welfare agencies, or in probation agencies, or in mental hospitals—where the behaviors and sometimes even the thoughts of clients *are of necessity* the interest of the organization. For example, what is a social worker to do with a communication from a welfare client that he is earning several hundred dollars a month "on the side"? Obviously the community would be outraged, as would most of his professional colleagues, if the worker treated this revelation as a privileged communication. It is the public welfare agency's business to know about the financial circumstances of their clients; for the worker to withhold such information from the organization as such would be unthinkable. However, when the stance of the agency is contrary to the professional position of the caseworker, the latter may find himself aligned with his client against the agency. Thus, it is not uncommon for caseworkers to look aside when public welfare recipients obtain modest sums of money from unreported sources. The rationale for such lapses is that the agency and/or legislation surrounding the financial benefit is so miserly that the caseworker feels morally justified in treating with confidence revelations of modest money accruals. The ethical dilemma is quite clear, however. To what extent does such complicity affect the moral tone of his client—and where is the line to be drawn?

By the same token, correctional workers are constantly faced with the problem of receiving from their clients information as to their violation of probation and parole conditions. Such conditions are, in many respects, quite restrictive. Does a probation officer take official note of his client's visit to a bar when indulging in alcohol is forbidden by the terms of probation?

Thus, in these two instances we find that certain "confidences," if revealed by the caseworker, would result in rather unpleasant consequences for the client. These consequences, however, follow immediately from the nature of the service and need not create any problem for either client or caseworker, unless, as was suggested, the latter finds himself in opposition to the purposes of the agency. The worker can say to his client, in effect: "There are certain things that I cannot keep in confidence and you must be aware of this. Therefore, if you reveal such things to me you do so at your own risk."

In other situations, however, the "risk" entailed in certain communications may not be at all evident to the client. Thus, in a mental hospital, the extent to which a patient "opens up" and reveals his paranoid delusional system or his suicidal thoughts may have the effect of insuring his continued commitment to the hospital. The ward social worker, if he hears such things from his patient, would be obliged to reveal this content to the patient's psychiatrist. The patient may thus find himself in a bind—he is advised that his successful treatment is contingent upon utter frankness, yet there are certain things that, if revealed, may work to his immediate disadvantage.

So too in work with children; the child client cannot presume upon the confidentiality of his relationship with the therapist. The child may reveal behaviors that should be brought to the attention of his parents. Indeed, his parents, as the bearers of legal responsibility for the child, may insist that such behaviors be brought to their attention. How then, can the clinician guarantee confidentiality to the child, especially when it is not always clear, a priori, what things can or cannot be kept confidential?

It is interesting to note that some facilities, be they mental hospitals or children's institutions, resort to dual therapists to accommodate such contingencies. Thus, there is the "administrative therapist," the professional who must make specific decisions as to the life of the client, be it in regard to discharge, cottage or dormitory transfers, punishments or privileges, etc. In regard to this therapist the client knows in advance that the concept of confidentiality extends primarily to the confines of the institution. The "therapeutic therapist," on the other hand, allegedly has no decision-making powers vis-à-vis the practical life of his client; therefore he may treat any or all communications as privileged. Despite practical difficulties involved in such arrangements, continued attempts have been made to employ this system. Thus, the Peace Corps was confronted with a situation where psychiatrists were placed in the dual role of screening and treating corpsmen. That is, during the training period for Peace Corps volunteers a given psychiatrist would have the mandate of both providing therapeutic service to the corpsmen and providing screening data to the Peace Corps administrators. Such functions were seen by the psychiatrists involved as mutually contradictory and they recommended the "dual therapist" model as heretofore described.

The problem with the system is that it does not solve the difficulty. The "therapeutic therapist" may yet become aware of certain client characteristics that *should* come to the attention of decision-making authorities. The Peace Corpsman who complains to his "real" therapist of homicidal impulses should hardly expect that such information will be kept in confidence. Or the child who presents his run-away plans to his "real" therapist should also expect that a phone call will come to his cottage parent, with the admonition to "keep an eye on Johnny tonight."

The discussion, thus far, brings to the fore at least three dimensions to the problem of confidentiality:

1. Confidentiality is a legal construction that bears on the notion of "privileged communication." In this sense, the social caseworker would ask that his client's communications to him be protected much as are the communications of a physician's patient, or a lawyer's client, or a priest's parishioner. The difficulty with this revolves around the fact that a large bulk of social work is practiced in public agencies that have protective functions. There are some things that organizational arms of the community must know about their clientele. Perhaps public welfare case records, or probation records, or hospital charts should be made available to certain people at certain times and for certain situations. In any event, it is not at all clear that the legal right of privileged communication is appropriate for all aspects of the social work profession.

2. Confidentiality is part of the therapeutic atmosphere. Here, the concept begins to take on aspects of a technique rather than of a value. Thus, there are no overriding considerations as to the ethical or moral imperatives implied by confidentiality. Rather, it is held that a spirit of confidentiality generates an atmosphere within which the client will be encouraged to reveal himself. For, it is further held, only if the client freely and without reservation communicates the troubling matters on his mind—no matter how intimate or morally offensive—can the therapeutic work take place successfully.

3. Confidentiality is a synonym for professional responsibility. It is here that the concept becomes more purely a value consideration. This aspect of the problem suggests that the worker should adopt a philosophical position that holds that all the confidences of a client are to be treated *responsibly* and, in the *judgment of the worker,* will not be used to the client's disadvantage. In effect the clinician says to his client: "Trust me. I will not blabber about what you say. I am a responsible person and will employ your confidence in a way that will be helpful to you. If I have to reveal to others what you say to me, I will do so with great care. But you must learn to trust me not to do anything that

will be harmful to you *in the long run.*" Such a stance, of course, puts a profound burden on the clinician, but, as we shall see, it is only one of many that inescapably fall upon the shoulders of the social caseworker.[8]

ACCEPTANCE, OR THE NONJUDGMENTAL ATTITUDE

This secondary value of social casework can be described in a number of different ways. Primarily, it should be seen as stemming directly from the fundamental value—it is, in effect, the operational form of that value. Clients are to be seen, it is held, as worthy human beings —irrespective of their behavior. That is, they are not to be assessed along any evaluative dimension of good or evil. The manifest employment of the value suggests to the client that no sin is so great, or no behavior is so despicable, that he cannot still be treated as a respected human being by his caseworker. Just as any man, in the eyes of God, is worthy of salvation—so too is any man, in the eyes of his caseworker, worthy of courtesy and understanding.

"Acceptance," in this sense, is a very noble ideal within social casework and developed out of a reaction to the moralistic machinations of the "friendly visitor." In the early years of the profession it was clear that there were two gross types of people—the worthy and the unworthy, or more directly, the good and the bad. The good people merited infinite care and respect—the bad people were scoundrels and could find little hope at the door of the social agency.

Two new assumptions permitted social casework to move away from this moralistic or judgmental framework. First, there was the development of an assumption about the basic nature of man, that is, that man was fundamentally good. Second was the assumption that behavior is determined, or at least explained, in terms other than of volition. Psychoanalytic psychology, with its premise of psychic determinism, provided the rationale for such an assumption. Thus, the caseworker could argue that man does not behave reprehensibly through his own malevolent choice; rather his behavior is a function of developmental and/or contemporary determinants. In essence, clients were not to be regarded as responsible for their behavior, hence there would be no basis for either condemnation or praise. The concept of acceptance rests on a theory of behavioral causality. Actions may be identified as morally reprehensible or praiseworthy, but the *person,* as such, cannot be so eval-

uated. Thus the shibboleth "It is not you that I object to but your behavior" becomes the operant principle. Obviously, specific *acts* cannot
be treated with moral indifference by the caseworker. Murder is murder
and brutality is brutality; the caseworker cannot by indifference con-
done such acts. But if the act can be divorced from the person, moral
neutrality and the nonjudgmental attitude become meaningful concepts.

The rub, of course, is in making the separation between an individual and his behavior. Some would argue that such a distinction is
patent nonsense; that a person *is* what he *does*. By subtracting his behavior from an individual the net result is zero—nothing is left but a
hollow concept. If this be accepted the caseworker finds himself in a
particularly difficult bind. He can, on the one hand, continue his adherence to the principle—in which case he must acknowledge the moral
equality of all behavior, throwing altruism and sadism into the same
moral pot. To a certain extent this alternative has great appeal, since it
follows so nicely from a completely deterministic psychology. Moreover, it spares the caseworker the profound dilemmas inherent in the
second alternative. This second alternative entails giving up the nonjudgmental attitude, in that the caseworker holds certain behaviors to be
morally superior to others. The problem, of course, is how to construct
the hierarchy. Shall it be left to the individual caseworker, with a resul-
tant moral anarchy? Should it be left to the prevailing middle-class culture, in which case there will reign a moral hegemony? And how will
this hierarchy of morality among clients and their behaviors blend with
the earlier-mentioned conceptions of self-determination?

These issues are particularly relevant in the light of earlier writings
on the role of psychotherapy vis-à-vis the moral life of clients. Mowrer, for example, argues that neurotic behavior is a function of gaps in
the conscience of the individual.[9] The neurotic suffers not so much from
a harsh and overdemanding superego as from one that is weak and fragmentary. In essence, Mowrer continues, the psychotherapist must deal
with the lapses of moral conscience that his patients display. Psychotherapy can no more stand aloof from moral concerns than can the physician stand aloof from the physiology of the human body. London pursues the argument even further when he suggests that the preponderance
of human distress confronting psychotherapists stems *directly* from
moral concerns.[10] That is to say, clients come explicitly with problems

as to what is right and what is wrong in terms of their behavior; what are the proper responsibilities entailed in marriage and parenthood, what responsibilities are entailed in employer-employee relationships, etc? London concludes that the present-day psychotherapist thus becomes a secular priest. Willy-nilly, without design or desire, the therapist inevitably finds himself thoroughly involved in the moral life of his client. The obligations thrust upon the therapist in this eventuality become quite horrendous. Since, it is argued, the caseworker must take a moral stand with his client, what stand shall be taken? Alas, neither Mowrer nor London provide a satisfactory answer to this all-important question.

In summary, then, we see that the concept of acceptance stems directly from the fundamental value of social casework. Clients are to be seen as worthwhile individuals irrespective of their behavior. Such a conception is viable to the extent that actions can be partitioned from actors and to the extent that client problems are not located in the domain of morals and values. If these presumptions do not hold, social caseworkers must make evaluative judgments of their clients and their clients' behaviors. These judgments can come from a variety of sources: the personal value system of the individual clinician, the values of the community, or the values of the profession. The first source, as we suggested, leads to moral anarchy, the second to a moral hegemony, and the last source probably does not yet have as explicit a value system as would be helpful. Which is to conclude that, again, a burden of uncertainty and ambiguity falls upon the shoulders of the hapless caseworker.

CONCLUSION

Social caseworkers may take justifiable pride in their preoccupation with the value assumptions of the profession. While psychiatrists and psychologists, for many decades, blithely proceeded without any major scrutiny of the assumptions underlying their activities, social workers were always cognizant of these assumptions. Perhaps the nature of social work's clientele provided the impetus for this awareness; the problems of poverty, criminality, child care, and family discord are inextricably bound up with moral issues and the belief system of society. Which is not to say that social casework has solved the issues arising out of its value premises—such a resolution is hard to come by. But the problems have not been ignored, and the cognizance of an issue is the necessary, even if not sole, prerequisite for its management.

In a very real sense, the value base of social casework serves to differentiate the social caseworker from a variety of other "healers." The astrologer, if he is a charlatan, may be quite as efficacious as the caseworker—he may even use similar methods—but he is bound by a radically different belief system. Thus, the witch, fortune teller, astrologer, or magician may use his client for his own purposes; in the process he may help the client, but such a contingency is not necessarily the prime consideration. The social caseworker may never do this. By the same token, the social caseworker does not indoctrinate an ideology— at least not a political or theological ideology—and hence is radically different from the brain washer or priest—who may also effect cures in their clients.

In the light of recent debate, the differentiation between the caseworker and his more ideologically committed "colleagues" is, admittedly, more difficult to make. But even so, a profound commitment to the sanctity of man, his worth, and his dignity; an ever-present desire to see his client make his own choices, where possible; a benign evaluative posture; and a respect for the privacy of his client's life and thought— all remain the hallmarks of the social caseworker.

CHAPTER THREE

VIEWS OF MAN IN SOCIAL
WORK PRACTICE

Casework practitioners often have disagreed about the place and importance of theory in casework practice. One side of the argument holds that theory should be left at the doorstep and not allowed to intrude into the encounter between worker and client, so that the worker presumably can approach the client unencumbered by the concepts and categories of a theory. In an important sense, however, the issue is a false one, and the atheoretical position is simply naïve.

The choice for the practitioner is not *whether* to have a theory but *what* theoretical assumptions to hold. All persons acquire assumptions or views on the basis of which they construe and interpret events and behavior, including their own. These assumptions frequently are not explicit but are more what has been called "implicit theories of personality." [1] Thus, the appeal for practitioners to be atheoretical amounts simply to an argument that theory ought to be implicit and hidden, not explicit and self-conscious.

It is difficult, however, to defend an argument favoring implicit theory that, by definition, is not susceptible to scrutiny and objective validation and therefore cannot be distinguished from idiosyncratic bias. The weaknesses of implicit theory are particularly serious for a profession in which a significant portion of the practitioner's activity consists in forming judgments and impressions about persons on the basis of which decisions are made affecting their lives in critical ways. The practitioner who can make explicit the empirical and logical basis for his judgment that a client is "psychotic" provides opportunities for test, verification, and thus appropriate modification of his judgment, all of which is not possible in the case of the worker who merely says he has a "feeling" or "hunch" that the client is psychotic.

Whether implicit or explicit, the social worker's particular assumption about human behavior can be expected to influence his professional actions and, therefore, to have important consequences for his clients. For example, the assumptions a caseworker holds regarding the *plasticity* or *malleability* of human behavior probably will be associated with the degree of optimism with which he approaches his clients and their problems. If the caseworker believes, as many do, that "basic character structure" is formed in early childhood and is rarely susceptible to profound change in adulthood, he is apt to respond pessimistically to the client who wishes to make a radical change in his way of life and, in fact, will very likely regard such aspirations as "unrealistic." (In fact, if dramatic changes do occur, they may be considered suspect, as implied in phrases such as "flight into health.") Similarly, the social worker's premises regarding *what* can be changed and *how* will largely determine what he will *attempt* to change in the situations confronting him in practice. For example, the practitioner who believes, along with Reiner and Kaufman,[2] that people live in poverty because they have a psychological need to do so, is not likely to regard changes in social conditions as an effective strategy for improving the lives of the poor.

An important point to be noted about such assumptions—in addition to the fact that they have tangible consequences for professionals and clients—is that they represent *choices* made by the practitioner, the profession, and educators in professional schools. Current knowledge in the social and behavioral sciences would permit the practitioner to adopt quite different assumptions about human behavior from those that have informed much of casework theory and practice. Consider, as only one example, the assumption—still relatively widespread among social caseworkers—that feeding and toilet training practices in infancy and early childhood play a critical role in the development of personality. In a review of the relatively voluminous research bearing on these assumptions, Caldwell concludes that the evidence simply does not support the presumed relationships between feeding practices, elimination training, and personality development.[3] A quotation from Hetherington and Brockbill, in a study cited by Caldwell, is representative:

From the data on toilet training, one can only conclude that analytic theory is not correct in maintaining that too early, too late, or too severe training leads to high degrees of obstinacy, orderliness, and parsimony. Since previous investigations using the scientific method have come to the same conclusions, one might suggest that it is time for psychoanalysis to reconsider its adamant perpetuation of this aspect of its theory. Most certainly it is time to discard the "anal" from "anal personality traits"—a term that has too long accepted as fact an unproved, perhaps untenable, hypothesis.[4]

Moreover, Caldwell suggests that continued emphasis on the presumed importance of feeding and elimination practices "may have led into a theoretical wasteland in which some of the more important transactions of the infancy period are not to be found." [5] Caldwell argues that the failure to make further advances in this area is attributable, in part, to the tendency of psychoanalytic theorists to remain "indifferent to the accumulation of empirical data." [6] *

The point of the above example is not simply that many assumptions held by social workers have not been verified scientifically, in any meaningful sense of the term "scientific," although this fact is important in view of the profession's explicit commitment to a *scientific* knowledge base. Rather, the point is that *because* many of the assumptions held by caseworkers have not been verified, it is possible for the caseworker to choose and be guided by other, equally tenable assumptions if they appear to be more *useful* to him in his practice. In other words, two general criteria should be considered in the evaluation of behavioral theory for casework practice: (1) validity or the degree to which the theory has been verified scientifically and (2) utility, or the pragmatic usefulness of the theory in relation to the realities and conditions of casework practice. Obviously, at present the caseworker cannot base all his actions on verified theories, but he should do so wherever knowledge permits, and the expectation is that over time his practice will be based increasingly on verified theory.

In this chapter we will examine and evaluate the underlying as-

* The preceding discussion is only an illustration, but it is not an isolated one. Nor do such criticisms apply only to the assumptions caseworkers have imported from psychoanalytic theory, as we will show later in this chapter.

sumptions about behavior in social casework theory, and we will begin an exploration of alternative and neglected theories and assumptions that may prove more useful than some current views. This exploration will be expanded and elaborated in subsequent chapters.

Certain aspects of theories about human behavior afford social work a basis for comparing and contrasting different theories. The following seven specific criteria bring into focus assumptions that in any theory of human behavior have particular significance for the utilization of that theory by an applied profession.

1. *Relative importance attached to past experiences versus present experiences versus expectations for future experiences as determinants of behavior.* Two polar examples are classical Freudian theory, which assumes that early childhood experiences are critical in the formation of adult personality and, at the other extreme, Kelly's personal construct theory, which holds that behavior is future-directed.[7] Even a theory that holds that all time perspectives are important will be comparatively useless to social work unless it allows for some assessment of the relative importance of past, present, and future influences on behavior. The position a practitioner takes on this dimension obviously will influence his notions about what factors are most important in understanding and treating his client.

2. *Relative plasticity of behavior—the nature-nurture issue.* Here the issue is not only the assumptions in a theory regarding the *extent* to which behavior can be changed but also those regarding which *kinds of behavior* can and cannot be changed, and the presumed *consequences* of specific changes in behavior. Notice the differences in theory between psychoanalysts and behavior therapists regarding the consequences of removing phobic symptoms, that is, specific fear of heights, closed spaces, snakes, etc. The psychoanalysts argue that if the phobia is removed without resolving the unconscious conflict that causes it symptom substitution will occur, that is, the underlying conflict will find expression in another form of behavior. The behavioral therapists disagree. They hold that there is no "unconscious conflict" behind the phobia, and therefore if it is removed no symptom substitution will result.

3. *Relative importance of intrapsychic versus social influences on behavior.* A comprehensive, fully integrated psychosocial theory of human behavior has not yet been formulated, and available theories of

behavior give greater emphasis either to psychological *or* to social influences on behavior. This aspect of their overall theory is crucial for social workers because of the extent to which environmental factors—and modification of them—enter into the practice situation in many social welfare agencies.

4. *The unit of behavioral analysis.* Theories of behavior differ in the unit of human behavior they select for analysis. For some theories, this unit is the individual person; others focus on human interaction or interaction systems; still others take the family as the unit of analysis; and, of course, there are theories that focus on larger units of analysis, such as organizations, communities, and societies. Some social workers have regarded theories that differ in this respect as competing and mutually exclusive (one example is the debate over a family *versus* an individual-centered approach in casework, as if one excluded the other) rather than simply as different perspectives, each of which may be useful in certain situations or which may illuminate different facets of the same phenomena.

5. *Is behavior knowable?* Theories differ on the question of whether or not it is possible to fully understand and explain the meaning and causes of human behavior. This issue has been of some significance in social work since it was one focus of a major theoretical dispute in social casework, namely the controversy in the 1930s between the Freudians and the caseworkers who became followers of Otto Rank.

6. *Amenability to scientific test.* This issue is related to, but should be distinguished from, the preceding one. Here the question is whether the concepts and propositions of the theory are or can be formulated in ways that will admit to scientific test. This issue has long-range implications for a profession committed to a scientific knowledge base. An untestable theory can never be more than a creed or an article of faith.

7. *Capacity to generate specific principles and guides for intervention.* This is a crucial point on which to evaluate a theory for use in social work practice. No matter how impressive a theory may be in relation to other criteria, if it does not provide guides for intervention it has no *relevance* for social work practice. It is important for social workers to keep this criterion in mind, since it is not always an important consideration to theorists in the social and behavioral sciences.

With these analytic measures as a backdrop, we turn now to review the major theories of behavior that influence current casework practice. In this review we will be concerned primarily with evaluating the adequacy of currently used theories as a basis for considering possible future directions for the advancement of practice theory.

INDIGENOUS TENETS AND ASSUMPTIONS
IN SOCIAL CASEWORK

Theories of behavior in social casework tend to be a pastiche of specific theories imported from other disciplines amalgamated with certain tenets and assumptions indigenous to casework. Before examining specific theories of behavior that have been imported by caseworkers, it is well to explicate the indigenous assumptions widely shared by caseworkers who nevertheless differ in their theoretical persuasions. It is important to be clear that what we have in mind here are assumptions about human behavior, not social work *values*.

One of the most widely held tenets in social casework is the concept of self-determination.[8] Actually, this concept has been used in at least three distinct ways, only one of which is of concern to us in this section. One usage regards self-determination as a value, a desirable goal of professional activity. This means that social workers believe it is desirable for people to be able, or to *believe* they are able, to shape their own destinies—or at least to make choices about the course of their lives. Self-determination in this sense is not an assumption about human behavior; it is an article of faith. A second usage, which to some extent is implied in the first, is based on the assumption that human behavior is, in fact, self-determined.[9] For example, this assumption sometimes is invoked in discussions of the use of authority in casework; the argument is that if the client makes productive use of the caseworker it is a sign that he chose to do so, or, in other words, that in the last analysis even the client who is forced into treatment chooses whether or not he will use it. A third usage of the self-determination concept is as a principle of intervention, namely, that the effectiveness of casework will be increased to the extent that the client participates actively in treatment.[10] While "participation" often is not defined in terms of specific behaviors, it includes the notion that the client should participate in making decisions about the course of treatment. All three meanings of this concept have in common the assumption that there is such a thing as "free will," or that individuals have the capacity to make "free" choices.

A second assumption prevalent among social workers is the notion that all behavior is purposeful.[11] As used in the social work literature, this concept usually means that all behavior is caused and that there are no accidental or random behaviors. This amounts to a commitment to a rather thoroughgoing determinism in which all events are assumed to have specific causes. It has often taken the form of psychological determinism, namely that personality factors are primary determinants of individual behavior.

A third assumption is that contemporaneous social, situational, and interpersonal factors are important influences on individual behavior. While historically caseworkers have given primacy to psychological determinants of behavior, social and situational influences have always been assumed to be important. Until recently, however, caseworkers lacked the theories by which to conceptualize situational dynamics with the same degree of sophistication they have been able to apply to psychological processes.

In addition to these three basic assumptions about individual behavior, caseworkers have developed, over the years, a set of more specific assumptions about the conditions under which casework treatment is effective. An example is the assumption, noted earlier, that treatment is more effective if the client participates actively in it. These specific assumptions about treatment, or more generally the conditions under which induced change can occur, will be discussed in later chapters.

The three general assumptions outlined above have certain characteristics that should be noted. In the first place, they do not constitute a theory. At best, they amount to a prescription for the kind of behavioral theory *desired* by caseworkers. That is, caseworkers are apt to be attracted to theories consonant with these assumptions. The assumptions, however, are not found to coexist in the theories of behavior that casework has borrowed from social science. A theory that is highly deterministic, such as classical psychoanalytic theory, tends to give less emphasis to the importance of individual choice as a determinant of behavior. Conversely, a theory that stresses personal choice, as does the existential approach, tends to deemphasize scientific determinism. As Nagel has shown, determinism and individual choice are not necessarily logically incompatible,[12] but few theories of behavior give strong emphasis to both of these assumptions.*

Each of the specific theories of behavior that caseworkers have imported from other disciplines has satisfied only some of the requirements of (1) the assumptions about behavior to which caseworkers are committed and (2) the realities of the practice situations in which social caseworkers find themselves. In other words, each theory imported thus far has contained some of the elements desired by caseworkers but has failed to supply others. We will attempt to show this in the next section of the chapter. This state of affairs raises a question that needs to be considered in relation to the future development of casework theory, namely were the theories casework has thus far drawn upon to inform practice deliberately selected because they are more useful and valid than alternative theories, or were they adopted by historical accident? If these theories were adopted and retained for historical reasons, now that a much wider range of theories of individual behavior are available the profession can take a more evaluative approach to the selection of theories for use in social casework. We will return to this point later.

In borrowing behavioral theory from other disciplines, social work sometimes has imported specific theories *in toto,* although in recent years the tendency has been to borrow more selectively and less systematically.

SYSTEMATICALLY IMPORTED THEORIES

FREUDIAN PSYCHOLOGY

Any discussion of theories of human behavior used in social casework must begin with classical psychoanalytic theory. To be sure, casework existed and developed prior to the influence of Freudian

* Cognitive theories of personality—with their emphasis on the notion that the individual's cognitive construction of his world determines his behavior—perhaps come closest to a strong emphasis on both determinism and individual choice in behavior.

psychology, but the behavioral theory employed by Mary Richmond and other pre-Freudian caseworkers was rather crude, unsystematic, and not well articulated. Mary Richmond was influenced by Adolph Meyer, but Meyer's formulations amounted more to an approach or a point of view on human behavior than to a theory in any systematic sense.[13] For example, one of Meyer's central ideas, which Richmond also followed, was that if one simply collected enough data about a case, an understanding of the case and how to treat it would emerge from the facts themselves. Thus, one of Mary Richmond's major contributions to social casework was her emphasis on the importance of a systematic approach to the collection and evaluation of evidence.[14]

It was not until the influence of psychoanalysis began to appear in casework in the second decade of this century that one begins to see the emergence of a systematic theory of behavior in the casework literature. For a number of decades to follow, the theory of behavior that informed casework was psychoanalytic, and predominantly Freudian; in fact, not until the 1950s and 1960s did the dominance of the psychoanalytic view of human behavior begin to be challenged seriously.* What assumptions did the embrace of psychoanalytic behavioral theory introduce into casework theory? Are these assumptions valid and useful or not, in light of the realities of casework practice and the value commitments of caseworkers?

It is particularly hazardous to make general assertions—as we do below—about psychoanalytic theory. In the first place, the protean extent of the theoretical literature in psychoanalysis makes it possible for diligent scholars to find passages in support of and in opposition to the same propositions.[15] And this characteristic of the theoretical literature is augmented by the extensive reliance on metaphors and analogies by psychoanalytic writers, permitting widely divergent interpretations of the same statements. And finally, of course, psychoanalytic theory has been subjected to revision and change—some of which we consider later in this chapter—although it is open to debate whether any fundamental changes have been made. In our view, the changes that have occurred are minor, in that they have not altered the character or structure of psychoanalytic theory. Despite these hazards, we can venture

* We are excluding here the functional or Rankian school of social casework, which is discussed later in the chapter.

some selective generalizations about the central assumptions that the importation of psychoanalytic theory introduced into casework.

First, psychoanalytic theory brought with it a heavy emphasis on the past. To be sure, quotations can be found in the writings of Freud to indicate that he recognized the importance of current "human and social circumstances" [16] and even of future aspirations in understanding behavior, but there certainly can be no doubt that the latter sets of influences received only occasional and unsystematic attention in the early literature of psychoanalysis; they are decidedly subordinate in importance to past, and particularly early childhood, experiences in explaining human conduct.[17] Once this assumption penetrated social work practice and education, caseworkers directed their efforts to activities such as collecting intensive historical data on their clients in order, for example, to trace the vicissitudes and anomalies of the client's psychosexual development.[18]

As a corollary to this emphasis on the past, psychoanalytic theory also brought a pessimistic, even fatalistic, orientation to expectations for psychological change, particularly in adults. If the major influences on personality are those that occur in childhood, and if the basic structure of a person's personality is set at an early age, it follows that subsequent influences on personality are comparatively weak at best and that the amount and type of psychological change that can conceivably occur following childhood are severely limited.* And if the primary roots of an individual's behavior and problems usually lie buried deep in his past, it also follows that what he can do about his behavior is limited. The past cannot be undone. At best it can be understood, and then, through the exercise of will, perhaps its influence can be weakened or reduced. As Luborsky and Schimek have put it:

Early levels of development never completely disappear . . . [and] it is likely that personality development, *especially after puberty,* consists not so much in completely new stages of development being added, but rather in changes in relationship between the already existing levels of personality structure . . . ; it is essentially this kind of change that analytic therapy aims to bring about [emphasis added].[19]

* "It is in these early years that the most basic and lasting personality patterns are established, *setting the general framework of all further change* [emphasis added]." Lester Luborsky and Jean Schimek, "Psychoanalytic Theories of Therapeutic and Developmental Change: Implications for Assessment," in Philip Worchel and Donn Byrne, eds., *Personality Change* (New York, Wiley, 1964), p. 85.

Moreover, the techniques that psychoanalysts have assumed to be necessary in order to bring about even these modest changes have been beyond the reach of more than a handful of social workers since they can be learned only in lengthy and arduous training in psychoanalysis, not to mention the fact that few clients of social agencies possess the resources and personality characteristics demanded of the person who would undergo psychoanalysis.

In addition to an emphasis on the past, and a pessimism that followed from this emphasis, psychoanalysis deemphasized, as we indicated earlier, the importance of current social, situational, and interpersonal factors, both as influences on behavior and as forces to be used for change. The corrosion of the attention social caseworkers previously gave to the social situations of their clients and to the use of social and interpersonal influences to bring about change is nowhere more dramatically seen than in the casework literature written at the time the influence of psychoanalysis began to appear. Numerous illustrations of this point could be cited, but perhaps one will capture the essential change in emphasis that occurred. Not quite two years after the book was published, Mary Richmond's *Social Diagnosis* was subjected to a reanalysis from a "psychiatric" perspective by E. E. Southard and Mary C. Jarrett.[20] They concluded that "fifty percent of the cases cited by Miss Richmond in *Social Diagnosis* present clearly psychiatric problems, and another fifteen percent strongly suggest a psychopathic condition." [21] The orientation of the "new breed" of psychiatrically oriented caseworkers was aptly expressed, during this same period, by Jessie Taft: ". . . casework is always fundamentally psychological or, if you please, psychiatric, even when it is applied to the so called normal person, and . . . environment is never external to the psychology of the client." [22] *

Three other related emphases carried over from psychoanalysis deserve mention here. One is the commitment of psychoanalysis to a particularly thorough determinism. Determinism had already caught hold in social casework—as in the work of Mary Richmond, for example—

* To be sure, these earliest influences on casework were from psychiatry rather than from psychoanalysis as such. However, it is virtually impossible to separate the two, since once the psychiatric emphasis was established, the introduction of psychoanalytic ideas simply amounted to a change in the content of that emphasis. Scott Briar, "Some Elements, Issues, and Problems in the Early Relations Between Social Casework, Psychiatry, and Psychoanalysis" (unpublished manuscript, 1957).

but psychoanalysis added the notion of biologically driven stages of development that unfold inexorably, and the curiously redundant concept that many behaviors are "over determined," as if the word "determined" were not strong enough to convey the supposed power of psychoanalytic principles to account for cause-effect relationships. Moreover, the primary determinants of behavior were held to consist of irrational, instinctual forces. While it is true that Freud rested his hopes for the future of mankind on reason, he believed that this "voice . . . is a soft one," [23] and there can hardly be any doubt that psychoanalysis "contributed to the discrediting of reason." [24] (In recent years, attempts have been made to strengthen the role of conscious, self-directing processes in psychoanalytic theory through an elaboration of ego psychology; these will be discussed later in this chapter.)

Second, psychoanalysts were preoccupied with phenomena and operations of little concern to caseworkers and of little relevance to the situations confronting them. As Heinz Kohut, a psychoanalyst, has observed, the basic operation of the psychoanalyst, the encouraging of introspection called "free association," influenced decisively the kind of theory that psychoanalysis evolved. Since this method and the behavioral phenomena to which it is directed do not and cannot occupy a place of similar importance in casework, theoretical importations from psychoanalysis to casework should, in Kohut's opinion, be marked "handle with care." And Kohut advised that "it is erroneous to assume that psychoanalytic theory is *the* theory of social work or that the practice of social work is an attenuated form of psychoanalysis." [25] What Kohut has emphasized is confirmed by studying the process of Freud's development of psychoanalytic theory. The theory was developed in an attempt to understand specific empirical phenomena, that is, certain psychiatric symptoms, and the evolution of the theory essentially consisted of a series of successive approximations tested and revised in light of observations made under a specific set of conditions, the psychoanalytic interview. Theory developed in relation to one set of empirical problems under one set of conditions cannot be assumed to be applicable to a different set of problems dealt with under a different set of conditions.

Thus social workers, who are concerned with a set of problems different from that of psychoanalysts, and who practice under a quite different set of conditions, need to develop their own theories, theories tailored to these problems and conditions. This is not to say that these theories must be developed *de novo*. On the contrary, the profession can and should borrow widely and heavily from ideas developed elsewhere, but these borrowings should be selectively and judiciously made, on the basis of their applicability to the realities and exigencies of social work practice. This, however, was not the approach taken to the use of psychoanalytic theory in casework. The hallmark of the most prestigious psychoanalytically oriented casework theorists—Annette Garrett, Gordon Hamilton, Beatrice Simcox Reiner—is the purity of their commitment to the whole of classical psychoanalytic theory and the lack of distortion in their reiteration of this theory, not a careful selection and transformation of psychoanalytic concepts in light of the practice situation in casework. Modification of psychoanalytic concepts was for psychoanalysts, not caseworkers, to make. As a result, the process of theory development in casework became the direct opposite of that followed by Freud and advocated here. Instead of beginning with the special problems and conditions of casework practice—as Mary Richmond had done—and searching for ideas (from various sources, including but not limited to psychoanalysis) that might usefully be applied to these problems, the approach taken by the psychoanalytically oriented caseworkers was to redefine the problems and conditions of casework practice so that they could be made to fit an unreconstructed psychoanalytic theory. If anything was to be changed in the attempt to reach an accommodation between psychoanalytic theory and casework practice, it was to be the practice situation, not the theory.* Nowhere are the problems created by this approach to the utilization of psychoanalytic theory more apparent than in the effort to construct a treatment therapy for casework from psychoanalytic principles of therapy.

It is generally recognized that the least well-developed aspect of psychoanalysis is its theory of treatment. The limited, inchoate literature on treatment theory, studded with a mixture of ad hoc prescriptions and mystical allusions to the therapeutic process, stands in sharp contrast to the elegant elaborations of psychoanalytic personality theory.

---

* This is not to suggest that Hamilton, Garrett, and their followers could have done otherwise. To them, psychoanalysis appeared to offer a more than satisfactory and welcome theory for casework practice.

This may be partly attributable to the persistent ambivalence Freud expressed about the use of the psychoanalytic method as a therapeutic rather than research tool. Although this quandary has been resolved pragmatically by the widespread use of the psychoanalytic method for purely therapeutic purposes, the theoretical issue remains. No less eminent an authority than Karl Menninger has argued, in one of the few books that have attempted to construct a theory of the psychoanalytic method, that the method should not be viewed as a therapeutic device but as a tool for education and research.[26]

In any event, the psychoanalytic method was used as a therapeutic tool, and the principles underlying that method have had a strong impact on the development of treatment theory in casework. The central, pivotal principle of the psychoanalytic method is insight, the development of intellectual and emotional understanding of the historical, largely unconscious forces that direct much of the analysand's behavior. It is only through such understanding that these forces can be attenuated and a redistribution of energy—or "structural change"—be affected among the three structures of the personality, the ego, id, and superego. Anything less than this amounts, by definition, to palliative or symptomatic therapy. To dispel any doubt about the primacy of insight as the goal of therapy, one need only consider the attitude toward symptomatic relief in the psychoanalytic literature to see clearly that alleviation of the specific problems that led the patient to seek therapy in the first place is secondary in importance to the development of insight and the structural changes presumed to result from it. The disputes in the psychoanalytic literature over the role of the transference neurosis, analysis of the transference versus analysis of resistance or of character armor, etc., are essentially arguments over the most effective means to create the conditions for development of insight.

It was inevitable that advocates of this method would encounter the problem of patients who could not be subjected to it because they lacked the personality attributes and strengths its effective use required. These problems could not be ignored entirely, partly because the society expects that the therapist's basic commitment should be to patients and their problems, not to methods and techniques, partly because the psychoanalytic *personality* theory purported to explain all types of social and emotional disorders, whether amenable to the classical psychoanalytic method or not, and partly because social workers and others were asking psychoanalysts to tell them how they should treat persons not suited for psychoanalysis, including persons and problems ordinarily not even seen by psychoanalysts. These pressures gave rise to several variations in therapy. First, modifications were made in the techniques employed in the classical psychoanalytic method, while still preserving its goal. For example, if use of the couch was too threatening, certain types of patients could be treated, in the early stages at least, in a sitting, face-to-face position. Second, the ambitious, extensive goals that characterized the classical method were relaxed, generating a broad range of therapies loosely labeled "psychoanalytically oriented psychotherapy." Typically, these therapies were conducted in face-to-face situations, and while they shared with the psychoanalytic method the central aim of achieving insight, the insight sought was more limited in extent and "depth" and, according to a frequently cited distinction by Eissler, resulted not in "structural" personality changes but changes in "content," the former supposedly achievable only in classical psychoanalysis.[27] Even these modifications, however, were not sufficient or appropriate for certain classes of problems, patients, and situations, nor for practitioners who lacked the training and experience considered necessary to attempt insight attainment in treatment. To meet such conditions, a third type of therapy was identified, which differed more radically from psychoanalysis in the sense that the central aim of insight development was abrogated and even purposely avoided. This type of treatment, called supportive therapy, was conceived to be essentially palliative in nature and sought primarily to reinforce or activate manifest and latent strengths already present in the personality.

Several characteristics of this threefold treatment typology should be noted. First, the reference point used to differentiate the three types is "insight"; in other words, psychoanalytically oriented psychotherapy and supportive therapy are defined, essentially, by how they differ from psychoanalysis. Second, by definition the three types imply a value hierarchy, in which psychoanalysis is the more powerful and preferred method and supportive theory is the weakest and most limited since its effects are superficial and palliative. Third, use of the psychoanalytic method is restricted to bona fide psychoanalysts—or professionals, increasingly physicians, who have completed long and arduous training in the method—while the more limited therapies might be practiced by a variety of professionals, including social workers. Thus, social workers were restricted from using the only method that could offer any assurance of producing a genuine and lasting "cure." And fourth, this typology, with all of its assumptions and implications, was fully assimilated into casework theory and became the dominant treatment classification in casework, unchallenged until recently.[28]

The above assumptions, which the reliance on psychoanalysis brought into social casework—that is, the emphasis on the past, a pessimistic view of change, a deemphasis of the importance of social, situational, or interpersonal forces, psychological determinism, the psychoanalyst's preoccupation with intrapsychic processes, and the assumption that insight is the most powerful therapeutic agent—have come to permeate casework theory to such a degree that for many they tend to be regarded as givens. The extent to which this is so can perhaps be seen more dramatically by examining—before we turn to a discussion of recent modification in psychoanalytic theory—another set of theories of personality and therapy that was introduced into casework during the psychoanalytic era, namely the theories of Otto Rank and the functional school of casework that grew up around them.[29]

Otto Rank's theory of personality was never as fully developed and elaborated as that of Freud. It might be accurate to characterize Rank's formulations more as providing an orientation toward personality than a theory in any formal sense. Nevertheless, the assumptions underlying the Rankian view differed radically from those embedded in Freud's theories.

First, in the place of the Freudian emphasis on the past, the Rankians substituted an emphasis on the present and, to a lesser extent, the future. It is in the present, the argument goes, that the person's psychological problems are manifest, and it is in the present, particularly in interpersonal relationships, that change is brought about. Insight into the past may be useful in some instances, but it is not essential, even for profound psychological change. In fact, too much concentration on understanding the past may impede progress and growth.

Second, and partly because of their emphasis on the present, the Rankians adopted an optimistic view of the *possibility* of change, even of the most profound and lasting sort. Rank's theory of personality is essentially a "self" theory. Each individual possesses a self with unique and basically positive characteristics and potentialities. Personality development is a process of self-actualization and self-realization. Expression and realization of the self are stimulated by social encounters, particularly interpersonal relationships. Thus personality functioning is a continuous process of becoming. Since each moment provides new opportunities for further realization of self, each moment also contains the potential for evoking radical changes in the course of personality development. Consequently, for example, there was no place in the Rankian view for the hierarchy of therapies that developed in the Freudian movement. The caseworker's therapeutic efforts in the social agency might produce effects as profound, "deep," and lasting as those of the Rankian psychoanalyst in his consulting room. The essential task of the therapist was to release the self so that its natural development could proceed with fewer impediments. The stance was not that of inducing change but of permitting change to occur by freeing the self. The functions and services of the social agency were used as tools in carrying out this task, although the primary tool was conceived to be the worker-client relationship.

And third, the Rankians rejected scientific determinism as a *modus operandi* for understanding personality. Since the essence of each personality is unique, that essence is ultimately unknowable except to the person himself and hence is inaccessible to external observation. The proper study of the personality is autobiography and art, and some functionalists have attempted to make a case for these forms as research. Scientific procedures of inquiry can, however, be applied to other phenomena, such as the society, the agency, and the helping process.

While the Rankian position never attracted more than a small fraction of professional caseworkers, the introduction of these ideas into the profession led to one of the most intense and heated controversies in its history. Theoretical controversies of this sort can furnish the life blood of a discipline by acting as a stimulus to thought and innovation. But in social casework, the prevailing attitude was anything but hospitable to this controversy. Battle lines were drawn, epithets were hurled, and one senses an urgent pressure for closure, as if casework could not tolerate more than one conception of its endeavors. This stance effectively prevented each side from using the other's contributions, because to do so publicly was to run the risk of being accused of going over to the other side. Thus, for example, when Herbert Apthekar attempted a rapprochment of the two camps in his book, *Basic Concepts in Social Casework,*[30] his work was rejected by leaders of both the diagnostic and functional schools as unrepresentative of either view.[31]

This controversy has since subsided, partly because of the waning influence of the Rankian position on the casework field as a whole, and perhaps partly because even more fundamental controversies began to loom on the horizon. Nevertheless, the Rankian school left an imprint on casework theory in the heavy emphasis on the worker-client relationship, the attention paid to the agency and its functions in casework practice, the clarification and perhaps excessive solidification of the diagnostic or Freudian school, and possibly in the more receptive attitude among caseworkers to some concepts currently appearing in the field that bear a strong resemblance to Rankian ideas.

Two characteristics these two schools of casework thought have in common should be noted. Both assume that the unit of attention in casework is the individual person and not, for example, the family or some other social unit. Second, both assume that the overriding variables in individual behavior and pathology are intrapsychic processes, not social and interpersonal factors. Thus, both encouraged a view that casework is essentially psychotherapy. Their difference had to do only with certain therapeutic principles and the nature of the intrapsychic processes to which these principles were applied.

RECENT DEVELOPMENTS

We can now turn from the two major views of man that dominated casework throughout most of its history to consider developments over the past ten to fifteen years.

EGO PSYCHOLOGY

The developments that have attracted most attention in recent years—as in the past thirty to forty years—have emanated from psychoanalysis. The increased emphasis on ego psychology in psychoanalysis, stemming from the work of Anna Freud [32] and more recently Hartman, Kris, Loewenstein, and Rapaport,[33] has received considerable attention among psychoanalytically oriented social caseworkers. This development has modified the assumptions introduced into casework by classical psychoanalytic theory in several respects.

The development of ego psychology has brought an increased emphasis on the role of conscious cognitive processes in behavior. One advantage of this emphasis, for the caseworker, is that it focuses attention on psychological phenomena that are more accessible to the caseworker than are the unconscious processes that were the central preoccupations of classical psychoanalysis. Moreover, the interest in cognitive processes has been accompanied by an increased emphasis on the individual's adaptation to situational conditions. The latter emphasis is most evident in efforts, such as those of Parad,[34] Sarvis [35] and others, to apply psychoanalytic ego psychology to crisis situations and to short-term, situationally oriented treatment. Implicit but unstated in this development is a heightened optimism about the individual's capacity to adapt and change without lengthy and radical therapeutic measures, such as classical psychoanalysis.

But the significance of this development should not be exaggerated. It does not represent a radical break with the psychoanalytic tradition. The shifting assumptions about the nature of man, summarized above, are only relative and less marked than this review of them may imply. Even Hartman, whose formulations could be construed as representing a fundamental departure from classical Freudian theory, took pains to show that his concept of autonomous ego energy was implied in the work of Freud, and his theories therefore represent an elaboration, not a revision, of psychoanalytic thought.

Moreover, the increased attention to the present and the situational context of behavior has not resulted, as one might expect, in the incorporation into these formulations of the more sophisticated concepts available in the social sciences for the analysis of social situations. Crisis theory, as formulated by Caplan,[36] Kaplan,[37] Parad,[38] Rapoport,[39] and others, presumably represents an effort in this direction, but this is no more than a vague and loosely defined perspective. The central focus remains on intrapsychic processes, and the approach therefore is psychological, not psychosocial.

Most discouraging, perhaps, is that although the shift to a focus on cognitive processes appears to be better suited in many ways to the situation of practice in casework, even the casework theorists who seem to recognize the value of this shift have not made an effort to draw upon the most sophisticated theory and evidence concerning cognition. The psychoanalysts are relative latecomers to the study of cognitive processes, and their studies of these processes still are minor compared to the more substantial work done by psychologists. Yet one rarely finds reference in the casework literature to the latter, not even to the impressive work of Rapoport, who attempted to bring some of this material to bear on psychoanalytic ego psychology.[40] Kadushin's harsh judgment more than ten years ago still holds: in spite of their interest in psychological processes, caseworkers are psychologically ignorant because they are familiar, at most, with but one small segment of psychological knowledge.[41]

More generally, one sees in the work of some of those caseworkers who have been attracted to ego psychology a disconcerting reluctance, even an unwillingness, to look beyond psychoanalysis for ideas and knowledge. This self-imposed provincialism can only have undesirable consequences, since it isolates these workers from exposure to potentially useful ideas developed outside of psychoanalysis where, in fact, the bulk of work on cognition is being done.

SOCIAL SCIENCE

One of the most important developments affecting the knowledge base of social work in the last two decades has been the extensive infusion of knowledge from the social sciences, especially sociology. A steady flood of articles and books on this subject has appeared, schools of social work have added courses covering this content, and concepts such as *role* and *social system* have become part of the daily vocabulary of social workers.

As Inkeles has pointed out, any sociological theory contains, at least implicitly, a theory of personality.[42] That is to say, when a sociologist makes assertions about the relationship between sociological variables and human behavior, he necessarily makes certain assumptions about the determinants of individual behavior and about the responses of individuals to social realities. While many sociologists often do not make these assumptions explicit, nevertheless some generalizations can be made about the assumptions regarding behavior frequently invoked by sociologists.

Many sociologists seem to view individual behavior as highly plastic and malleable, especially in response to social forces. For example, it frequently is assumed by sociologists that people act in accordance with social expectations, and if these expectations are modified the behavior of the individual—or at least of most individuals—changes accordingly. Thus, individual behavior varies directly with social context or, put the other way around, social context profoundly determines and controls individual behavior. Probably the most familiar and dramatic examples are the profound effects that institutions (prisons, hospitals, etc.) exert on persons living in them. These assumptions have rather far-reaching implications for the practice of casework. Although, as we shall see later, these implications do not appear to have been recognized widely by caseworkers, they undoubtedly have contributed to the increased emphasis on social-change activities in social work in recent years.

The most valuable contribution of sociology to casework practice, beyond empirical generalizations about the relations between social factors and phenomena of concern to caseworkers (e.g., the relationship between social class and treatment), probably will reside in the conceptual tools sociologists have developed for analysis of the kinds of social situations with which caseworkers are concerned. For example, the concept of role, and the theory that has been built up around it, abstracts a set of social phenomena that includes the individual actor, his perceptions and dispositions, the expectations of relevant others, and social structural aspects of the situation.[43] The foci of analysis are social units, not individual organisms. The implications of this type of analysis for the caseworker's definition of his "client" and for intervention strategies are only beginning to appear in the casework literature. One example is the view in family diagnosis that individual pathology is a manifestation of systemic disturbance in the family.[44] Another example is Purcell and Specht's discussion of the importance of distinguishing between the *locus* of a problem brought to the caseworker by an individual and the *target* of intervention.[45] The tendency among caseworkers has been to assume that the locus of a problem—typically an individual in casework—should also be the target of intervention.

In general, however, social-science materials have not had an integral effect on casework theory but have been treated as a set of additional "factors" to be somehow taken into consideration within existing individual-centered, psychologically oriented social casework. For example, although Helen Perlman devotes a chapter in the first part of her book on social casework to a presentation of role theory, neither the concepts of role theory nor the kind of situational analysis they permit appear in the second part of the book where casework methods and processes are discussed.[46] Similarly, role and other concepts for the analysis of social situations are interlarded with an otherwise conventional psychoanalytic approach to casework in Florence Hollis' *Casework: A Psychosocial Therapy*, but the author seems to regard the sociological concepts essentially as a set of new labels for certain psychological concepts.[47] Dr. Hollis concludes that the latter are more useful, thereby missing the point that these sociological concepts were designed for and permit a different *kind* of analysis than is possible with psychological concepts. Even though, as these two examples indicate, efforts have been made to "put the social back into social casework," a genuine and fully integrated psychosocial casework theory has yet to be formulated. Recent calls for caseworkers to perform advocacy, social broker, and other socially directed functions may presage the development of new methods for social intervention by caseworkers.[48]

EXISTENTIALISM

Anything that affects psychoanalysis is bound, sooner or later, to affect social casework because of the long dependence of the latter on the former. In recent years, existentialism, or *Daseinanalysis,* has become a major movement within psychoanalysis. The leaders of this movement, notably Boss,[49] May,[50] and others, have made a determined effort to contain the movement within the mainstream of psychoanalysis. These efforts have been relatively successful, even though the existentialists have been critical of certain aspects of traditional psychoanalytic thought.

As its exponents frequently have emphasized, the existential movement is an orientation and an ideology, not a new theory of personality or therapy. The central tenets of this orientation—not to be confused with existential philosophy—are relatively simple, even though the terminology used is vague and the precise implications of these tenets for the therapist are not clear.

Such an orientation favors, first of all, a radical subjectivism: the true meaning of an experience is to be found only in its unique meaning to the individual. Thus, for example, accurate interpretations in psychotherapy cannot be derived from theory but can only be built up from an understanding of the specific, idiosyncratic existential meaning to the patient of the experience being interpreted. The existential orientation emphasizes the present and the future and is critical of previous inattention to these time perspectives in psychoanalysis. It relies heavily on the notions of "being," "becoming," and related concepts, the essential point being that personality is viewed as a continuously emergent process—much as it is conceived in other self theories, such as those of Carl Rogers [51] and Otto Rank, for to the extent that the existential orientation implies a theory of personality it is a self theory.

The preoccupations of the existential therapists are personal identity, isolation, and alienation. They emphasize personal choice and individual responsibility, but in their insistence on the personal, subjective character of values and morality, they deemphasize and perhaps even, as London has argued, undermine the notion of social responsibility.[52]

The ideology of this movement is stridently antiscientific, in terms of the accepted meaning of science, although the existentialists would like to redefine science to fit their purposes and their conception of knowledge.

Although the existential movement has attracted the attention of many caseworker practitioners, this orientation has not yet found much expression in the casework literature.[53] It seems likely that it will have an increasing influence on social casework, if for no other reason than its close connections with psychoanalysis. Yet its influence probably never will be dominant, because its antiscientism, undeveloped conceptual framework, lack of an articulated theory of treatment, and deemphasis on social responsibility militate against use of the orientation as a base for an adequate theory of social casework. Its introduction into casework is ironic in the sense that it represents a reappearance of some of the central ideas in Rankian casework, but expressed in different terms and promulgated under the legitimacy of psychoanalysis.

LEARNING THEORY AND BEHAVIORAL THERAPY

Currently looming into view in casework is a school of thought that already has had a profound impact on clinical psychology and psychiatry. This school of thought, to which the rubric "behavior modification" has been applied, represents an effort to apply experimentally derived theories and principles of learning to clinical practice. Remarkably successful results have been rigorously documented for a wide range of clinical problems.[54]

The behavior therapists view human behavior as learned responses, which can be modified by altering both stimuli and the rewards and punishments that follow the person's behavior. Rejected is the psychoanalytic assumption that symptoms are sustained by unconscious conflicts that will seek other forms of expression if the symptom is removed. For the behavior therapist, the "symptom" is not different from other behavior—its removal simply means that the person no longer evinces the behavior some call a "symptom."

Therapy, for the behavior therapists, is essentially to specify precisely the behaviors to be extinguished, modified, or acquired and then to apply relevant principles of behavior modification to bring these specified changes about. The therapeutic task is not, however, as simple as this brief description of it may imply. The application of behavior-modification principles to change complex sets of behaviors—as compared to single symptoms—is not a simple task. Behavioral therapy appears, nevertheless, to be an extremely promising development for social casework, and for that reason we will have more to say about it in later chapters. One of the most promising features of this school of thought is that its conceptualization of the task and process of therapy is much more amenable to rigorous investigation than are those of any other theory of therapy. The long-range implications of this advantage are obvious since research is essential to the development and improvement of any system of treatment. In fact, more systematic research already has been conducted on behavioral therapy and the theories on which it is based than on any other theory of treatment.[55]

PROSPECTS FOR THE FUTURE

Casework's long and heavy dependence on psychoanalytic thought is evident in the preceding discussion of the views that have informed casework theory. It seems clear, however, that the dominance of psychoanalytic theory is waning and in the future will at least have to coexist with alternative theories of behavior and treatment. In our view, this state of affairs will be beneficial for casework in the long run, although it means that caseworkers will have to learn to live with greater uncertainty and to accept greater individual responsibility for the theories they follow than has been the case in the past when it was assumed that one theory and one method were sufficient.

As casework enters an era in which it is confronted with an array of different theories that can be drawn upon to inform and shape casework practice, it needs to give careful thought to how it should relate itself to these bodies of knowledge if it is to avoid the problems associated with excessive dependence on schools of thought developed in other disciplines. Three broad courses of action are open to the profession. One is to continue to import schools of thought *in toto*. This would mean that in the future there would be, for example, existential caseworkers and behaviorally oriented caseworkers, just as now there are psychoanalytically oriented caseworkers. This course could be defended on the ground that the profession could fully explore and exploit the utility of each school of thought for casework. But such a path has obvious hazards, including perpetuation and extension of the kind of dependent relationship casework has had with psychoanalysis for the past thirty to forty years. A second course would be to encourage an unrestrained eclecticism in which caseworkers would be expected to draw freely and selectively from the range of theories available, with the responsibility placed on each caseworker to reach his own integration of these materials. And a third course is for casework to examine the tasks and realities confronting practitioners and to begin the laborious effort of *developing* theories suited to those tasks and realities. In this effort, casework still would draw widely and heavily from knowl-

edge developed elsewhere, but the knowledge imported would be selected and evaluated in light of an explicit conception of the mission
and tasks of the casework enterprise.

We favor the third strategy, primarily because it puts casework in
charge of the shape and content of its knowledge base and does not del-
egate this responsibility to other disciplines. To some extent, the concerns of caseworkers do overlap with those of related professions and
disciplines, and yet in other central respects caseworkers have concerns
not shared to any considerable extent with other professions. In these
latter areas, caseworkers can expect no one but themselves to develop
the knowledge and methods needed by the profession. We are calling,
then, for casework to conduct a frank examination of the realities that
characterize casework practice and to consider the implications of these
realities for current casework theory and for the kinds of knowledge
and methods needed by the practicing caseworker. This book represents, in part, a beginning effort in this direction.

CHAPTER FOUR

THE SCIENTIFIC METHOD
IN CASEWORK PRACTICE

It is important to note that a commitment to the scientific method is a value premise of social work. There are many conceivable avenues toward the accumulation of knowledge and, in the span of mankind, the method of science is a relative latecomer to the roster of alternatives. Thus, one may argue that a precise knowledge of man and his universe can best be obtained through divine revelation, or through the authority and tradition of society, or through common sense and intuition.[1]

The choice of which alternative is more rewarding is, in the final analysis, a value judgment, although rational arguments can be presented in support of the method of science as the most productive and potent. Appeal to rational argument is, in itself, a partial commitment to science, as is the basic premise that knowledge is valuable.

The foundation for a belief in the scientific method, then, is two premises: first, that knowledge is valuable and worthy of discovery and second, that rational procedures are the most productive for the accumulation of knowledge. Social casework, by virtue of its claim to professionalism, has incorporated these two premises. To the extent that the caseworker is forever engaged in serving his client well, he is also engaged in an unceasing quest for new knowledge that will enable him to understand his client and perfect his techniques. Further, the very fact that the profession has singled out education and supervision as vehicles for the improvement of practice implies a commitment to rational procedures. The caseworker does not go to a priest or a sacred text for guidance in the proper treatment of his client; he goes to a *teacher*.

It is probably unnecessary, in this day of the laboratory and the scientist, to belabor the point that social casework and social work rest on a belief in and commitment to the scientific method. In the hierarchy of social casework's value system, this belief ranks on a par with the fundamental value premise: the worth and dignity of the individual human being. This being so, social casework is immediately set apart from a large variety of endeavors that fall under the rubric of ameliorative therapies. Apart from the accepted disciplines of psychiatry, psychology, and social work, there are many different kinds of practitioners involved in working with distressed people. Astrologers are not quaint memories of an ignorant past—they abound today, in twentieth-century America, as do palmists, faith healers, fortune tellers, wizards, and other kindred souls.* Social caseworkers cannot take comfort in a belief that they are more efficacious in the treatment of clients than these "peculiar" therapists; indeed, in later chapters we will show that the astrologer and witch probably serve their clients as effectively as do the psychiatrist, psychologist, and caseworker. Further, it is possible to conceive of wizards and fortune tellers who are deeply committed to the worth and dignity of the individual; these people are not necessarily hard-hearted charlatans and gougers of the ignorant.[2] The professional caseworker can be differentiated from the aforementioned healers, in part, by virtue of his commitment to a method of inquiry and a means for improving his practice. Thus, although techniques may, at root, be similar, although goals and objectives may be identical, and a frame of mind toward the client may be the same—and, for the moment at least,

---

* Young people today are only newcomers to the fascination with astrology and the casting of horoscopes and the Tarot. In most newspapers throughout the land can be found classified advertisements that hawk the "therapeutic" skills of many diverse types. One such example from the Pittsburgh *Courier* (June 15, 1966) reads as follows:

YES FRIENDS
Contact this man, get what you want. If trouble seems to stand in your way, let me help you. . . . I will bring happiness into your home with money in your hand. No matter what trouble you are having, I will remove it in 3 days. If you have a cross condition or a money problem or want your loved one back, call me at once.

even results may be pretty much the same—an attitude toward the nature of his knowledge and his technique sets the caseworker apart from his more "unenlightened" therapeutic brethren.

The belief in the method of science carries with it certain implications and concomitants that further define the nature of this "attitude." The social caseworker, like the scientist, must be skeptical of his knowledge and procedures. Theory, even within the so-called "hard" sciences, is always partial, tentative, and subject to revision. Social work knowledge is seen by the professional as temporary, and techniques, to the extent that they follow from knowledge, are always being supplanted by new and different ones. Skepticism toward existing procedures and an open-mindedness toward new conceptions, then, become the hallmarks of the social caseworker. For him, there is no inviolable therapeutic regimen or sacred text; there is only an incessant and chronic uncertainty coupled with a humility in the face of an infinite ignorance, even if such a frame of mind, which is a necessary consequence of a commitment to scientific method, is not without its difficulties.

A subscription to the method of science carries with it not only an attitude of mind but a commitment to a methodology of inquiry. Many books have been written on science's philosophy of methodology.[3] Suffice it to say that there have been formulated certain canons of logic and proof that enable an observer to reach conclusions as to the relationships among a series of variables. Stripped of their precise phraseology and mathematical symbolism, such canons can be thought of as disciplined and rigorous thought processes that, again, are the hallmarks of the truly professional caseworker.

Stemming from the tradition of science is the paradigm of observation-hypothesis-experiment. This model is analogous to the traditional social casework formula of study, diagnosis, and treatment. A social study is merely a special instance of careful observation on the basis of which certain hypotheses (diagnoses) are formulated. The diagnostic assessment is put to test during the course of treatment. To the extent that the therapeutic laboratory casts doubt on the diagnostic formulation or hypotheses, the latter is revised and put to the test again. Thus, in outline, the model of study, diagnosis, and treatment becomes, for every caseworker, similar to the operations undertaken by any scientist who attempts the solution of a problem.

To this extent any dichotomy between research and practice is false. Some have felt that, in some way, clinical practice and clinical research are separate if not antithetical endeavors.[4] In part, this conception arises from a mistaken equation drawn between "true" research and methodological sophistication. Modern social research is, indeed, enhanced by the development of a growing methodology and, to the uninitiated, a mysterious statistical apparatus. But, Chi squares and correlation coefficients are merely devices that are handy and useful. They are not to be confused with sound research, which, when stripped of its methodological surplusage, is primarily logical and penetrating thinking. Every clinician, to the extent that he subscribes to the value of scientific method, is a researcher and any dichotomy between research and clinical practice is thus artificial.

Finally, the commitment to the method of science requires that one's professional thought and work be made open to examination within a professional arena. New theory and new techniques are of no value if such developments perish with their creators. The accumulation of knowledge is not a private effort, and a professional ethic demands that such accretions become part of the public domain. Further, practice must be open to the scrutiny of colleagues in order to get new perspectives and in order for "error" to be corrected and brought to light. In summary, skepticism, open-mindedness, critical thought, writing, talking, and an incessant scrutiny of one's practice are the necessary and inevitable by-products of the scientific method. Indeed, they serve to define it.

Although the above attitude is necessary for *any* professional who subscribes to the scientific method, it is particularly vital for the social caseworker. Social casework is a relatively young profession that is characterized by an inimitable lack of knowledge and technical imprecision. Thus it is that the question so often raised by beginning students and laymen, "But what is casework anyway?" causes so much embarrassment and even annoyance to practitioners and educators. Casework is, in fact, hard to define, and it is hard to define simply because it is a nonspecific, amorphous endeavor. Casework is many things at the same time, and what it is depends upon many different variables, the most important of which is the person who is constructing the definition.

That the definition of an allegedly professional activity is contingent upon what is essentially the *opinion* of individual practitioners says a great deal about the state of its technical maturity. If there were a consensus there would be no problem, but alas, there is no consensus. One might prefer to define casework not in terms of what practitioners *say* it is but in terms of what practitioners actually *do*. But the same result arises with this criterion—different caseworkers do different things.

It is also true that whatever casework is, it is changing. There is a veritable explosion of new conceptions and techniques within the field of casework—and the extent and confines of this movement cannot yet be predicted. Indeed, it is probably true that an ever-accelerating rate of change will be with the profession for many decades to come. The professional method of casework is amorphous and imprecise and is changing in the direction of becoming more diverse. This state of affairs was not as acute a relatively short while ago. There was an era—and a comfortable era at that—when social casework was predicated upon the theoretical base of psychoanalytic theory. This base was viable not so much because it was true but because it seemed to be *more* true than other available conceptions. One could then propound a casework theory; it was never clear-cut or easily identified, but it was a relatively realistic endeavor. This is no longer possible. The fact is that there are presently viable alternatives to psychoanalytically oriented casework that cannot be ignored. The trouble is that of competition, and the competition, in some instances, comes from reasonable, well thought out, and *empirically derived* alternatives. The above considerations are equally applicable to all professional disciplines that are predicated upon the one-to-one relationship. Psychiatry and psychology are also becoming more diverse and ambiguous, and these professions are agonizing about their knowledge base as much as we are.

The major thrust of the above argument is that casework can be characterized more easily by its uncertainties than by its certainties. In summary, what is its state?

1. A growing awareness that casework predicated upon the psychoanalytic method has yet to demonstrate its effectiveness.[5]

2. A proliferation of alternative treatment models that are generating great interest in the field of psychotherapy and that are based on

fundamentally *different* premises than is the psychoanalytic model. (In this connection it is only fair to note that none of these alternative approaches has satisfactorily demonstrated a *superior* effectiveness.) [6]

3. A proliferation of alternative treatment models that go beyond the one-to-one relationship. (We need only take note in this regard of a multitude of family and group therapies that increases in number with each passing year.)

4. A growing awareness that the value base of social casework can generate dilemmas and paradoxes for the professional that are not easily resolved. [7]

5. A rethinking of the place of social welfare in American society, of social work within social welfare, and of casework within social work. [8]

6. A reconsideration of the ultimate objectives of casework practice—what do we want to accomplish with our clients and what is proper for us to want to accomplish. [9]

7. A proliferation of bits and pieces of "hard" and "soft" knowledge that is presently fragmented and disjointed and that comes from a host of professional and academic disciplines.

It is our contention that the above dimensions characterize the present nature of casework knowledge and will continue to characterize it.

The uncertainty that adheres to social casework generates a difficult condition for the practitioner, and this difficulty can be outlined by the following questions: How can one doubt one's effectiveness and still be effective? And how can a professional induce a feeling of confidence in his client while remaining unconfident about what he knows? When a professional is faced with the necessity of communicating an aura of expertise to his client, while at the same time he is cognizant of his own ignorance, indeed, of his own lack of expertise, a paradox obtains. The paradox cannot be resolved unless a commitment to the scientific method is a basic part of the professional's equipment. In that event, he can say to himself, in effect: "I will try everything I know to help my client. I am too ignorant to truly know which way is best, but I will think carefully about my procedures. I will not be blinded by preconceptions. I will draw upon every bit of knowledge that is available, and this becomes my solemn credo in regard to my client. Thus, if I fail, I and my client can take solace in the fact that everything possible, within the content of our present state of knowledge, has been done." Such an attitudinal stance, it would seem, should be sufficient to enable the professional to come to terms with his dilemma.

Further problems face the social caseworker as he incorporates the scientific attitude into his value system. These problems revolve around what may be termed the "science-art" dimension of psychotherapeutic acitivity. A good deal has been written in this regard.[10] Essentially, the problem can evolve from either of two different assumptions:

1. Since so little is actually known about human behavior and means for its change, the caseworker must fall back upon some intuitive "artistry" in his therapeutic manipulations. The therapeutic interchange is extremely complex, and we do not yet know in detail what these complexities entail. Thus, in the absence of precise knowledge, the caseworker functions as an artist in that he proceeds, by and large, through his creative instinct and intuition.

This assumption is implicitly a provisional operating premise. Caseworkes are artists because they do not *yet* have the precise knowledge to be otherwise. In time such knowledge will be available and the amount of artistry contained in the casework process will diminish until it will vanish altogether (the millennium). The second assumption is different.

2. Human behavior is, at heart, unknowable and therefore science will *never* be able to explicate fully the mystery of human functioning and change. Thus, although science can make some contributions to the understanding of life, these will always be peripheral. Man and his behavior will forever be an unpredictable and mysterious phenomenon.

This second premise is, of course, not at all temporally bound. The therapist is not merely an artist because of historical accident, he must always be so by virtue of the inherent nature of man.

These two assumptions emanate from completely divergent beliefs as to the knowability of man and the ultimate predictability of his behavior. Depending upon which belief is held, therapeutic activity may take on important colorings. On the second assumption, the paradigm of study, diagnosis, and treatment becomes quite irrelevant. To the extent that man is unknowable and his behavior unpredictable, diagnostic formulations are logical absurdities, and treatment activities flowing from such formulations compound the absurdity. Indeed, one of the fundamental differences between the so-called diagnostic school of thought in social casework and the functional school revolves around this issue.

The diagnostic school, premised on the explicit determinism of Freudian psychology, holds that man is preeminently a predictable organism. His behavior follows lawful processes, and no facet of it can be attributed to random or capricious events. The diagnostic procedure then becomes crucial and has direct ramifications, in principle at least, for a regimen of treatment. Functional casework, on the other hand, is oriented toward Rankian psychology with its direct renunciation of this view of man and the explicative role of science. The flavor of functional casework is well illustrated by Jessie Taft, who writes:

Intellectualized organization of the therapeutic experience must take place after the fact. The therapeutic value of the hour lies in its immediacy and spontaneity, but the spontaneity of the therapist must of necessity be unfailingly oriented and re-oriented with reference to the patient, as the central and dominating figure of the relationship, with a prior, never to be forgotten claim. Which is one reason, perhaps the reason, why therapy is non-scientific, and the therapeutic relationship not open to research at the moment.[11]

In discussing how change comes about through therapy, Dr. Taft writes:

How is this possible? If one thinks of an exact scientific answer to the question, I must confess that I do not know; that, at bottom, therapy of this kind is a mystery, a magic, something one may know beyond a doubt through repeated experience but which in the last analysis is only observed and interpreted after the fact, never comprehended in itself or controlled scientifically any more than the life process is comprehended and controlled.[12]

Thus, Taft and the functionalists reject the method of science as a component of the professional therapeutic equipment, and this exclusion creates a radically different atmosphere within which their therapy is practiced. Treatment becomes an act of spontaneous creation and diagnosis an exercise in futility.

The science-art dilemma can thus yield two markedly different approaches to the casework endeavor. But there are yet further complications.

A commitment to the method of science involves a commitment to the construction of theory. Theory, in turn, implies classification—the identification of commonalities among individuals so that they can be cast into classes. How is this process of theory building to occur within a philosophical context that pays homage to the uniqueness of man? As Eaton has suggested, to the extent that all men are like all other men, the construction of theory can occur. To the extent that a given man is like no other man, the predictable (or scientific) aspects of casework endeavor must give way. Just as theory building is caught in this bind of commonality vs. uniqueness, so too is the prerequisite of theory construction—research investigation. Empirical research, by its very nature, requires an a priori theoretical simplification. All the relevant variables in a given behavioral phenomenon cannot be examined at once. Thus simplification, which includes selection, control, and even simulation, may result in distortion of what is probably an extremely complex event. The profession of social work would maintain, and rightfully so, that human behavior and therapy are extremely complicated phenomena, and in the process of investigating these events the empirical model does not do justice to their complexity and gives rise to conclusions that are artificial and unreal.

Thus, a commitment to the method of science with its concomitants of empirical research and the elaboration of theory comes face to face with an ethic that, in part, claims man is unique and with a reality that holds that the nature of the study problem is awesomely complex. But these considerations do not exhaust the paradox for social casework vis à vis the scientific method. A large segment of able casework practitioners would maintain that the spontaneity of the clinician is an essential ingredient in the process of casework. How is this factor of spontaneity to be reconciled with the notion of careful case planning? Further, "the third ear" of the clinician is thought by some to be a basic part of the effective caseworker's equipment. How is this to be reconciled with the controlled and thoughtful observation demanded by the logic of scientific procedures?

These dimensions of the rather paradoxical relationship between scientific method and the realities of clinical practice can be elaborated endlessly. But perhaps the point at issue has been sufficiently illustrated. A commitment to the method of science carries with it certain philosophical and clinical dilemmas. Many of these can be subsumed under the rubric of the science-art dimension and can be discussed and rediscussed in terms of a variety of polarities: determinism vs. free-will; case planning vs. "spontaneity"; controlled observation vs. "the third ear"; Freud vs. Rank; the diagnostic school vs. the functional school; theory building vs. the uniqueness of man; the complexity of the process vs. the need to simplify it for empirical investigation.

In some instances these issues may be rather remote from the demands of the day-to-day casework practice, but more often than not they become very real and vital in that a stand on a given issue sets in motion an entire series of attitudes toward practice and procedures within practice. They become immediate and real concerns for the clinician. Throughout this volume we will have occasion to return to these problems and illustrate what practical consequences follow from given positions in regard to them.

Well, what of the science-art paradox? Is social casework an art or a science? It is too simple to say it is, of course, both a science and an art. Casework's ultimate character, in this regard, depends upon a prior question—is man basically a knowable organism? Clearly, there is no answer to this question; perhaps there may never be one. But in the meantime, on what premise is the caseworker to proceed? To the extent that we adhere to the values inherent in a commitment to the method of science and to the extent that we hold as an overriding ethic the improvement of the quality of our services, we must assume that man is knowable and that the casework procedure will become primarily scientific. By doing so, all aspects of our work become open to study— nothing is closed on a priori grounds as unknowable. And, by doing so, we may learn something of what we are about.

PART II

Social Casework Practice

CHAPTER FIVE

REALITIES AND EMERGENT TASKS
IN CASEWORK PRACTICE

The mission of the social caseworker, as we view it, is to help individuals and families make desired changes in their lives through the application of knowledge and skills in a manner consistent with the values and objectives of social work. In this the caseworker is influenced by certain circumstances inherent in the practice situation, circumstances that shape and constrain his activities and sometimes even threaten to subvert his aims.

Two sets of realities in the situation of practice pose especially critical and perplexing problems for the caseworker. The first consists of certain characteristics of the clientele served by caseworkers. A second set of problems stems from the fact that most caseworkers practice in bureaucracies. Any attempt to develop an adequate formulation of social casework must not only take these realities into account but must, in fact, include careful examination of them.

With some exceptions, however, much of the literature in social casework is written as if many of these factors do not exist, or as if they are contingencies that do not affect casework practice in any fundamental way. Thus, for example, the advocates of "generic" casework have argued that the casework *method* is not affected fundamentally by the agency setting or the client group served.* We believe that the useful-

* For example, even though Perlman gives prominent attention to "place" (her term for agency setting) in her discussion of casework, she argues that the basic

ness of such a view, which ignores basic realities confronting casework-ers is significantly limited.

THE SITUATION OF PRACTICE IN SOCIAL CASEWORK

The typical setting for social casework is an institution, be it a public or private organization. Here a client (an individual, or one or more persons in a family) and a social worker interact with each other within an organizational context. Thus, there are three principal actors, or sets of actors, in the casework situation: the *client,* the *caseworker,* and an organization, the *agency.* Each of these influences the casework process in significant ways, and it is therefore important to examine their general characteristics.

SOCIAL CASEWORKERS AND CLIENTS

Who are the clients of social caseworkers? This is a difficult question to answer, for two principal reasons. First, consensus is lacking about who deserves to be called a social caseworker. Is the designation to be restricted to persons possessing a master's degree in social work, or should it include all persons who function as social caseworkers, regardless of the amount of formal professional education they have received? In practical terms, this question is a matter of deciding whether to include or exclude the comparatively large number of social workers performing direct service functions in public assistance and corrections programs, since the proportion of social workers without master's degrees in other social welfare programs is negligible. This issue, posed in different terms, was debated without resolution for many years, but now there are signs that a consensus may be emerging, as seen in the recent action by the National Association of Social Workers (NASW) extending membership to person's without the master's degree,[1] in the increasing efforts directed to in-service training (training on the job) in social welfare programs,[2] and in attempts to induce trained social workers to enter public welfare and corrections.[3] Setting aside the problem of dis-

---

method of casework (which she conceives to be a "problem-solving process") is fundamentally an invariant process with respect to "place," "person," and, for that matter, "problem." Helen H. Perlman, *Social Casework: A Problem Solving Process* (Chicago, University of Chicago Press, 1957).

tinguishing between professional and subprofessional responsibilities in these (and, for that matter, *all*) fields of practice,[4] one notices that there are social casework functions to be performed in these programs, and consequently that the conditions of practice found in these fields must be taken into account in formulations of casework theory and practice.

The second obstacle in the way of obtaining a precise description of the clients of social caseworkers is the lack of adequate statistics regarding the number and characteristics of the client groups in different fields of practice. This is a serious obstruction, especially if we are justified in claiming that casework theory must start from an analysis of the clientele served. It is possible, however, to approach the question another way, by asking what assumptions about clients are evident in theories of casework and then considering whether these assumptions are empirically valid.

In much of the casework literature, the typical client is assumed to be: (1) an individual, who (2) brings himself to the agency, (3) asks, directly or indirectly, for help with psychological problems and not simply for concrete services, (4) meets with a caseworker in counseling sessions over an extended period of time, and (5) seeks and continues in casework treatment voluntarily, so that his continuance or discontinuance in casework can be construed as an indicator of motivation for casework treatment.

Although these assumptions are central to the foundations of most major casework theories, the empirical evidence suggests that they apply to no more than a small fraction of the clients seen by caseworkers! An examination of each of these assumptions in light of some of the relevant evidence will illustrate this point.

Clients are individual persons. Most of the casework literature is written as if the object of casework treatment is an individual person, not a family group, a marriage,* or some other social unit. To be sure,

---

* As one example, in *Scope and Methods of the Family Service Agency* (New York, Family Service Association of America, 1953), which had wide acceptance as a statement of casework practice, it is assumed throughout the text that casework interviews are conducted only with individuals, and the treatment classification given in this monograph is applicable only to individuals. The same observations can be made about Perlman's *Social Casework: A Problem Solving Process* and Florence Hollis' *Casework: A Psychosocial Therapy* (New York, Random House, 1964), but it is especially striking that this should be true of a document addressed to settings called *family* service agencies.

the caseworker always works only with persons; moreover, many of the clients of social caseworkers are individual persons (either unattached individuals or members of family groups) in the sense that they present themselves to the caseworker as individuals with individual, personal problems. The point is, however, that in many other instances the client who appears is a family group, a married couple, or a mother-father-child triangle. But there is a more important issue here than the simple fact that many clients do not arrive singly: how is it decided who the client is? This question is important because it matters—in the sense that the decision has real consequences in treatment—whether the caseworker takes as the object of his attention an individual, a family group, or some other social unit. The usual approach has been, however, to assume that all clients either are individual persons or—in the case of some advocates of family treatment—family groups, with the result that, in the former case, all problems are reduced to individual treatment problems or, in the family approach, all problems are construed to be manifestations of disturbances in the family group. Neither approach can be appropriate for all clients in all practice settings. An approach more consistent with the realities of the practice situation, one that we discuss in more detail elsewhere in this volume, is to view the answer to the question "who is the client" as a range of alternatives to be selected on the basis of professional judgment.[5]

The client brings himself to the agency. Many clients seek out the agency on their own initiative, but many others—possibly a larger number in fact—do not. Large numbers of clients—in the corrections field, for example—initially go to see the caseworker because they are required to do so.* That clients do get to caseworkers in a variety of ways has two related implications. First, and most important, casework theory cannot be predicated on a treatment model that requires, explicitly or implicitly, clients who seek help on their own initiative. Second, to the extent that casework theory is predicated on such a model, its applicability might be limited to clients who meet this requirement.

Clients seek help with psychological problems. Just as clients come to caseworkers by a variety of pathways, so do they vary in what they

---

* In 1965, for example, the average daily population in all corrections agencies in the United States was 2,239,000. *Statistical Abstract of the United States, 1968* (Washington D.C., U.S. Department of Commerce, Bureau of Census, 1968).

want or expect from the caseworker. To decide in advance what clients seek—for example, to assume that a request for financial aid or homemaker service masks a desire for help with psychological or family problems—increases the risk of alienating the client. As a variety of studies have shown, if there is a discrepancy between what the client wants and what the caseworker believes he wants (or *should* want), the client is likely to drop out of treatment.[6] Briar found that most AFDC applicants interviewed went to the welfare agency seeking financial aid and nothing more.[7] The intake workers, on the other hand, operating on a broader conception of their own role, made considerable inquiries designed to provide them with a diagnostic picture of the case as a whole. One consequence of these discrepant expectations was that clients regarded many of the worker's questions as irrelevant—sometimes irritatingly so—to the kind of help they were seeking. Thus it is possible to claim that this assumption is valid only for some clients, and if the caseworker errs in his perceptions of the client's expectations the error may have undesirable consequences. There is some evidence that caseworkers prefer dealing with clients who ask for help with social-psychological problems and disdain providing help of an allegedly more mundane nature.*

Clients continue in casework over extended periods of time. Among the assumptions identified above, this is perhaps the most pervasive and least accurate. The fact is that in the settings with reference to which the central stream of casework theory has been developed and elaborated—namely the voluntary family agency and the psychiatric clinic—only a small proportion of the clients continue in treatment for more than a few interviews.[8] And yet, traditional theory conceives of casework treatment as a process extending over a period of several months, at the very least.† In assuming that casework treatment is an

* Note, for example, that in many schools of social work more students prefer field placements in psychiatric settings than in other fields of practice. While some students voice this preference before they enter graduate school, many do not develop a preference until after they enter the program, which at least suggests that these preferences are acquired from exposure to the culture of the schools and the profession. See *Statistics on Social Work Education* (New York, Council on Social Work Education), published annually.

† For example, a review of three major works—Gordon Hamilton, *Theory and Practice of Social Case Work* (New York, Columbia University Press, 1951);

extended process, casework theorists have adopted and elaborated a treatment model that—according to some statistics—is applicable to not more than one-fourth of the persons applying for help in "voluntary" agencies. Accordingly, concern about the remaining three-fourths, the clients who discontinue treatment prematurely, has tended to focus on finding ways of getting them to remain longer in treatment, rather than, for example, on developing methods for briefer treatment. To be sure, some efforts are being made to develop such methods,[9] but for the most part these have been considered experimental; they have been advocated as a means of alleviating specific problems—for example, long waiting lists—rather than as a response to the fact that a large proportion of clients are not disposed to continue in treatment for more than a few interviews. Furthermore, they have not been viewed as a viable and adequate alternative to long-term treatment but more as "first-aid." Continued adherence to the assumption that an extended time period is a necessary condition for successful casework treatment is all the more striking in view of (1) the results of the Community Service Society follow-up study,[10] which showed that outcome was unrelated both to duration of treatment and to whether termination was planned or unplanned, and (2) the impressive results reported for some extremely abbreviated treatment approaches, results that compare favorably with studies of the results of long-term treatment methods.[11]

Client continuance in treatment is voluntary and reflects client motivation. This assumption reflects a belief, as expressed by Hollis, that "the truth . . . is that it is not only inadvisable but impossible to impose treatment upon a client." [12] Clearly, if it is "impossible" to impose treatment on a client, and if treatment is administered and the client uses it, then he must be doing so because he wants and is motivated for it. Unfortunately, this assumption is untenable for a variety of reasons.

Hollis, *Casework: A Psychosocial Therapy;* and Perlman, *Social Casework: A Problem Solving Process*—in relation to this point reveals that although specific references to the usual duration of treatment are rare or nonexistent, the assumption is that casework treatment extends over several months, at least. Hollis, for example, describes six cases as illustrations of casework treatment (pp. 33–49, 246, 264). In three of the cases, treatment lasted from one to five years; although precise information about duration of treatment is not given for the other three cases, it is clear that they were carried for at least several months.

For one thing, as noted earlier, a large proportion of the persons seen by caseworkers are "captive" or involuntary clients. One may argue that the public-assistance recipient can refuse the caseworker's help, but to say that this is a "free" choice or that the choice to use the worker's help reflects a desire for help is to ignore the fact that many recipients feel refusal would jeopardize their assistance grants. Nor is the state of affairs regarding client choice in voluntary settings clear-cut and simple, as social workers are coming to realize. In a passage immediately preceding the one quoted earlier in this paragraph, Hollis notes:

It is the agencies that make the choices, deciding what services to offer, and what constitutes eligibility for them. A client is not given a foster home for a child just because he wants one, nor is he allowed to choose the type of foster home his child is placed in, *any more than he can decide that he should be given financial assistance.* Certainly, it is not up to him to determine whether his superego needs strengthening or liberalizing, or whether he should be helped to see his children's needs more clearly or should work on the question of why, even though he does see them clearly, he cannot put the understanding he already has of them into constructive action [italics supplied].[13]

Thus, for example, if a man goes to a family service agency seeking homemaker service and learns that homemaker service is given only as part of a total casework treatment plan, it is naïve to conclude that his decision to accept casework treatment invariably represents a free choice based on his desire for treatment. Of course, it can be argued that while such a client might go through the motions of accepting treatment simply in order to obtain homemaker services, his motivation (or lack of it) would be indicated by his "use" of treatment: he will use (i.e., respond favorably to) treatment only if he is motivated to use it. Here we return to the assumption that people will respond to (i.e., be affected or changed by) treatment only if they want to be. But this version of the assumption is not persuasive either, for persons can be induced to change even when they are not motivated or do not want to change.

Caseworkers also recognize—although usually the recognition is implicit—that persons can be induced to change even when they lack a desire to change. To cite Hollis once again: ". . . no treatment can be successful if the client lacks *motivation* to use it. Motivation sometimes exists spontaneously in the client. At other times, the *creation of moti-vation* [italics supplied] becomes an early task of treatment during the exploratory period." [14] To "create" motivation where it did not exist before is to change people in the absence of motivation to change.* To put social work theory on a sounder footing, it would seem preferable to recognize the fact that people can be changed even when they do not will it—that people can be manipulated—and to question the utility of self-determination as a practice principle, since the concept, as currently defined, is too much subject to interpretation to serve as a reliable guide for practice.

ORIGINS OF THESE ASSUMPTIONS ABOUT
THE CASEWORKER'S CLIENTELE

What accounts for the emergence and persistence of a set of as-sumptions about the clients of social caseworkers that are not consistent with the realities of casework practice? The principal and most immedi-ate source of these assumptions is not difficult to identify, namely the field of psychotherapy and, historically and in particular, psychoanalyt-ically oriented psychotherapy. For, as the reader already may have noted, these same assumptions also pervade the literature and practice of psychotherapy, but with one crucial difference: by and large, these assumptions *are* consistent with the realities of the practice situation in psychotherapy. That is, the psychotherapist—in private practice and even in public psychiatric clinics—can and does selectively *limit* his practice to individuals who voluntarily come for treatment with psycho-logical problems and who are disposed to continue in psychotherapy for extended periods of time. Unlike the psychotherapist, however, the caseworker, at least in many social agencies (e.g., public welfare and corrections), is not free to select his clientele according to these criteria, because the agency is required to accept all clients entitled to its ser-vices, regardless of their motivation for and understanding of casework services. In agencies where caseworkers have been able to exercise dis-

* Steiper and Wiener—Donald R. Steiper and Daniel N. Wiener, *Dimensions of Psychotherapy* (Chicago, Aldine, 1965), p. 123—have argued that: ". . . in an effort to view this problem freshly . . . we consider the essence of psychotherapy to be the task of changing motivation from *weak* to strong relative to rationally conceived goals. The most vital test of the therapist then becomes his skill in so shaping or modifying motivation."

cretion in the selection of clients (e.g., private family service agencies), it has been claimed that the workers tend to select clients who fit the psychoanalytically oriented treatment model and to exclude groups of persons who do not satisfy these requirements, including notably the poor.[15] In any event, it is clear that further elaboration and refinement of a treatment model carrying the assumptions identified above cannot be expected to yield approaches that will help clients for whom these assumptions are inapplicable. Since caseworkers cannot and should not ignore persons in need of help simply because they do not fit existing conceptions of treatment, efforts must be made to develop different methods of treatment based on assumptions that do not require people to change before they can be helped. It may be that as some psychotherapists become more concerned with persons they have not reached in the past, they will modify their procedures in ways that also will offer new possibilities for caseworkers. However, it is likely that the primary responsibility for developing more appropriate and effective methods for casework practice will have to be carried by caseworkers themselves.

THE ORGANIZATIONAL CONTEXT OF
CASEWORK PRACTICE

With minor exceptions,* social caseworkers practice in bureaucratic organizations, and this is another important element that must be taken into account in casework theory. The sometimes profound influence of organizational factors on professionals, clients, and the conduct of treatment in *institutional* settings have become well known through studies such as Stanton and Schwartz's *The Mental Hospital.*[16] That some of the same influences operate in noninstitutional settings—such as social agencies and clinics—has not been as widely recognized.

In certain respects the aims of the professional caseworker and the needs of the bureaucracy conflict.[17] One of the essential ingredients of professionalism, as the professional sees it, is freedom to base his judgments and actions on professional knowledge and experience, taking action that varies with the individual case. Yet some of the requirements of bureaucracy, for example, achievement of organizational goals, ad-

---

* The most conspicuous exception is private practice; at present, however, the proportion of caseworkers engaged in private practice is quite small.

ministrative control and accountability, preservation of organizational stability and continuity despite personnel changes, and efficient utilization of the division of labor, make *standardization* of decisions and procedures desirable. Interests of the caseworker and the bureaucracy are not necessarily incompatible. Thus, when a caseworker says with pride that, based on his assessment of what is needed, in his agency he is free to provide intensive service and carry a very small caseload, his statement indicates that work norms in the agency coincide with his conception of professional norms.

But such harmony is by no means universal. In many instances, the conflicts between organizational needs and professional norms are trivial and are experienced by the social worker only as a minor irritation or annoyance, as in the case of a request that he keep a record of his activities for a cost analysis of agency operations. In many other instances, however, organizational demands on the worker seriously threaten workers' professional commitments. In most public welfare departments, for example, social workers must devote considerable time to paper work required by the agency. Since a substantial portion of the administrative rules that keep workers at their desks in public welfare agencies are designed not so much to facilitate service to clients as to serve the need for public accountability and to mollify those segments of the society who believe that welfare clients cannot be trusted, these requirements not only make heavy inroads into the time available to the worker for providing service to clients but they have purposes that run counter to the professionally oriented workers' commitments. A striking example is the practice in many public welfare agencies of instructing caseworkers not to inform recipients about certain benefits and rights to which they are entitled. In one such agency, a worker who violated such instructions was fired on the grounds that his belief that the needs and rights of clients should come first was deemed unprofessional!

In the face of such conflicts, some workers become committed to the agency and its needs, consequently reducing the intensity of their commitment to client interests. Many others leave the agency or, if forewarned, avoid it in favor of settings where such conflicts are less intense or less obvious. This seems to be the preferred solution for professionally trained social workers,[18] and it has the unfortunate consequence of retarding improvement of service in agencies where such improvement is most needed. A few workers attempt to solve such conflicts by openly opposing agency demands—for example, by refusing to follow an order to conduct night raids—thereby creating a public issue and calling attention to the problem. And finally, of course, there are workers who attempt to ameliorate these conflicts by trying to introduce appropriate changes in the organization. Apparently few caseworkers have followed either of the latter two strategies; until recently the predominant attitude toward such issues among practitioners has been to deny or overlook them and to aver that administrative matters are the concern of administrators, not practitioners.

Some of the most pervasive and important influences that organizational needs exert on the situation of practice appear so subtly that practitioners often are unaware of them. The need for consistency in bureaucratic organizations,* for adherence to a common set of policies and procedures, creates a pressure toward uniformity in therapeutic ideology, diagnostic classification, and treatment methodology.[19] Thus, in some agencies diagnostic categories and treatment classifications are formalized, and workers are expected to adhere to these categories in their practice, or at the very least in recording what they do.[20] Although the adoption of uniform treatment norms satisfies certain needs of the agency, and perhaps even certain needs of the social workers in the agency, it hampers the profession by acting as a brake on innovation and experimentation at a time when—in view of the current state of knowledge in the field and the unsatisfactory degree of effectiveness achieved by existing methods of intervention—experimentation is sorely needed. The worker, for example, who attempts family group treatment in an agency where the norms are that definitive treatment can be conducted only in individual interviews runs the risk of being regarded unfavorably by his supervisor and his peers.†

* This arises not only from the organizational needs of bureaucracy but also from the universal tendency of groups to develop norms governing the behavior of their members.

† The omnipresence of supervision, a prominent characteristic of social work practice, is partly a result of the organizational need for administrative control. The supervisory system, however, tends to develop needs of its own, which affect the situation of practice. For example, in a study of case recordings, Frings— John Frings, Ruth Kratovil, and Bernice Polemis, *An Assessment of Social Case Recording* (New York, Family Service Association of America, 1958)—found

It should be noted that since organizational influences affect the *situation* of practice, they impinge not only on the worker but on the client as well (the client role in the organization is discussed more fully in the next chapter).

We have discussed two broad constraints in the situation of practice that are little acknowledged by the social casework theory still predominately employed by caseworkers: (1) the characteristics of the caseworker's clients and (2) the fact that the worker practices in bureaucratic organizations. We can now attempt to outline a framework for social casework that takes these and other often-unacknowledged circumstances of the practice situation into account.

A FRAMEWORK FOR SOCIAL CASEWORK PRACTICE

The task of conceptualizing casework practice can be approached in two fundamentally different ways. One can begin with an already developed theory and then redefine practice in terms of the theory. By and large, this was the approach followed by both the Freudian and the Rankian caseworkers and still is being followed by, for example, those who currently are attempting to reformulate the problems of casework practice in terms of ego psychology as developed by psychoanalysts. A second approach is to begin with the realities of practice—the phenomena and tasks confronting the caseworker—and then to search for those concepts and theories that best fit these realities. Although this was essentially the approach followed by Mary Richmond, it has not been widely used by casework theorists.* Each approach has its own advan-

---

that detailed "process" recording, expected and desired by the supervisory staff, served no clear function for workers or for the agency. Moreover, it was not even clear what function such recordings served for the supervisors, since the recording typically was completed too late for use in supervision. Despite such anomalies and despite studies indicating that the present supervisory system is implicated in social agency morale problems, it is striking that no systematic, empirical study of the supervisory system in social work has been conducted. William Tollen, *Study of Staff Losses,* Child Welfare and Family Service Agencies, Children's Bureau Publication No. 383 (Washington D.C., U.S. Department of Health, Education and Welfare Children's Bureau, 1960).

* It is of interest that Freud followed this approach, at least in the years when he was developing his theories. The account of his discoveries is the story of a man

tages and limitations. While the first is more likely to yield a systematic, internally consistent formulation, this is achieved at the expense of ignoring or distorting some phenomena in order to preserve the integrity of the theory. The second approach brings less elegant and formal results, but it has the advantage of remaining closely tied to the realities of practice. At the present stage in the development of social casework, the empirical relevance and pragmatic validity of theoretical propositions seem more important than their formal properties; elegance, though desirable, can be deferred. The selection of one approach, of course, does not completely preclude the other. An approach that begins with the pragmatics of practice should lead to an examination of available theories and evaluation of their relevance for specific practice problems.

Accordingly, the framework outlined below takes its elements from the situation of practice in social casework. It is not, in any sense, a theory. Rather, it is an assembly of the crucial questions confronting the caseworker in his practice, questions that casework theory must address. It is therefore a set of criteria for the comparison, evaluation, and development of casework theories.

As one closely examines casework practice, it becomes apparent that there are certain tasks inherent in the practice situation that the caseworker must perform in each instance. Each task also can be stated in the form of questions the caseworker must answer for each case—or rather, he must *select* answers, since for each question a variety of different answers can be found. We turn now to a discussion of these tasks and some of the questions associated with them.

Identifying the client. In each case the caseworker must answer the question: Who is my client? He must be clear about the person or persons on whose behalf he will work. The answer may be an individual, a couple, a child, or all the members of a family group, but regardless, his commitment is to serve the interests of his client.

Communication and the worker-client relationship. One of the first

---

who was attempting to find ways of explaining phenomena of concern to him. The process of discovery was one of successive approximations in which a variety of formulations were developed, found wanting, and replaced by others—the test was whether the formulation fit the data confronting him. In other words, psychoanalytic theory was the result, not the starting point, of Freud's work.

tasks confronting the caseworker, and one that continues throughout his work with a case, is that of effectively communicating with his client(s) and understanding the latter's attempts to communicate with him. Closely related to this task is the necessity for the worker to determine how to create a relationship with his clients that will be of maximum benefit. If a common base of communication is not established, the caseworker will not accurately understand the needs and wishes of his clients; and he will not be able to convey to his clients his own intentions and the meaning of his interventions. Clients often are not clear about the precise nature of their problems, needs, and wants, and even if they are, it frequently is difficult for them to express their needs and wishes clearly. While the caseworker may be clear about what he wants to get across to his clients, he often finds it difficult to do this in a way that is understood by them. The extent and importance of this problem is indicated by a recent study in public welfare agencies showing that in *most* of the cases studied the caseworkers and their clients failed to achieve a common understanding even about the nature of the problem on which they were working; moreover, the caseworker's interventions were effective, from the client's perspective, *only* when a common understanding about the problem was reached.[21] And failure to develop an effective relationship with a client will vitiate the caseworker's attempts to influence him.

Diagnosis and assessment. In every case, and repeatedly in the same case, the caseworker must determine which problems, behaviors, or social conditions will be the focus of his interventions in the interest of the particular client. In order to make these decisions, the caseworker must make a number of sometimes complex diagnostic assessments about the problems confronting the client and the factors affecting these problems.

Goals and objectives. In mapping a treatment strategy, it is not enough simply to arrive at a diagnostic assessment—that is, to decide what the problems are—it must also be determined what the outcome of treatment should be. If change is not to be aimless and haphazard, the caseworker needs some conception of the specific goals that he and the client are attempting to achieve. And these goals should be defined in specific, behavioral terms. For example, in the case of an unemployed man who wants a job, is the goal to help him locate a job suited to his skills, to help him acquire new job skills, to modify his job-seeking behavior, or any of a number of other possibilities? Thus, establishing the goals of treatment involves answering questions such as: What does the client hope for and expect? What can be changed? What should be changed?

Strategy and tactics of intervention. The development of a specific treatment plan is another task confronting the caseworker in each case. Under what set of conditions can the changes desired in this case be induced? What procedures within the resources available to the caseworker will produce this set of conditions?

Termination and outcome. When should treatment end? How is treatment to be terminated? What constitutes a successful outcome? Failure to answer these questions in advance can lead to interminable treatment and abortive terminations by the client.

These tasks can be and are approached by caseworkers in a variety of ways. The approach taken varies not only in relation to differences between cases but, with the same case in relation to differences in the caseworker's theoretical orientation. More generally, the various existing theories of casework practice can be viewed as different approaches to the above tasks. In subsequent chapters, detailed discussion of these tasks will include analyses of the different consequences of alternative approaches to them; only in this way can a basis be established for rational choice among these alternatives.

The fact that there are different ways of approaching the same task is not in itself desirable; ultimately, it is to be hoped that one set of solutions will be found for each type of case. But until the knowledge base of casework has advanced to that stage, we will have to contend with a variety of beliefs about how the caseworker should approach the tasks of practice. The uncertainty inherent in this state of affairs is uncomfortable and burdensome. The practitioner can avoid the discomfort by adopting one set of answers to these questions and regarding them as the "true" answers, but in doing so he runs the risk of following an approach that, at best, will be helpful only to a portion of his clients— those in circumstances served by the theory he employs. No theory now in use equally serves all problems of clients.

CHAPTER SIX

WHO IS THE CLIENT?

Confronted with a "case," that is, a situation in which he has a professional responsibility to help one or more persons, one of the first tasks facing the caseworker is that of selecting a *focus* of attention from among the array of possible foci. To what aspects of the case situation should he direct his attention? This question can arise repeatedly throughout the course of his work with the case, for the focus of intervention may shift at different stages.

The focus selected in a case derives essentially from the caseworker's answer to two questions: (1) Who is the client? (2) What are the units of attention; that is to say, what are the salient phenomena that need to be considered in order to assess the case situation and develop an effective intervention strategy? Closely related, these questions concern the central aspects of diagnosis and assessment. We begin consideration of these processes by discussing the problem of defining the client and examining the alternatives involved in selecting units of attention.

DEFINITIONS OF "CLIENT"

The term "client" can be said to refer to a social role. As such, "client" possesses the characteristics of roles generally imputed to the term in social psychology, for which field it was formulated, namely (1) a set of expected behaviors and norms associated with the role, and (2) a set of labels applied to incumbents of the role.

A person who becomes a client is confronted with role expectations emanating from four sources. One is the social agency. An agency's "eligibility" rules, for example, express normative expectations that must be met before a person can occupy the role of client in that agency and thereby acquire the rights and obligations associated with the role. In family service agencies that provide homemaker services, for example, a person frequently cannot obtain that service unless he conforms to certain agency-defined norms, such as participation in casework treatment.

A second source of normative expectations is the caseworker and his reference groups. The caseworker's definition of his *own* role implies a reciprocal definition of the role of the client. Thus, the caseworker who conceives of his role as that of helping clients acquire increased self-understanding will define and assess differently clients seeking help only with concrete situational problems than will the caseworker who views the provision of concrete services as a central part of his role.

The self-image of the client and his reference groups comprise a third source of normative expectations. The public welfare recipient who sees himself as the fortunate beneficiary of agency largesse will conduct himself quite differently in relation to the agency and the social worker than will the recipient who regards himself as a citizen properly seeking the benefits to which he is entitled by law.

And finally, other persons and groups in the community whose expectations affect the client, the worker, and the agency constitute a fourth source of norms defining the client role. The permissible actions of both staff and clientele in probation and parole agencies, for example, are directly affected by the expectations of the police and the judge in the community. Thus, a parole agent may be required to revoke parole in a case for the sake of relations between his agency and the police, even though in his professional judgment revocation is not in the best interests of the parolee.

The fact that expectations about client behavior are held by a number of different persons and groups has important consequences. One is that the expectations may be incompatible and confusing to the client. Examples of such conflicts are familiar to most social workers. The social worker in a parole agency, for example, is expected by his professional reference groups to develop relationships with his clients such that they will feel free to discuss with him their most private feelings and actions. Such relationships are assumed to be essential for therapeutic effectiveness, and the social worker may be evaluated negatively if he is not able to establish them with a significant number of his clients. At the same time, in many parole agencies, the worker also is expected by agency administrators and/or by outside groups (e.g., the police) to reveal certain information he obtains in his relationships with parolees, in order that this information may be used as a basis for official action, for example, revocation. In other words, the professional norm dictates, for therapeutic ends, a relationship in which the parolee may be expected to reveal self-incriminating information that may be used against him by officials. Attempts have been made to rationalize this conflict by arguing that use of information in this way also serves therapeutic or rehabilitative ends, but this argument rests on rather dubious assumptions, including an assumption that the persons and groups seeking the information will use it in the best interests of the client.[1] In any event, it is unlikely that parolees would find this rationalization convincing. On the contrary, at least in some parole agencies, parolees appear to perceive and experience both sets of expectations and find them a source of conflict and confusion.[2]

The above example is only one instance of a larger problem, namely the strain between professional and administrative authority, a particularly acute problem for social workers, nearly all of whom practice in bureaucratic organizations. The distinction between the two types of authority has been described by Etzioni:

The ultimate justification for a professional act is that it is, to the best of the professional's knowledge, the right act. He might consult his colleagues before he acts, but the decision is his. If he errs, he still will be defended by his peers. The ultimate justification of the administrative act, however, is that it is in line with the organization's rule and regulations, and that it has been approved—directly or by implication—by a superior rank.[3]

The strain between these two types of authority, coupled with the administrator's power to invoke sanctions to enforce compliance with administrative decisions, generates a tendency to substitute administrative decisions for professional ones, to rely on agency policy and rules for decisions that social work values specify should rest on professional judgment.[4] When this occurs it can seriously compromise the relationship between the caseworker and his client, since it undermines the legitimate right of this client to expect the professional to base his actions on what is best for the client and not, for example, what is best for the agency. The professional should resist efforts to persuade him to identify himself fully with agency policies and rules and to present them to his client as "our" policies. The client who is told at a number of points that "in this agency *we* do this or do not do that" begins to feel that he is dealing with a bureaucrat and not a professional person.

The client's opinions are critically important, and expectations of his own role and the social worker's behavior are critically important for the worker to understand and use. One of the few variables that in a variety of studies has been found to be related consistently to continuance in treatment is the degree of consensus between worker and client in their conceptions of what they are to do together. The greater the consensus between them regarding what is to transpire in the casework situation (e.g., what problems are to be worked on) the more likely the client is to continue in and therefore make use of casework.[5] The caseworker, if he is to be perceived as helpful by the client, must minimize discrepancies between his own and his client's conception of what they are doing together. To do so requires that the caseworker make an effort to discover his client's conceptions and expectations and be prepared, accordingly, to modify his own behavior and his expectations of the client, or else educate the client to the worker's views. Many persons cannot comprehend that the process of sitting and talking with a caseworker about their problems could possibly help them. To expect such persons to sit in the caseworker's presence for fifty minutes every week, and then to interpret their silences as resistance, is to substitute custom and ritual for professional judgment.

A number of such rituals have developed in casework and are perpetuated simply because of tradition or in the interests of administrative efficiency. *Any element in the casework situation that can be varied by the caseworker is potentially a therapeutic tool.* Thus, the duration, spacing, location, and frequency of interviews, the reliance on verbal versus nonverbal communication, and the determination of which services in a case are "appropriate" for a professional rather than a nonprofessional to provide ought to be matters of professional discretion, to be decided anew in each case and not relinquished by the caseworker to administrative simplification and routinization. Not only does the client role vary from agency to agency, but the role also *ought* to vary from case to case within the same agency. The expectations of clients in public welfare agencies, for example, differ in quite fundamental ways from the expectations of clients in child guidance clinics. Some of these differences are beyond the control of the caseworker or client, since they have to do with public attitudes and formal constraints on the agency, but to the degree that caseworker and client are two important sources of expectations for the worker-client relationship, the caseworker should deliberately structure this relationship in the way that seems most likely to achieve therapeutic ends. If, for example, it seems to the worker that the best place to interview Mr. X. in order to establish the rapport necessary to help him is the neighborhood bar, then this is what he should do, unless it can be shown that there are reasons why he should not see Mr. X. in a bar that are more compelling than helping the client. These structural aspects of the worker-client role relationship and its social context that are left to the discretion of the caseworker should be viewed as points to which informed professional judgment should be applied. Attempts to reduce or constrain these areas of discretion should be carefully evaluated and resisted if they restrict the worker's use of an important variable in treatment.

Bureaucratic pressure is not the only constraint that can impede the caseworker's efforts to flexibly and imaginatively structure the client-worker relationship to serve therapeutic ends. Treatment theories and ideologies imply an "ideal" or at least modal conception of the client role, for each theory imposes explicit expectations that the client presumably must meet if treatment is to succeed. Verbal therapies require articulate clients; introspective therapies require clients with the capacity and disposition to be introspective; and family therapies that assume troubled families really want to stay together may complicate rather than ameliorate the problems of a family whose members are seeking separation. Similarly, casework theories suggest conceptions of the "ideal" client, as implied in Helen Perlman's criteria of "workability" [6] and Hollis' assumptions about anxiety in clients,[7] both of which specify attributes the client must possess if the casework method is to be successfully employed; in chapter 5 we examined certain assumptions about the model client that pervade much of the case-work literature.

The solution to such problems is not to dispense with treatment theories, a step that, in any event, would simply substitute implicit assumptions and expectations of the client for explicit ones. Rather, the caseworker should acquire as full and accurate an understanding as possible about what the client wants and expects in regard both to the outcome and character of his experience with the caseworker, and this understanding ought to be at the center of the worker's attention as he formulates his intervention strategy. Clearly, the caseworker frequently cannot do what the client expects, in which case he may have to modify the client's expectations; but if the worker proceeds without a clear understanding of what the client wants and expects he seriously risks estranging the client. Thus, the client's subjective view of the casework situation is an extremely important perspective for the caseworker to recognize.

Another crucial variable affecting worker-client relations is the pathway by which the individual or family becomes a client. A basic distinction appears between voluntary and involuntary client roles, the latter ascribed to the person because of some other status he occupies (e.g., parolee) or because of some acts he is judged to have committed (e.g., child neglect), the former achieved by the person because of some benefit he hopes becoming a client will bring him (e.g., reduction of marital conflict).

Involuntary induction into the role of client is typically associated with "authoritarian" settings, such as corrections agencies, but this pathway is not limited to agencies that have formal authority over their clients. The person who seeks financial assistance from a public welfare agency and then accepts casework counseling because he fears that to refuse it would jeopardize his financial assistance is as much an involuntary client as the parolee who fears revocation if he does not cooperate with his caseworker. By the same token, the husband who goes to see a caseworker at a private family agency because his wife has threatened divorce if he does not go is hardly a voluntary client.

The distinction is not, however, a sharp one and is best viewed as a continuum. Etzioni has identified three points on this continuum, expressed in the form of client orientations toward the worker and the agency.[8] The first is what he calls a *moral orientation,* in which the client and worker share the same values—in effect, the client wants what the worker wants to provide, and the client willingly cooperates with the worker. The second is called a *calculative orientation,* in which the client overtly cooperates with the worker in order to get something he wants. Examples would be the welfare recipient who participates in personal counseling not because he shares the worker's convictions about its value but because he believes that by cooperating he can gain more liberal financial benefits from the agency, or the person who complies with the private family agency's expectation that he participate in regular interviews with the caseworker and does so only to obtain homemaker service for his family. Finally, Etzioni identified an *alienative orientation,* in which the client not only does not share the worker's values but actively opposes them and complies only when coercion is applied or threatened. A case in point is the parolee who attends group counseling sessions only because it is a condition of parole and is silent or antagonistic in the group meetings.

It is evident that all three of the above orientations can be found in any social welfare agency, though their distribution probably varies greatly in different kinds of settings. Mental hygiene clinics and private family agencies, for example, can and generally do avoid clients with alienative orientations, while corrections and public welfare agencies must work with them frequently. It is also evident that these orientations. sometimes arise from circumstances independent of voluntary *or* involuntary induction into the client role. Some parolees present a moral orientation to the caseworker; that is, they want and seek help from a caseworker. And some persons who voluntarily present themselves to the caseworker in a private family agency manifest an alienative orientation, although their encounter with the agency is apt to be brief.

These orientations have not, of course, gone unnoticed by caseworkers, but usually they have been construed as personality types or as manifestations of motivation. The value of Etzioni's analysis is to show that while the client's orientation may be related to personality patterns, it also is a function of context, reflected in the expectations of the worker and the agency. Moral orientation—or, to use terminology more familiar, high motivation for treatment—is not so much an attribute of the client as it is a consequence of the degree of congruence between

the values and norms held by the client on the one hand and the caseworker on the other. The client who wants and expects direct advice on
his problem will be construed quite differently by a nondirective practitioner than by a more directive one who is willing to give direct advice
to his client. While the latter will see the client as being highly motivated (moral orientation), the former will perceive him as being manipulative or even as resistant or alienative in his orientation to treatment.
Similarly, the client with a calculative orientation may appear so only
because the agency has interposed a set of rituals between the client and
the service he wants, rituals that seem meaningless or irrelevant to him.
An example is the practice, common to some agencies serving skid-row
residents, of requiring clients to participate in religious services before
they can get the meal that attracted them to the agency. And this illustration is only a somewhat more obvious example of a type of practice
that, in a variety of more subtle forms, agencies and caseworkers impose upon their clients.

The general problem with the preceding discussion is that the values and norms of both the caseworker and the agency are implicated in
the definition and structuring of the client role, in the way that persons
enact the role, and in the personal characteristics that are attributed to
persons for the manner in which they perform the role. In effect, the
client who shares the caseworker's diagnostic and therapeutic ideology
will be seen as motivated, while the client who does not will be construed as lacking motivation for treatment, even though they may have
equally strong wishes to be helped. And the worker's differential attri-
bution of motivation to the two clients will appear (superficially) valid
since the "motivated" client will continue in treatment after the "unmotivated" client has "dropped out."

What is the practitioner to do in the face of these complexities?
How is he to chart a course through the field of forces that impinge
upon him and his clients? In a sense, this always is the central question
confronting the practitioner, complicated now by our discussion of the
constraints on practitioner and client emanating from the social context
in which their encounter takes place. To answer this question is one of
the aims of this book. To answer it more specifically is the concern of
the next seven chapters.

If we are to deal with this question more concretely, it is necessary to break it down into the specific questions or tasks facing the case-worker. The only alternative would be to rely on broad principles, such as "develop a relationship" or "begin where the client is," which are too vague and general to serve as specific guides to action for the practitioner.

The first specific task facing the practitioner in a case is that of determining where and upon what to focus his attention. Each case, no matter how simple, presents a great variety of possible foci for attention by the caseworker, ranging from subtle aspects of the client's personality to his spending habits, or from his early childhood experience to the way he feels about the caseworker at the moment, and so on ad infinitum. The caseworker cannot attend to all of these things. He must be selective. He must, whether he does so deliberately or not, decide which foci are salient and relevant and which are to be ignored. He must, in short, construe the case.

THE PROBLEM OF FOCUS—SOME ALTERNATIVES

It is clear that the caseworker's attention will be guided, to a considerable extent, by the assumptions he adopts about human behavior. Some dimensions along which these assumptions vary—and shape the caseworker's attention accordingly—were identified and discussed in chapter 3. The caseworker's attention, the cognitive structure within which he perceives and construes case situations, will vary depending on the extent to which the behavioral assumptions held by the caseworker emphasize, for example, present versus past influences on behavior, overt behavior versus subjective experience, social versus psychological determinants, or an ideographic versus a nomothetic approach to the analysis of human behavior. Thus the caseworker who is committed to an intrapsychic determinism, and who believes that most behavior reflects individual psychological predispositions, will be less interested in and pay less attention to the social factors in the case situation. While it is probable, as Haworth's research suggests, that few caseworkers are committed to an extreme position on these assumptive dimensions, caseworkers do differ relatively in their positions on these issues and these variations lead to differences in the focus and direction of attention.[9]

It can be claimed that theoretical differences of this sort do not have tangible consequences in practice, that caseworkers tend to differ much less in what they do than in their allegiances to theory. The research of Strupp has often been cited in support of the latter argument. Strupp found little differences among psychotherapists in what they said they would do as a function of their varying theoretical orientations, and moreover the similarities in response among therapists of different theoretical persuasions were greater among those with more experience.[10] Strupp has been criticized, however, for sampling only those aspects of therapist behaviors on which most schools of thought would agree and of failing to include behaviors on which these schools explicitly differ. Some subsequent research has shown systematic differences of action between clinicians as a function of their theoretical orientations.[11] And on an anecdotal level, one has only to listen to the debates among caseworkers about technical matters such as the use of family group interviews, or the use of direct advice—to cite only two examples—to be aware that caseworkers differ in what they do and that these differences are related to divergent theoretical convictions.

It may seem that we have led the caseworker into a morass. Any theoretical orientation, we have said in the preceding discussion, confers bias: it limits and directs the caseworker's attention and, consequently, his actions. But, as we argued in chapter 3, the caseworker cannot dispense with theory; if he tries, he simply submerges his assumptions, for he cannot proceed without them: the "facts" do not speak for themselves as Meyer and Richmond hoped they would. Moreover, this dilemma—the necessity of theory and its inevitable effects of bias on his understanding of the work with a case—is compounded immeasurably by the reality that the caseworker is confronted with a variety of radically different theoretical orientations. This is one of the most difficult dilemmas facing the modern caseworker, one that could hardly arise in an earlier era when it was assumed that there was one theory that was basically "true"—for if a theory provides a "true" account of behavior, there is no need to be concerned about bias.

The way out of this seeming morass is to regain a clear understanding of (1) the points at which caseworkers can find stable anchors for their practice and (2) the nature of theory and its uses in practice. The points of anchorage for the caseworker are the goals and values of the profession and the central tasks that inhere in the practice situation, not a particular theory of behavior. In concrete situations the specific implications of the commitment to self-determination may be extremely ambiguous, but the *general* intention of that value is clear. Similarly, it may be difficult to know how to communicate most effectively with a particular client, but there can be no doubt that communication with the client is a central, unavoidable, and persistent task confronting the caseworker.

Theory, on the other hand, is for the caseworker a tool—an essential one, but still no more than a tool. It is a tool that helps the caseworker to see, to understand, to anticipate, and to plan and implement his interventions. Therefore, beyond the question of validity, or the "truth" of a theory, the test of a theory for the practitioner is pragmatic: is it useful in meeting the tasks he faces? The practitioner cannot afford to ignore a theory that has attained a high degree of scientific or pragmatic validity nor retain an invalid theory, and he must also be prepared to discard an idea when a more useful one comes along. Thus, the caseworker's stance toward theory should be one of skepticism about the validity of a particular formulation for any specific case (i.e., his question should be "does the theory fit this situation?" not "how does this situation fit the theory?"), and he should combine this with an active search for more adequate and effective formulations.

A theory is an attempt to describe, explain, and predict events. Theory simplifies events in order to reduce them to a set of abstract principles, and the validity of a theory depends on the extent to which the principles it invokes account for variation in the events the theory purports to explain. Most theories in the social and behavioral sciences that might be useful to the caseworker have been found capable of accounting for only a small portion of the variance in human behavior and thus contain substantial error or bias. The problem of bias—the dilemma that prompted this discussion—can be reduced if the caseworker is sufficiently familiar with a range of theories and perspectives to be able to apply any or all of them in his analysis of a case. The limitations of a purely psychological analysis of a case can be compensated to some extent if the worker is able to conduct an equally sophisticated social analysis of the same situation. This requires the worker to be familiar and at home with a variety of divergent, even contradictory, theories of behavior, much as the physicist uses both wave and particle theories of light—although the two theories are contradictory, at present both are necessary to account for the behavior of light. For the social worker confronted by a variety of theories about people and their problems, the task is more difficult.

This approach to the problem of theoretical bias—one that calls on the worker to recognize that theory is only a tool and to become familiar with and use a wide range of theoretical tools—can be extended to two other major considerations guiding the worker's attention in a case. These considerations we discussed earlier in the chapter, namely the caseworker's conception of who or what a "client" is and his view of the role of the caseworker.

In social work, as we have noted earlier, the term "client" may have a variety of meanings. It may be used to refer to an individual, a dyad, a family unit, a group, a neighborhood, an organization, and a variety of other units or systems. While there have been debates about whether, for example, the caseworker's client is an individual or a family, such debates seem rather pointless since this decision need not be made a priori. The caseworker can, and should, entertain a range of possible answers to the question "who is the client?" to be selectively applied depending on the nature of the case.

In an exercise used in first-year casework courses, students were given a written case and asked to write responses to a series of questions, including one that asked who the client should be and others that asked about the caseworker's activities in the case. The case is that of a fifty-five-year-old Black man whose wife had been paralyzed by a stroke several months before. The husband had been attempting to care for his wife at home, even quitting his job in order to do so. When the husband appeared at a private family agency to ask for help in making other arrangements for the care of his wife, he was physically, psychologically, and financially exhausted. It was clear in this case that the marriage, which was childless, was extremely important to both husband and wife, and therefore that the wife's illness represented a deep loss to both of them. The outcomes of casework were specified as placement of the wife in a nursing home and restoration of the husband to his occupational role. Only students who defined the client as the family unit considered or advocated work with the wife to help her as well as the husband with plans for placement and the separation it entailed. Those students who defined the husband as the client considered only work with him, as did the worker in the written case report whose only direct contact with the wife was a brief telephone conversation. In class discussion of the student's papers, the students who defined the husband as the client typically had an "ah ha" experience when they discovered that a different definition of the client opened new dimensions of the case and additional intervention alternatives.

Similarly, a variety of conceptions of the caseworker role have been advanced, criticized, and defended. These conceptions have included: the therapist, who treats the client's psychological problems; the enabler, who helps the client help himself; the problem solver, who tries to increase the client's ability to find better solutions to his problems; the counselor, who counsels and advises his client; the aggressive caseworker, who reaches out to persons who do not seek his help; and, more recently, the social broker and the advocate, two conceptions about which we will have more to say in later chapters. Although at times these different views of the caseworker's role have been debated as if only one viewpoint could be tolerated in the profession, we see no justification for a unitary conception of the worker's role. On the contrary, we think the caseworker may need to do quite different things to help client X than to aid client Y. In other words, we favor a comprehensive view of casework intervention, in which the caseworker possesses a role repertoire with sufficient range to permit him to vary his stance from that of therapist to that of active advocate according to what it appears may most effectively help the client toward specified goals.

Caseworkers need a variety of conceptions, not only of their own role but of theoretical orientation and view of the client. We have yet to deal with the crucial question of where and under what conditions the worker is to use specific alternatives from the array in his repertoire. When is it useful to construe the client's problem in psychological terms? Under what conditions is the family group to be defined as the client? When should the caseworker adopt an assertive stance and "reach out" to the client? The process by which these decisions are reached has been called diagnosis or assessment. We shall turn to these matters shortly, but first we must discuss a more immediately pressing task in casework, that of communicating with the client.

CHAPTER SEVEN

COMMUNICATION AND THE
WORKER-CLIENT RELATIONSHIP

OVERVIEW

In all of the social work literature no concept appears as frequently as that of "the casework relationship." Social workers have long known of the power for good or evil that inheres in an interaction between two human beings. The credo of the caseworkers prototype, the friendly visitor, during the heydey of the COS—"Not alms, but a friend"—is testimony to the profession's early preoccupation with such interchange. Exactly what transpired in the intimacy between friendly visitor and client was unknown, but it was obvious that *something* of importance to the client was taking place.

Knowledge that behavioral change can occur through one person's acting upon another in an association of some kind is not unique to the social work profession. That one person can engage with another in a relationship of intimacy and emotion is probably one of the most notable and remarked upon characteristics of man's humanity. Thus, although social work can take pride in attending to and employing the human relationship in a conscious and deliberate way for the *benefit of the client,* the profession cannot claim to have discovered this attribute of mankind nor to have preempted its investigation. All human beings form relationships with other human beings but, it is held, there is something special about the relationship formed by a caseworker with his client. The development of social casework could be chronicled in terms of the evolution and elaboration of this concept without doing gross disservice to an historical understanding of the method as a whole. In the prehistory of "social work," the one-to-one ministrations of family members to other needy family members, of friend to friend, and of priest to parishioner, were probably of the same order as any interpersonal interchange. More recently, the friendship of the friendly visitor was in fact a friendship colored only by a missionary spirit and directive zeal. Economic aid was seen as insufficient; character building and moral reform had to accompany the dole, and what better way to accomplish these ends than the time-honored technique of establishing a cordial relationship with the recipient, thereby making him amenable to up-lifting influence.

Mary Richmond's *Social Diagnosis* was an elaboration of procedures to gather meaningful and reliable data about a client.[1] Interestingly enough, there is no specific discussion in this work of the relationship between caseworker and client; it is as though the development of a warm human association was so elementary and basic to data gathering that it hardly merited detailed attention. But this omission would not be tolerated in a discussion of casework matters other than those that were purely "fact finding." In *What is Social Casework,* Miss Richmond based the entire therapeutic rationale of casework on the relationship between helper and helped.[2] Her definition presupposes this when she speaks of "adjustments consciously affected, individual by individual," [3] as does her treatment of "direct action of mind upon mind." [4] Alas, Miss Richmond could go no farther than to indicate that this interchange is important; she could not explicate the details of the interchange. In her discussion of the Young case she comments feebly: ". . . *something* passed between mind and mind that made for permanance of relation and of influence." [5] We should not judge Miss Richmond too harshly for this evasion; the problem of explicating the human interchange remains the central problem of psychological and social science to this day.

With the publication of *Social Diagnosis* and of *What Is Social Casework*—the culmination of a noble beginning to the profession— new winds began to blow over the discipline. A psychological revolution was fomenting in Vienna. Freud had been both enraptured and troubled by his Parisian experience. The near miracles that seemed to occur as a result of hypnosis in Charcot's clinic were so dramatic that they could not be ignored. Charcot and his associates exerted a powerful influence over their patients, but understanding the influence was another question. Ignorance of such an obviously powerful phenomenon was not compatible with the deterministic spirit of Freud's work.[6] Although he played with hypnosis in his early work on hysteria, it was quite in keeping with his style that he would soon give it up. Freud's beginning development of psychoanalytic theory and therapy could be characterized as an unceasing effort to objectify the relationship between himself and his patients. Hence, the "blank screen": the couch, the passive analyst, the avoidance of face to face contact, all relics of the early years that still survive. The idea was simple: neurosis was to be understood as an aberration of the contents of the unconscious mind; its resolution resided in an intellectual struggle, by the patient, to lay bare the contents of this instinctual reservoir. Originally, the relationship between analyst and patient was seen as an encumbrance to the work at hand—to the extent that such a relationship could be avoided, so much the better. It did not take Freud very long to realize that such a relationship between his patients and himself could not be avoided and with some chagrin, he came to see the complexities of the interchange between doctor and patient as the heart and soul of the analytic work. Hence, the development of theory around "tranference" and all that it implies. As Anna Freud was to observe several years later, resistance, which was once seen as being only a nuisance, became, in fact, the central concern of therapy.[7] Instead of an analysis of the instincts, psychoanalysis became an analysis of the resistances, and ego psychology was born.

Despite acceptance of early psychoanalytic concepts, the casework relationship remained a mystery. What was absorbed by the casework theoreticians of the time was the original "blank screen" concept; to the extent that the caseworker could function as an impersonal machine, so much more could the intellectual struggles of the client for self knowledge be facilitated. Fortunately, the client would not permit this, nor could the caseworker disavow his humanity and operate in such a manner. The concepts of transference and counter-transference returned the human element to the transactions of worker and client but, as we shall see, did not fully explicate that enormous complexity subsumed under the rubric of "the casework relationship."

Primarily because of basic theoretical differences as to the etiology of neurotic behavior, but also partly as a result of a distaste for the mechanization of the therapeutic interchange, Otto Rank developed a "psychology of will" that had an important impact on casework theory. Thus the crucial importance of the worker-client relationship, long seen by social caseworkers as the prerequisite and means for treatment, became, for the functionalists, the end of treatment. Virginia Robinson's book brought into focus the incredible therapeutic powers that inhere in a relationship in and of itself.[8] Casework treatment was seen as providing for a client a powerful, current, reality-oriented experience with a helping agent. "The treatment relationship itself becomes the constructive new environment," wrote Miss Robinson.[9] But this relationship was not to be the patronizing friendship of the friendly visitor, nor the manipulation of transference that characterized the "diagnostic" practitioner; rather it was to be a highly charged, emotional interchange that would provide a unique and never-to-be-forgotten experience between two people. Social casework must always be grateful to the hearty souls of the so-called functional school who, without trepidation, plunged into their client's interview with heart, soul, and mind and engaged themselves with their clients.

Although the "diagnosticians" rejected the theoretical and philosophical assumption of the Rankian caseworkers, they acknowledged, at least implicitly, the emphasis on the relationship itself. Thus, attempts at constructing typologies of treatment—efforts thought irrelevant by the functionalists—subtly incorporated the relationship concepts: hence, the "experiential treatment" (or relationship therapy) of Lucille Austin,[10] the "psychological support" of Florence Hollis,[11] and the "type A treatment" of the Family Service Association of America.[12] In spite of these concessions, however, the diagnostic school of thought in social casework still holds that the casework relationship is primarily a *vehicle* of treatment rather than treatment itself.

Efforts have been made to describe this important medium in some detail. Garrett offers a definition that incorporates transference and counter-transference phenomena as well as all those things that can be subsumed under a "reality" relationship.[13] Although transference and counter-transference events have been more or less explicitly formulated in psychoanalytic writings, the reality components of a relationship leave a wealth of unknown phenomena yet to be explicated. In any event, it is recognized in casework that the relationship between worker and client, while including many components that inhere in any human relationship, has certain unique features. Thus, any human friendship contains transference and counter-transference elements as well as "reality" or objective elements. The unique features of the casework relationship are thought to reside in its professional purpose. In the casework situation the beneficiary of the relationship must be the client, whereas in the garden variety of human intercourse there is a mutuality of benefit. That is to say, the caseworker enters the professional relationship without expectation of personal gain. From this vantage point, Biestik persuasively defines the casework relationship in terms of its purpose: ". . . helping the client achieve a better adjustment between himself and his environment." [14]

A further distinction between the casework relationship and an ordinary human relationship can be found in the "business" quality of the former. It has a purpose, but it also has an implicit (and in some cases, explicit) point of termination. It is not to be a permanent association as friendships may sometime be—both parties are aware that it will be restricted to "business hours" and will eventually end. It is, in effect, a contractual association that could read as follows: "For a certain unspecified, albeit limited, period of time, I, the caseworker, agree to enter into a human relationship with you, the client. The purpose of this relationship will be for your benefit; I will not use it to further my own ends nor seek gratification from it at your expense. Further, I will, during the course of this contract, treat you with respect and courtesy. I will have compassion for you and your problems, and I will accept your feelings and self without prejudice. Your communications will be held in confidence, subject to the limitations of civil and agency policy. In return for these commitments, you will agree to confine your contacts with me to such times and places as I prescribe."

The above "contract" in essence sets the terms of the casework relationship, as they are held to be in present casework thinking. It does not, however, address itself to the basic question: "What, in fact, *is* the casework relationship?" That it is important, we have attempted to establish. That it is the definition of treatment for one school of thought at least, we have suggested. Garrett identifies some of its components, but unfortunately under gross rubrics. Biestik provides some of the terms of the contract. We have, thus far, talked around the casework relationship, not directly to it.

THE COMMUNICATION TASK OF THE
CASEWORKER AND CLIENT

In a very general sense, the communication of ideas and emotions between caseworker and client is the fundamental business of the casework enterprise. Various theoretical persuasions differ as to what the *content* of these communications should be, but all agree that something must be communicated. Thus, the Freudian therapist would hold that the communication of thoughts and feelings surrounding the early developmental years are to be preferred, while the behaviorists or action therapists will seek out the manifest content of the symptom itself. Adler will nurture communications of protest and power; [15] Kelly of construct versatility; [16] Jung of archetypes and mystical experience; [17] but all will insist upon communication of some form. Without communication there can be no treatment. A possible exception to this might be the Rankian and Rogerian therapists, who would hold that the act of communication itself, irrespective of the content, is the essence of treatment.[18] But even in this instance something of a communicative nature must transpire between worker and client.

Social casework provides the one true exception to the above when it offers, as a treatment method, therapeutic services that do not involve any direct contact with the client. Thus, those activities that are directed toward the well being of the client without his involvement in the process itself do not require communications of the kind implied above. A phone call to a housing official arranging living accommodations for a dispossessed family, arranging a summer camp experience for a child, arranging an adoption or foster home for a week-old infant—indeed, many of those activities that can be subsumed under the concepts of "environmental manipulation," "the administration of a social service," or "social therapy"—do not necessarily involve communications between a caseworker and his client. Of course, the need for such services must be ascertained in some way, and usually it is communicated to somebody by the "client"; but that somebody need not be the caseworker. In any event, we will restrict the rest of this discussion to casework transactions other than these.

Obviously communication can occur by means of a variety of symbols. Not all communications are verbal—indeed, some would argue that the most important communications, for therapeutic purposes, are nonverbal. Thus, the language of the body—posture, gesture, facial expression, even dress—is communicative. But in some ultimate sense, verbal communication is the most elegant and useful type. Language is the hallmark of the species and, in the final analysis, must carry the burden of the therapeutic work. Grunts and gestures—though sometimes eloquent—more often convey the complexities of thought and feeling only in the most primitive ways.

It should not be assumed, however, that word symbols are precise. Indeed, their very imprecision and the problems that this presents has given birth to a new field of study: semantics. The communicative task facing both caseworker and client is essentially one of insuring that the intended meaning of the communication is received and understood by the other party. The ambiguity of language and the inevitable private meaning that people attach to words make this task problematic. An example can be offered to highlight the problem. One of the authors interviewed a Black mother who recounted the trials she was having with her fifteen-year-old son, a large, husky youth. In the course of the account she mentioned the boy's attendance at a local medical clinic and said: "I carried Seth to the clinic yesterday." At this point, the worker's diagnostic mind spun into motion and the following private formulation was reached: "What a sick woman this must be who carries a 150-pound boy to a clinic as though he were an infant!" The outcome of the brief interactive vignette was quite benign; very shortly it became clear that the use of the phrase "to carry" was an idiom of the southern dialect and meant simply "to take" or "to accompany." The error was a function of the worker's ignorance—in this case a rather unimportant and temporary error that was soon corrected. But the haunting fear remained that perhaps there were other such erroneous receptions of meaning that went unnoticed and served to confound and distort the communications uttered by this and other well-intentioned clients. Words, then, are the most useful tools of the communicative process, but at the same time they are responsible for important errors within the process.

The communicative process is, of course, reciprocal. It is not only that messages or packets of meanings are being transmitted from client to worker; messages are also flowing from worker to client. The first has, as we have intimated, been seen as a diagnostic problem, "how am I, the caseworker, to understand the communications of my client?" More will be made of this later. The second problem, "how can I, the worker, be sure that what I have to say will be understood?" is essentially a diagnostic problem for the client, who must continually attempt to decipher the verbalizations and gestures of the clinician.

HOW ARE THE COMMUNICATIONS
BETWEEN CLIENT AND WORKER
TO BE UNDERSTOOD?

Many sensitive caseworkers would reject the idea that the face-value, dictionary meaning conveyed by the client's words is the preferable interpretation of his communications. That is to say, if a client were to utter the statement "I love my boss," many clinicians would not be content to accept this as a statement of objective fact—even if they could be sure that "love" really meant love. Now this is a curious state of affairs, for, at first blush, why shouldn't the statement be accepted for what it says? After all, one might argue, the client should be in the best position to know what he feels, and there is no reason to suppose that in this particular context he would attempt to deceive the caseworker.

This line of argument could be challenged in the following way: True, the client does not deliberately attempt to lie. However, human emotion is powerful, and people generally are often not aware of their true feelings. Thus, the client may *think* he loves his boss, but in reality he may hate his boss—or, at least, have mixed or ambivalent feelings about him. It is most important to note that the refutation is based on a series of propositions that, in effect, constitute a theory of personality. Indeed, several theories of personality would assume concepts of an unconscious mind and ambivalence. But we must also realize that several other theories—equally tenable by empirical and clinical test—do not make such assumptions.[19]

Thus, if the dictionary type meanings of a client's verbalizations are not to be accepted at face value, the interpretation a clinician gives to word symbols will be a function of his theoretical allegiance. For example, suppose a client were to appear twenty minutes late for his interview and were to accompany his breathless and hurried arrival with a flood of verbal protestations as to the uncontrollable events that caused his tardiness. The question confronting the clinician then becomes "how am I to understand the meaning of this behavior and the verbalizations surrounding it?" Obviously, if this is seen as a clinical problem worthy of solution (it must be remembered many clinicians would not so see it), information would be solicited about the events surrounding the late arrival. But the nature and direction of these solicitations would be determined by the clinician's theoretical orientation—in fact, the questions put to the client would be a consequence of hypotheses already formulated as to the possible meaning of the behavior. Hence the psychoanalytically oriented therapist would attempt to extract meaning in terms of the transference; the Rankian in terms of an expression of counter-will; the Adlerian in terms of power motives; the behaviorist (if he bothered at all) in terms of prior conditioning; and so on.

Thus, to the extent that the client's word symbols are not taken at face value, an important problem of interpretation faces the clinician. He must decide what theoretical system best serves to interpret the communications. How is he to do this?

A final answer to this problem awaits the development of a comprehensive theory of personality and clinical judgment. The best that can be offered at this point is an injunction that the clinician continually engage in a process of testing to validate his interpretation. This injunction, of course, is implicit among all schools of thought; the Freudian therapist knows that his interpretations are valid only if they work or somehow resonate sympathetically with his client. But all too often the process of test is neglected, and the clinician insists upon the accuracy of his interpretation simply because of his affection for the hypothesis. If the client's reactions belie the validity of the interpretation, it can easily be attributed to another cluster of hypotheses variously labeled "resistance" or "lack of motivation" or perhaps even "psychosis."

As a paradigm of strategy for the caseworker when he faces the enormous problem of understanding his clients' communications, we would suggest that the face value, dictionary type of meaning be entertained as a first working hypothesis. After first ascertaining that he and his client are both using the same dictionary, such meaning merits primary consideration until such time as evidence indicates that it is not valid. At this point, a series of alternative hypotheses can be generated and put to the test. Obviously the "strategy" outlined is not unique or earth-shaking; its simple-minded purpose is to emphasize the need for a constant and unceasing scrutiny of the hypotheses upon which the caseworker operates. Such scrutiny should be the hallmark of professional practice.

But we have been discussing only one side of the reciprocal phenomenon, communication. Assuming that the clinician can understand the utterances of his client, how is the client to understand the clinician? Either the worker can learn the client's system of communication and, thereafter, both parties "talk the same language," or the same effect can be reached if the client is taught the caseworker's system.

The first alternative embodies what is the essence of the psychologist George Kelly's personal construct system.[20] To oversimplify what is an enormously rich and novel theoretical structure, Kelly holds that each person construes the events of the world in his own unique way. It behooves the therapist, Kelly maintains, to learn the construct system of his client, for therein lies the entry to the difficulties faced by the client. To a certain extent, social casework has anticipated Kelly. The literature is replete with homilies that bear on this conception: "begin where the client is," "acceptance," "put oneself in the client's shoes," and "talk the client's language." But in a larger sense, these appeared for reasons of expediency; one begins where the client is only so as to be able to take him where he should be. Within the context of communication, which is our present concern, the injunctions contained in the above homilies suggest that the client is not to be frightened off; he is to be accepted and empathized with—the caseworker is to enter his language system, but only as a temporary expedient. The end, it would seem, is to gain time so that the client can eventually be induced to talk the language of the caseworker.

The second alternative underlies the preponderance of therapeutic activity. The reader should note that we are referring not merely to words but to the meaning of words, and this implies a system of thought. In essence, then, the clinician may attempt to cultivate within his client not only a new language but a new outlook. The Rankian therapist becomes satisfied with his therapeutic work when his client begins to *think* of himself in terms of the separation-unity dialectic. The Freudian therapist is likewise gratified when his client begins to understand his own behavior within the constructs of defensiveness, the oedipal system, aggression, and the like. It is as though the clinician were to say: "We must talk about something during our interview. I have a theory as to what may be responsible for your difficulty; alas, you do not know this theory, but I will teach it to you. At the beginning I will demonstrate that I understand you; I will not treat your own explorations lightly (imperfect though they may be). As time proceeds, we will talk together in a language that is new to you but old to me." What is unsaid, however, is that the treatment is deemed successful when the client becomes fluent in the new discourse.

It is difficult—perhaps even impossible—for the clinician to avoid superimposing his own thought system, that is, language system, on the client. Research on verbal conditioning suggests that man will respond to the subtlest of cues as to what a therapist may expect from him in the way of verbalizations. For example, if an experimenter were merely to respond with an "un huh" every time a plural noun is uttered by a subject, the frequency of such plural nouns will increase significantly without the subject being aware of it.[21] If this be the case in the relatively indifferent atmosphere of the laboratory, how much more likely is it to occur within the highly charged environment of the therapist's office? It is well known that analytic patients report their dreams—and perhaps even dream—more often during the height of their analysis than before or after. This may be explained in a variety of ways, but a simple explanation would hypothesize that the dreams result from a perceived expectation of the analyst. Dreams are one of the major components of the analytic work; if the analyst expects them, the patient obliges. There is nothing malicious or otherwise "wrong" with this. It simply suggests that the client or patient is ready to "go along," to cooperate, as it were. The danger inheres in a misperception of what is actually taking place.

Thus, the clinician must not be deceived into thinking that the production of content relevant to his own theoretical system is evidence for the validity of the system. Freudian therapists will elicit—in spite of themselves—Freudian content; but Sullivanians will elicit Sullivanian type data. Perhaps the followers of Rank and Rogers, who, by design, ignore the content of communication have accidentally found a means of avoiding this problem.

Thus, the client may learn the caseworker's language system, but the "learning" takes place at one of several different levels. First, he may simply translate his own language into that of his caseworker. If the therapist prefers the word "ambivalence" to the client's phrase "all mixed up," the translation can be easily accomplished. Second, the client may use the verbal symbols of the caseworker, not for the purpose of communicating but rather to be liked, accepted, or otherwise thought well of. Finally, the client may actually begin to think like the caseworker and use the new symbols as his own.

In any case, the communication of thoughts, ideas, and emotions becomes the prerequisite for the therapeutic work. The client who refuses to communicate may well be written off, not as a therapeutic failure but as an uncooperative or unmotivated client. In the voluntary agency where self-propelled clients are the rule, few clients refuse to communicate—at least on a superficial level. But what of the involuntary client? This question has been addressed by casework theorists for many years under a variety of topical headings: "reaching the unreached," "aggressive casework," "work with the multiproblem family," and other similar concepts. The central question could be: "how can the unwilling, involuntary client be encouraged to enter into a contract wherein he will communicate and share his ideas and his feelings?" Again, there is no direct answer to the question. We will discuss in some detail peripheral facets of this question that focus around the expectations of the client and the characteristics of a professional role. For the time being, let us be content with the knowledge that the presence of a climate for uninhibited communication along with the actual fact of communication between clinician and client serve to define a casework relationship. Thus, the relationship can be more fully explicated by identifying five prerequisites of the communicative process:

1. What is said—either verbally or nonverbally—by one party is understood by the other.

2. What is said by one party is accepted as a valid communication by the other party; that is, the communication is accepted as truthful or sincere.

3. What is said by the client will be treated responsibly by the worker; what is said by the worker will be treated seriously by the client.

4. Both parties will have an expectation, during the entire course of the relationship, that the above prerequisite will obtain.

5. There will be some sort of contract or bargain that services are to be rendered to the client in return for certain investments by the client—either in time, money, or emotional energies expended.

Given these components, one can assert that a therapeutic relationship exists. But why should a potential client subscribe to these prerequisites and enter into such an unusual contract? And why do some clinicians seem to be so much more successful than others in establishing such contracts? Before addressing these issues, we must first consider certain technical problems that confront the caseworker as he deals with a few more or less exceptional types of clients.

TECHNICAL PROBLEMS IN COMMUNICATION

Our discussion of communications thus far has failed to consider problems that are perhaps unique to certain identifiable populations of clients. There are at least three such groups of clients that make up a most significant part of social work's clientele: children, psychotics, and lower-class people and ethnic minorities.

The young child speaks a different language than does the adult: in the preverbal age group he of course has no articulate language at all; during the latency years he is more likely to act than to speak. The unique difficulties that the child client presents to the caseworker are described by Fraiberg:

There is a certain type of client who creates special problems in the administration of social agencies and in the interviewing situation. This client seems totally unable to comprehend the function of a social agency. He frequently creates disorder and chaos in the waiting room. Often he talks loudly and shrilly, demanding numerous attentions, and has been known to look boldly over the shoulder of a typist as she transcribes confidential reports. In the initial interview with the caseworker, this client states more or less positively that he has no problem and he does not know why he has come to the agency. Further difficulties are encountered when it appears that he cannot sit in a chair for more than five minutes. He tends to concentrate on irrelevant matters like the operation of the Venetian blinds, the counting of squares on the asphalt tile floors, the manipulation of paper clips into abstract forms.

The client has neither marital problems nor employment problems. He is not in need of relief, although he will gladly take a hand out. The sex of the client may be male or female. The age is roughly 5 to 15 years. What shall we do with him? [22]

What shall we do, indeed, since he either cannot or will not talk about his problems; how is the caseworker to communicate with him? To resolve this dilemma, psychotherapists who specialize in work with children have evolved a new dialectic: play therapy.[23] The play of children is thought to be equivalent to the language of adults; whereas the adult will put into words his perception of his difficulty, the child will act out the parameters of his problem with the paraphernalia of play. Following this line of thought, modern child guidance clinics have ingeniously constructed a wide assortment of playthings in the hope of facilitating and understanding play language—hence, puppets, doll houses, little toilets, and dolls with removable appendages around the genital area. The child, in the comforting medium of his own familiar discourse, speaks through his manipulation of these objects; the caseworker responds in turn, perhaps supplementing his actions with a verbal accompaniment: "Let's take the bad mommy doll out of the oven now." The subtleties of such a discourse require special skill and understanding on the part of the clinician and cannot be discussed here. Suffice it to say that communication with a child requires, in many instances, recourse to a new language.

Part of the difficulty in communicating with children is that they have not been socialized to the extent where they can enter into a contractural relationship with the caseworker, hence, the troubles outlined by Mrs. Fraiberg. They are still learning the norms and expectations surrounding not only the therapeutic relationship but everyday social relationships. Thus children do not know that rummaging through a "stranger's" desk drawer or sprawling out on an office floor is inappropriate behavior and in gross violation of the therapeutic contract. Caseworkers have, by and large, learned to adapt themselves to such violations and interpret these behaviors within the context of typical child behavior. With the next group of clients to be discussed, however, such violations are, unfortunately, interpreted in a less benign fashion.

Whereas children may violate the contractural norms with impunity, adults may do this only with great risk—the risk inhering in a possibility that the behavior will be seen as indicative of gross pathology. A simply example may suffice: An orthodox, male Jew interviewed by a female caseworker disregarded a proffered hand of greeting in the waiting room, refused to sit down in the offered chair, and throughout the initial interview stood by the door wretchedly uncomfortable and in an acutely anxious state. He refused to talk about his marriage and never returned for a subsequent interview. Partly on the basis of this behavior the client was seen by the caseworker as an extremely disturbed individual, possibly psychotic. The behavior described above can only be understood within the context of an orthodox Jewish culture, which provides its own norms for contact between men and women. Within this frame of reference, the above behavior is not ominous: orthodox Jewish men do not closet themselves with strange women, they do not talk about their personal affairs with them, and they do not even touch them in so benign a way as shaking hands. These taboos are very powerful and can be broken only with much distress and anxiety. In the above situation several lessons can be learned: the client should, if at all possible, have been seen by a man; if that were impossible, the woman caseworker should not have offered to shake hands in the reception room, and above all, should have left the office door open during the interview.

Thus, although the child client may be unsocialized, the client from an ethnic minority or lower socioeconomic status may be too well socialized—but to a different system. Verbal and nonverbal cues in these instances, if viewed outside of their context, can convey erroneous meaning, and it behooves the clinician to be sensitive to such a possibility. A wealth of literature bearing on the expectations of lower-class incumbents suggests that such clients will see the casework process as a rather puzzling enterprise, and they may be extremely loath to enter into a contractual relationship.[24] The problem for the caseworker is, again, to understand the meaning of his client's communications and behavior; ignorance of the cultural and class matrix within which the behavior is imbedded precludes such understanding.

Whereas the communications and relational behavior of lower-class clients, ethnic minorities, and children may be understood from the vantage point of socialization, the communications of the schizophrenic may present a hopeless jumble of nonsense and cognitive disarray.[25] How is the word-salad of the psychotic to be understood and his elaborate delusional system to be explained? Alas, all too often the clients of social agencies communicate in such language, and unfortunately we still lack a valid system of theory to interpret this behavior.

The schizophrenic is unable to form mature relationships with fellow human beings. When the clinician expects him to enter into a communicative relationship, he essentially asks the impossible—he asks that the illness be cured before the treatment starts. Skillful therapists who work with psychotics are prepared to spend a great deal of time and employ extremely unorthodox methods in gaining access into the mental life of the patient.[26]

But it is time to return to the questions left unanswered earlier: Why should a client enter into a casework relationship? Why are some clinicians more able than others to engage reluctant clients? And what is this relationship anyway?

CONCEPTIONS OF THE COMMUNICATIVE RELATIONSHIP

All societies have certain functionaries singled out and designated as healers of the mind, soul, and body. The simpler the society the more likely it is that mind, soul, and body are seen as inseparables, although in the supposedly highly sophisticated culture of the contemporary Western World there are prophets who hold that these facets of the human being are indeed interrelated—if not inseparable. But generally, in our world, physicians heal the body, priests the soul, and psychiatrists, psychologists, and social workers heal the mind. Prior to the wonders of the twentieth century, the division of labor among healers was not so clear, and a host of sanctioned and unsanctioned functionaries were involved in the healing enterprise—as, indeed, they still are, despite the above observations. Fortune tellers, astrologers, wizards, witches, priests, shaman, and even God were directly involved in healing.

It would be too easy to suppose that these people were ineffective in their ministrations to the ailing; they were probably as effective as our current specialists. How could this be? Obviously, diagnoses based upon the vagaries of the spirit world, the violation of taboos, the spells of witches, the configuration of planets, and the machinations of the Lord could not be correct diagnoses. And yet, by and large, the "patients" recovered—and still do recover. Since the rationale for the recovery cannot be found in the particular theory of the disease—which is patently absurd—it must be located within the expectations of the afflicted vis-à-vis the appropriately designated healer and in the relationship between patient and healer.

If we restrict ourselves to consideration of afflictions that today would be subsumed under the notions of functional disorders—schizophrenia, neuroses, neurasthenia, malaise, and general miseries of the psychic life—we could conjure up the following model: an individual senses that he is ill and suffering and he then turns to an acceptable healer. At that moment, and without further ado—indeed, without even seeing the healer—he has partially recovered. Turning to the healer implies expectation of relief; in other words, he has hope or optimism that his difficulty will be resolved. And such optimism, in itself, serves to restore the individual to his former healthy state. Lack of hope is, in part, a characteristic of his illness—the hope that he will be cured fills the lack. The healer can be charlatan or saint, magician or scientist; it is irrelevant to the patient so long as he *expects* that succor will come. A vicious circle can ensue: "I expect to be helped and I feel better; hence, my expectations were correct and I should soon feel even better; that is, I expect even more," and so on.

The efficacy of the "prescientific" healers may be attributed to this very human characteristic of mankind—in despair there is death, in hope there is life. The healer, be he shaman or psychiatrist, has many things going for him. He has, first, the sanction of a culture to play the role of healer; the patient and the people whose opinions matter to him regard the healer as competent to effect a cure. Secondly, he fosters a dependency in the patient; the patient needs him desperately. To the extent that the healer is the *solely* santioned healer, the greater the dependency. Finally, but not least importantly, the healer may have a large array of healing accoutrements—rattles, bones, drums, incense, icons, couch, books, or stethoscopes. It is these, the dependency of the patient and the accoutrements of skill, that Frank suggests offer an explanation for the efficacy of religious healing. Thus he writes:

The core of the effectivness of methods of religious and magical healing seems to lie in their ability to arouse hope by capitalizing on the patient's dependency on others. This dependency ordinarily focuses on one person, the healer, who may work privately with the patient or in a group setting. In either case, the patient's expectation of help is aroused partly by the healer's personal attributes, but more by his paraphernalia, which gains its power from its culturally determined symbolic meaning.[27]

Frank also argues that the placebo effect—"cure" resulting from the administration of inert agents—can be explained in the same way: some people are predisposed to react favorably to the culturally defined symbols of healing.

The fact that the personal attributes of the healer are important in evoking the optimistic expectations of his patient merits further consideration. What are these personal attributes? Surely it would seem that confidence, certainty, unshakeable faith in one's theoretical system, a certain missionary zealousness—in short, those attributes of the authoritarian personality—would do well to inhere in the mental healer. And in fact, the prototypical healer is an authoritarian: he is privy to the secrets of the supernatural (or intrapsychic) world; he has usually gone through a prolonged and arduous initiation into his craft; he is both feared and respected; he has status in his community; he is, in short, a formidable and powerful figure. It is difficult to picture a Casper Milquetoast as a shaman; a passive and uncertain Billy Sunday; a reticent John Wesley; or a cowering Sigmund Freud.

The problem for the modern day clinician becomes enormously complex. First, by his very training in the discipline of science he is uncertain (see chapter 4). The dogmatic (hence authoritarian) clinician is seen as an anachronism in present-day professional circles. Second, his client, also raised in the modern age, is likely to be skeptical of the healer's efficacy, and the clinician's tentativeness may increase his skepticism. The problem for the social worker is even more difficult. Whereas the psychiatrist, by and large, deals with patients who have come to him of their own volition and hence, in spite of some skepticism, see him as *the* defined healer, the social worker's client may be sent by someone else, and the client may have other "healers" in mind as more appropriate. Thus the psychiatrist's patient may have some hope, albeit feeble, to start with; the caseworker's client may have no initial hope. Indeed, he may feel a good deal of antagonism toward the caseworker. Further, the caseworker usually lacks the paraphernalia of efficacy: his office is typically shabby; there is no white coat or stethoscope of the "real" healer; no pills; no hypodermics; and for the not infrequent client of another intellectual world, no charms, amulets, or "know-how" with the important powers of the universe.

In spite of these obstacles, the caseworker treating the involuntary client must somehow generate an initial hope in the client, that hope that seems so essential in motivating a client to return and enter into a communicative interchange with the caseworker. Perhaps the caseworker would be well advised to ascertain what people are seen as the appropriate healers by his particular client. If the proper healer is a priest, the caseworker can take on priestly attributes; if he is a *curandero,* then the caseworker takes on the characteristics of a medicine man. This is not to say that the caseworker actually pretends to be a priest or medicine man, rather it is to say that he assumes the personal attributes of such people, usually attributes of authority and expertise. The almost magical ability of many caseworkers to involve reluctant clients is, we suspect, due to their intuitive ability in generating a charisma: "I want to help you—I can help you—I know how to help you —I have powers of which you are unaware—and, in spite of your objections I *will* help you." There is no monkey business with this caseworker; he is a person with power and ability.

The above "strategy" for involving a client in a therapeutic relationship raises certain obvious ethical considerations. As outlined above, it is a ruse, a pretense. The caseworker deliberately attempts to ascertain what role he may play to best foster optimism in his client and then proceeds to play the role. If the client wants magic, the caseworker puts on his magician's robe. The ethical questions do not differ, however, from those posed in chapter 2 and are resolved, by each caseworker, as he decides how far he can go in deciding what is best for his client.

We have, thus far, identified three components that are prerequisites for a healing relationship: the hopeful expectations of the client, his dependency, and the charisma or authority of the caseworker. Given these conditions, the client is highly susceptible to influence and the persuasive powers of the clinician. Indeed, Frank argues that the highly efficacious brainwashing techniques of historical and modern times can be explained in this manner. And it is not to be assumed that the *method* of brainwashing differs in principle from current psychotherapy; the difference resides only in the objectives of each.

From an entirely different perspective, Haley conceives of the therapeutic relationship as a struggle for the control of the communication process.[28] In this struggle, the voluntary client is at a distinct disadvantage: if he is too successful in wresting control he may lose by forfeiting treatment. The control exercised by the clinician is accomplished by means of paradoxical communications: to the extent that the client *obeys* the clinician—no matter what he does—he is obviously in a subordinate relationship to the clinician. The full flavor of Haley's conceptions can be indicated by the following passages:

When one person communicates a message to the other, he is by that act making a maneuver to define the relationship. By what he says and the way he says it he is indicating, "This is the sort of relationship we have with each other." The other person is thereby posed the problem of either accepting or rejecting that person's maneuver. He has a choice of letting the message stand, and thereby accepting the other person's definition of the relationship, or countering with a maneuver of his own to define it differently. He may also accept the other person's maneuver but qualify his acceptance with a message that indicates he is *letting* the other person get by with the maneuver.[29]

Further:

Any two people are posed [sic] the mutual problems: (a) what messages, or what kinds of behavior are to take place in this relationship, and (b) who is to control the definition of the relationship. It is hypothesized here that the nature of human communication requires people to deal with these problems and interpersonal relationships can be classified in terms of the different ways they do deal with them.[30]

Most everyday human relationships are, in Haley's language, symmetrical; that is, both parties have agreed to exchange much the same kind of language and to resolve the problem of control by stalemate.

The therapeutic relationship, however, is complementary—one gives and the other receives; one is "superior," the other is "subordinate."

The most effective means available to the therapist for sustaining control in the complementary relationship is, as we have suggested, the paradoxical communication. Thus a request to "do a certain thing—but don't obey my order" presents a paradox for the respondent—whatever he does he conforms to the request of speaker. A similar example within the context of the therapeutic relationship is: "You don't have to talk about it if you don't want to." Implicitly, of course, is a dictum that he should talk about it—whatever the client does, he submits to the control of the therapist.

Haley goes on to construct a rationale for both symptomatology and therapeutic change on the basis of these concepts, but these elaborations do not concern us here. What we are concerned with is Haley's rather novel consideration of the complexities of the casework relationship, and with this last conception of the therapeutic relationship we bring the chapter to a close.

The mystery of human interchange is not solved and it will not be solved for a very long time. But therein lies the crux of all therapeutic work. Whether it be means or end, the relationship between helper and helped remains a central concern for psychotherapeutic research.

CHAPTER EIGHT

DIAGNOSIS

Three uses of the term diagnosis can be found in the casework literature.[1] One use refers to classification and categorization. This type of diagnosis may employ categories such as neurotics and psychotics, neuroses and character disorders, and multiproblem and nonmultiproblem families. A second usage refers to understanding the dynamics of a case, in what might be called the *verstehen* conception of diagnosis. The caseworker who says, "this man's problem with his wife is a reenactment of his unresolved conflicts with his mother" is making a diagnostic statement of the second type, which has sometimes been called "dynamic" diagnosis. And third is the usage we recommend, by which diagnosis refers to the process, or the procedures followed by the worker in order to construe the case. These three uses are not equivalent alternatives; the third use, in particular, is more general than the other two. The other two definitions—classification and meaning—touch on important issues in diagnosis that need clarification.

CLASSIFICATION VERSUS VERSTEHEN

The view that the major purpose of diagnosis is classification of cases or problems is one that casework probably adopted from medicine, although it has other sources as well. As Greenwood and others have noted, for example, the development of a classification scheme is an essential step if casework is to base its practice on a scientific footing.[2] The basic idea here is to generate a set of relatively discrete categories under which one can reliably group together similar and separate dissimilar cases or problems. If this can be done, the assumption goes, then it should be easier to derive effective intervention strategies specific to each category.

Medicine provides one of the most conspicuous illustrations of a successful application of this approach. For example, pneumonia, tuberculosis, and lung cancer are clinical categories that can be reliably differentiated even though all are lung conditions. Differentiation of these categories was instrumental for the development of increasingly effective therapies specific to each diagnostic category.

Understandably, psychiatry sought to emulate this approach, from the early efforts to construct typologies by Kraepelin [3] and Freud [4] to the descriptive nomenclature today in the official diagnostic manual of the American Psychiatric Association.[5] Unfortunately, psychiatric typologies developed thus far cannot be applied reliably [6] and have not yet led to the development of definitive and clearly successful therapies specific to the categories of these typologies. One suspects that if these efforts had been more successful there would be fewer objections in social work to "pigeon holing." Some of those who object most strenuously to the allegedly dehumanizing effects of categorizing clients do not seem to mind being categorized by physicians—in fact, they are apt to complain if their physicians cannot unequivocally locate their symptoms in a specific diagnostic category. We all expect the physician to be able to do this, because we have come to believe that if he can he will be able to treat us more effectively, a belief for which there is considerable empirical support. But this belief has not yet acquired a comparable degree of support in psychiatry, clinical psychology, and social casework, because the diagnostic categories used have not yet generated clearly successful methods of treatment. However, the lack of success thus far does not alter the argument that the development of some classification of behavior is essential if intervention is to become rational and scientific.

The recognition among caseworkers of the need for some classification system has been a persistent theme in the casework literature from the beginning.[7] Although some early attempts were made to construct typologies within social work, those results never found wide use. For the past thirty years or more, apart from the superficial descriptive categories used by agencies for statistical purposes, by far the dominant trend has been to rely upon the categories developed in psychiatry, and especially psychoanalysis.* For several reasons, however, dissatisfaction with the heavy reliance on psychiatric nomenclature in casework practice has been mounting. For one thing, as we already have indicated, psychiatric typologies have low reliability and validity, even in the hands of psychiatrists. Second, caseworkers have been uneasy about using these categories because they are not trained psychiatrists. And third, typologies developed for the classification of mental illness are inadequate for the caseworker's diagnostic task. At most, psychiatric nosology only identifies personality types—the categories are not psychosocial and do not define situations or units larger than the individual, such as the family. When a caseworker classifies his cases within a typology of mental illness, he is reducing the problems these cases present to "varieties of mental illness." To say that Mr. Jones, who is unemployed and having problems with his wife and son, has a character disorder is to imply that "character disorder" is the problem, thereby minimizing other salient aspects of the situation that may be more important and/or more amenable to remedy.

In recent years, renewed efforts have been made to develop classification schemes more relevant to the caseworker's task, as in the work of Buell and his associates [8] and Warren,[9] and in Ripple and Alexander's work on the motivation, capacity, and opportunity scheme.[10] The most sophisticated of these efforts has been the work on the motivation, capacity, and opportunity (MCO) scheme at the University of Chicago. However, attempts to validate these schemes—including MCO—have not produced impressive results, and relations between these schemes and interventive strategies are not so far demonstrated; consequently, these typologies now have little, if any, immediate applicability for the practitioner.

The *verstehen* view of diagnosis appears to oppose the conception that the function of diagnosis is classification. The *verstehen* approach

* Caseworkers have made little use of the classification scheme provided by the official manual of the American Psychiatric Association but have relied rather on Freudian categories.

says that the important thing is to comprehend the individual or the case in all its uniqueness and in fact, to avoid classification, which, according to this approach, reduces the person simply to another member of a class of persons. Thus, to use an example introduced earlier, saying that Mr. Jones is unemployed, has conflict with his wife and son, and has a character disorder is not meaningful, precisely because it does not convey the unique characteristics of Mr. Jones' unemployment, family conflict, and character disorder, and this criticism still would apply even if we were to specify the *type* of character disorder, the *type* of unemployment, and the *type* of family conflict presented by Mr. Jones.

On closer analysis, however, the opposition between the two conceptions of diagnosis turns out to be only apparent. "Individualized" understanding of a case is essentially the result of an extended if implicit process of classification and categorization. That is to say, we "individualize" a person by classifying him along certain dimensions, thereby distinguishing him from persons occupying other categories on these dimensions. Thus a person walks into the caseworker's office and the worker begins to "individualize" him by making distinctions of the following sort: the person is male, not female; he is Caucasian, not Negro, or Mexican-American; he is sixteen, not seventeen, or twenty, or seventy; he is psychologically rigid, not flexible; he evokes in the worker feelings of hostility, not warmth; and so on. By this process of progressive categorization and discrimination the worker "individualizes" this young man, that is, determines in what respect he is similar to and differs from other persons in a large number of dimensions.

Thus the issue is not about categorization, since categorization is inevitable if one is to make statements about persons and situations. Rather, what the issue does seem to concern is the *number* of categories to be used in classifying a person or situation. Consider the following examples:

MISS A.

I	II
Miss A. is petite, attractive, vivacious and was somewhat flirtatious in the interview. She described the presenting problem as follows: She has been engaged to a young man for one year and is eager to marry him, but whenever they attempt to set a wedding	Miss A. is narcissistic phobic seductive uses denial uses repression

date she is overwhelmed by anxiety and
fear, which she can overcome only if she
"stops thinking" about the wedding. She is
deeply in love with her fiance and has no
idea what could cause her anxiety. She is
not aware of any fantasies associated with
her anxiety ("I don't want to think about
it.") Later in the interview, she brought out
another fear, namely that she will be attracted to another man (other than her
fiance). She added that she likes to have
men admire her or even whistle at her, but
if they approach her, she rebuffs them—
this pattern has bothered her for many
years.

Both of the above descriptions are attempts to classify or identify
Miss A. *I* is no less a classification than *II* but simply uses many more
concepts and categories. The question "which is better?" is a matter of
which is more useful, but before that question can be answered we need
to analyze more carefully the function of diagnosis and its relation to
intervention.

RELATION OF DIAGNOSIS TO INTERVENTION

Diagnostic efforts are justifiable only insofar as they contribute to the
effectiveness of intervention. Clients generally do not come to caseworkers simply to be diagnosed—they want and legitimately expect to
be helped. Caseworkers are not paid to write biographies or to seek out
the arcane subtleties of the client's experiences unless they can demonstrate that these activities increase their effectiveness in helping clients.
It is important to be clear on this point since there is much confusion
about it in the literature and in the field. In many social agencies, it is
not uncommon for staff conferences convened to discuss cases to devote
fifty-eight minutes to "diagnosis" and two minutes to intervention planning, with little apparent connection between the two discussions. Such
a practice reflects a means-ends confusion in which diagnostic activity
and speculation is regarded as an end in itself and not a tool for in-

creasing effectiveness. Such confusion can be avoided if one achieves a clear understanding of the relationship between diagnosis and intervention.

Diagnosis is a tool for differentiating among cases for the purpose of determining which of the intervention strategies is most likely to be effective. As in the example given earlier, diagnosis may be used to make crude (e.g., "phobic") or highly specific (e.g., "setting a specific wedding date evokes severe anxiety") discriminations. Whether the discrimination mode *should* be crude or refined depends on the complexity of the intervention system. If there were only one method of intervention to be applied in all cases, diagnosis would be superfluous, since discrimination among cases would be unnecessary—all cases would be treated with the same method anyway. Thus, Carl Rogers' client-centered therapy required no diagnostic activity, since the same therapeutic approach was used with all clients. To present this problem in another way, if there were a unique diagnosis for each person—as the critics of classification seem to imply—then we would need three billion treatment methods, or one for every person, if the diagnostic discriminations are to be useful. In other words, there is, or at least there should be, a direct relationship between a diagnostic typology and the intervention alternatives available to the practitioner. If, as we noted above, the practitioner has only one treatment approach in his repertoire, then diagnosis is not only unnecessary but meaningless. Since the issue of monolithic versus differential conceptions of treatment is discussed more fully in a later chapter, it is sufficient for this discussion simply to note that our reading of the evidence indicates that a differential model of treatment, that is, one in which the practitioner has a repertoire of different intervention methods from which he selects a method(s) to be used in a specific case, is more likely to increase the effectiveness of casework in the long run than a monolithic or single-approach model.

The differential model of intervention requires a diagnostic typology linked to the intervention alternatives in order that the practitioner can choose among them. Thus, if the practitioner has two different methods of intervention (A and B) at his command, he needs a two-category diagnostic typology, one to identify those clients who should receive method A and a second for those who will be helped more by method B. And additional categories would be redundant since in any event they would have to be reduced to *the choice* between A and B.*

Construction of a diagnostic typology ideally requires (1) identification and definition of the alternative intervention methods available to the practitioners and (2) knowledge about the differential effects of the alternative methods. While knowledge about these requirements is far from complete, information is accumulating that makes it possible for caseworkers to make some of their intervention decisions on the basis of reasonably firm evidence about the effectiveness of certain methods of intervention. Some selected examples illustrate this point:

1. We now know that for certain kinds of clients, and possibly for many others, brief intervention is more effective than extended treatment.[11]

2. Agreement between caseworker and client on the problem and what they are doing about it appears to be essential for intervention to be effective.[12]

3. The presence of an advocate for the client at fair hearings in public welfare substantially increases the chances that the decision will be in the client's favor.[13]

4. The application of social learning principles to the modification of behavior has created highly effective, quite specific, and therefore preferred methods of intervention for a wide variety of problems, including phobic reactions,[14] public speaking anxiety,[15] stuttering,[16] and behavior problems in general.[17]

For purposes of this discussion, however, we want to emphasize that it is important for caseworkers to be aware of the requirements for constructing useful and effective diagnostic typologies, so that they will know how to evaluate and make discriminating use of the knowledge available to them. The implications of this point will become more clear as we discuss the problem of constructing diagnostic typologies.

* To be precise, three additional diagnostic categories would be relevant and useful, depending on the nature of the treatment approaches and their known effects. These are: a category for those cases that would benefit equally from method A *or* B; a category for those cases that would benefit most from a combination of methods A *and* B; and a residual category for those cases where one cannot reach an opinion about which of the two methods would be more effective.

CONSTRUCTING A DIAGNOSTIC TYPOLOGY

Two general approaches or strategies can be followed in developing a diagnostic typology.[18] In what might be called the *descriptive-genetic* approach, one attempts to group together cases with common descriptive characteristics (e.g., unmarried mothers) or preferably common etiologies (e.g., pneumonia). The central assumption of this approach is that if one can group similar cases together he will be able to develop an intervention strategy specific to that type of case; moreover, if a common etiology can be discovered for a group of cases, it may be possible to devise a method of intervention directed to causes rather than symptoms. This strategy has dominated efforts to construct diagnostic typologies in social casework, psychiatry, and clinical psychology. Virtually all of the typologies familiar to social caseworkers—such as the Ripple-Alexander motivation, capacity and opportunity scheme, the multiproblem family concept, and psychiatric nosology—were developed within this approach and predicated on its assumptions.

There are a number of problems in the descriptive-genetic approach, problems that raise serious doubts about the capacity of this approach to generate useful typologies for casework practitioners. It does not necessarily follow that the identification of common characteristics or even a common etiology among a certain group of cases will simplify the task of devising an effective method of intervention for these cases. To discover, for example, that a certain type of individual problem invariably has its origin in events that occurred in the first three years of the individual's life does not, in itself, provide guides for the practitioner who is attempting to deal with the problem; he cannot undo the past. And the most compelling question for the practitioner always is "what can I do to reduce the problem now?" not "what caused the problem?" unless the latter question clearly helps him answer the first one.[19] A second difficulty in the descriptive-genetic approach is that of determining which are the most salient and potent variables for grouping cases or persons. That is, should one group individuals by their presenting problem or personality characteristics, or age, or . . . ? Actually there are two aspects to this. One is the matter of selecting relevant variables for classification, and this is largely determined by theory. A specific theory of delinquency, for example, identifies the salient variables for distinguishing different types of delinquents. The second aspect hinges on the question "relevant to what?" The primary preoccupation of social scientists when they address problems of concern to the caseworker, such as juvenile deliquency, is explanation. That is, they are searching for variables that will answer the question "under what conditions does the phenomena (e.g., delinquency) occur?" As we have argued, there is no assurance that the answer to this question will also answer the question of more immediate concern to the practitioner, namely "under what conditions can the phenomena be changed?" since an answer to the latter queston must include conditions not relevant to the first.* At the very least, changing a problem involves the introduction of conditions (e.g., a change agent) that logically could not have been implicated in producing the problem. What the practitioner most needs to know are the predictable effects on the problems of the various intervention tools at his disposal. Thus, to the extent that social work scholars and researchers adopt the social scientist's preoccupation with explanation, their conclusions are less apt to be of direct and immediate use to the practitioner than if scholars were to direct their efforts to the question "under what conditions can the practitioner induce change in specified directions?" †

The latter question points to the second strategy for constructing diagnostic typologies, which might be called the *pragmatic* approach. Here typologies are constructed by classifying cases on the basis of their responses to intervention methods rather than by characteristics selected a priori. In principle, the approach would be to randomly assign clients

* Even when change involves manipulation of the same variables that "caused" the problem, the relative importance of the same variables may differ in the two contexts. For example, if a constricted opportunity structure was found to be an important variable in the etiology of delinquency, it does not necessarily follow that presentation of an open opportunity structure will change delinquents into nondelinquents.

† There is no intent in this discussion to discount the importance of explanatory knowledge. Clearly, the more we know about the problems that concern social work the more effective the profession will become, and explanations of problems can stimulate new possibilities for intervention. Our concern here is simply to make clear the kind of knowledge most needed by the practitioner.

to the known methods of intervention, assess outcomes, and use the outcomes to construct a diagnostic typology for these interventive methods.
A hypothetical example may clarify this principle. Suppose that there
are two known methods of intervention, A and B. Clients are randomly
assigned to these methods and measures of success at the conclusion of
treatment yield the following results:

	Percent Success	Percent Failure
Method A	50	50
Method B	50	50

The practitioner's problem is to choose between the two methods in
specific cases. Clearly, if the above results comprised all the information
available to him, his best strategy would be to flip a coin, since neither
method shows any clear superiority. However, is it possible that some
of the clients who benefited from method B failed to respond to method
A? And do such clients have some characteristic in common that is not
shared by the other clients? To answer this question one would collect
data about clients on a large array of variables and attributes, including
those drawn from theory, clinical hunches, or even wild guesses. The researcher's aim would be to find variables that would increase the practitioner's ability to select the method most likely to benefit a client or, in
other words, to make effective diagnostic discriminations. Assume this
approach produced results of the sort illustrated in the hypothetical
table on page 150.

The tabular results (it is important to emphasize that an initial exploratory study would include a much larger array of variables than
shown in this table) reveal three things important for the practitioner.
First, if one chooses between methods A and B on the basis of marital
status alone he improves substantially the client's chances of benefiting
from treatment. Second, the results indicate that age, character disorder,
ego strength, and education are diagnostically irrelevant since they essentially provide him with no information for choosing between the two
methods. And third, clients with high anxiety levels are unlikely to benefit from *either* method. Through further permutations and combinations of the client variables and their associated outcomes, the

Variables	Percent Successful	
	Method A	Method B
Age		
Less than thirty	50	50
Thirty and over	50	50
Oral character disorder	50	50
Ego strength		
Weak	50	50
Strong	50	50
Education		
Less than high school graduate	50	50
High school graduate	50	50
Marital status	50	50
Married	70	30
Single (including widowed,		
divorced, and separated)	30	70
Anxiety		
High	20	20
Low	50	50

researcher could create empirically three *types* of clients, described by the variables that define them:

TYPE I   Variables associated with a higher rate of success with method A than with B, for example, married clients.

TYPE II   Variables associated with a higher rate of success with method B than with A, for example, single clients.

TYPE III Variables associated with low rates of success with both methods, for example, high anxiety.

Identification of the third type is especially important because it provides a focus for efforts toward discovering new methods that would be effective with cases in this group.

Only recently has this approach to the construction of typologies begun to be used in social work. An example would be the studies of continuance in casework, which have attempted to identify the variables that differentiate clients who continue in casework from those who do not.[20] This research has highlighted the importance of such factors as the congruence between the expectations the worker and client have of each other, the client's social class status, and the unimportance of some variables that had been assumed a priori to be diagnostically relevant.

Medicine has made some impressive advances on the basis of knowledge about the effects of therapeutic procedures and has done so without a full understanding of the causes and dynamics of the illness—cancer treatment is an example. Behavior therapists, whose approach requires a precise definition of desired outcomes in behavioral terms, are explicitly attempting to construct typologies based on client responses to specific intervention procedures.

Through these and other efforts mentioned earlier, the knowledge base necessary for pragmatically constructed typologies is gradually accumulating. The development of such knowledge can be expected to increase as the importance of this approach is recognized more widely and as practitioners and researchers increase their capacity to define intervention methods and desired outcomes with the specificity this approach requires. Such developments will ease the difficulties most casework students encounter as they attempt to grasp the meaning and importance of diagnosis in casework, for given the state of knowledge in casework, the linkage between diagnosis and intervention frequently has been unclear at best.

THE AIMS OF DIAGNOSIS

To return to a more specific examination of the task of diagnosis, we have indicated in the preceding discussion that *the aim of diagnostic activity is to answer a series of questions assumed to be essential for planning and implementing a successful intervention strategy.* And *which* questions are essential depends on what is known or perforce assumed about the available intervention methods—in other words, which kinds of cases respond more favorably to method A than to method B? The practical implications of this conception of diagnosis can be suggested by examining the questions currently held to be essential, together with some questions raised by our discussion of the function of diagnosis.

WHAT IS THE PROBLEM?

Identification and classification of the problem(s) that the case presents clearly is needed, if for no other reason than to focus the caseworker's diagnostic and interventive activities; in any differential model of casework intervention, the client's particular problem obviously has implications for making at least gross choices among interventive strategies, for example, financial assistance versus psychotherapy for an individual who is destitute. For other types of problems, however, whether defined by the client ("I don't know what's the matter—I just feel unhappy"), or the community ("he is a delinquent"), or theory applied by the worker ("the client has a weak ego"), identification of the problem does not in itself suggest what should be done, primarily because it is not known with any certainty what procedures will remedy the problem. It is known that the problem of destitution will be alleviated promptly by financial assistance, at least temporarily. It is not known with equal certainty, however, what will relieve unhappiness, end delinquent behavior, or strengthen an ego.

HOW SERIOUS IS THE PROBLEM?

Judgment of seriousness, or what caseworkers have called "assessment," has at least four aspects. One is the *pervasiveness* of the problem(s). Is it an isolated problem, localized in one area of the life of the individual or family, or are there multiple problems in different life areas? The relevance of this question to intervention is simply that the more pervasive the problems, the more likely it is that intervention strategy will need to include multiple methods directed to different levels of the case situation. A second aspect is the degree of *impairment* or disablement associated with the problem(s). To what extent is the person prevented from performing his social roles or the family its functions? Answers to this question have less direct relevance to intervention than to the assessment of the social seriousness or cast of the problem(s). To society, the man who is unable to hold down a steady job represents a more "serious" problem than the man who works steadily but is unhappy or in conflict with his wife. These social values may influence the caseworker's activities. A third aspect of seriousness is *persistence* of the problem(s). Did the problem have a recent and relatively sudden onset or has it existed for a long time? What is the relevance of this question to intervention? Although direct evidence is scarce, a variety of studies of acute crises suggests that many if not most crisis situations are self-resolving—the resolution may or may not be adequate, but the acute stage of a crisis typically cannot be tolerated very long. This is analogous to the physician's recognition that his greatest ally is the fact that most people who become ill will improve without treatment, as recognized in the folk saying about the common cold: "If you don't get treatment it will take you a week to get over it, but if you go to a doctor, you'll be well in seven days." In other words, as staff members in psychiatric hospitals long have recognized, a high proportion of acute problems "improve" in a short period of time, regardless of what practitioners do about them, a fact that probably accounts at least for some of the success reported with short-term crisis-oriented treatment in casework. Finally, a fourth aspect of seriousness is *prognosis,* or the probability that the problem will respond favorably to intervention. This assessment clearly derives from what is known or assumed about the effectiveness of intervention methods. The ambulatory schizophrenic who is able to work and manage his own affairs is considered to have a more serious illness than his neurotic counterpart only because schizophrenia is assumed to be less responsive to treatment than neurosis. Were the situation to be reversed, that is, if a dramatically successful "cure" for schizophrenia were developed, neurosis would be viewed as a more serious diagnosis than schizophrenia.

WHAT ARE THE DYNAMICS OF THE PROBLEM?

This question represents the search for an explanation of the problem. There are instances in which explanation is essential in order to make certain decisions about intervention, and in such cases this question becomes diagnostically important. For example, it is important, in planning intervention, to know whether the problem of unemployment in a case represents a lack of available jobs or an inability to hold a job, or whether marital conflict reflects lack of affective commitment or misperception of intentions and motives. And in some cases the search for an explanation becomes a central aim and theme of intervention, either because that is what the client is seeking or because it is instrumental to bringing about other changes in the client's behavior. But a search for explanation that has no clear implications for intervention—a popular pastime in case conferences—should be recognized for what it is: an academic exercise, and one that can displace attention from more relevant questions. It may be interesting to speculate about the meaning of Mr. Jones' slips of the tongue, but if his problem is unemployment these speculations are not likely to help him find a job, although it may be relevant if what he is seeking is an explanation of his covert wishes and feelings. The heavy emphasis that caseworkers (and psychotherapists) have long attached to explanation is shifting now that the assumption that self-understanding is an essential prelude to change in behavior is yielding in the face of evidence that behavior change can occur without prior attitudinal change.

The search for *cause* is part of the Western scientific tradition with which social workers, along with most professionals, are imbued. In fact, the question "why" is so deeply ingrained in the professional-scientific culture that it arises naturally, and it is difficult for the caseworker to think about a case without searching for causes. Since we discussed at length the relevance of cause to intervention earlier in this chapter, at this point it is sufficient to summarize some of the problems associated with the search for causes in diagnosis. First, the causes of many of the problems confronting caseworkers are complex at best and often indeterminate. Yet, perhaps because it has been assumed that identification of cause is an essential component of diagnosis, many caseworkers seem compelled to make categorical causal statements from which most social scientists would shrink. Second, as the behavioral therapists and others have shown, the identification of cause is not necessary for effective treatment. And as we argued earlier, not only have effective treatment strategies been developed in the absence of knowledge about cause but knowledge of cause may not be sufficient, or even in some instances useful, in devising intervention measures. These considerations suggest that the search for cause in casework diagnosis should be carefully circumscribed and closely related to the specific focus of change efforts. It is possible to make useful causal inferences at low levels of abstraction. The fact that Mr. Jones has a long, stable work history and is currently unemployed *because* the plant where he worked was shut down suggests an approach to the problem of his unemployment different from that needed for Mr. Smith who was fired, once again, for drinking on the job. Similarly, the impression that Johnny's temper tantrums are reinforced and perpetuated by the rewards they evoked from his parents is a low-order causal inference that points to a condition that, if modified, might lead to the extinction of the tantrums, regardless of what originally gave rise to the tantrums or "why" his parents reinforce them. In general, to the extent that causal inferences concern variables that can be influenced by the caseworker and are at a sufficiently low level of abstraction to be tested empirically in the practice situation, they may be useful in the planning and conduct of treatment.

WHAT ARE THE CLIENT'S EXPECTATIONS OF TREATMENT?

As we emphasized in our discussion of the client role in chapter 4, the client's expectations of treatment and his conceptions of what treatment entails provide at least the initial focus for the caseworker's diagnostic and therapeutic activities, and the basis for the contract between them. This is so even when the problem and the desired outcome have been defined by someone other than the client, for *that* conflict then becomes the focus of their initial encounters. To interpose foci or objectives outside the range of the client's views and expectations is to risk alienating him, as Sullivan repeatedly emphasized; a shift in focus and goals should be made only with clarification and establishment of consensus between worker and client.[21] It is this principle that is implied in caseworkers' emphasis on "beginning where the client is" and "moving at the client's pace."

WHAT CAN BE CHANGED?

To establish goals and to evaluate the client's expectations of outcome, it is important to assess which aspects of the case can be and which cannot be changed. This may be rather difficult since the limits of behavioral and attitudinal change are not known, but experience and available knowledge provide some basis for discriminating among events according to the probability that they can be changed with available methods. Explication of the elements in the case that are amenable to change and control, and those that probably are intractable, helps to identify alternatives to be used as a basis for developing an intervention strategy.

WHAT IS TO BE CHANGED?

This is perhaps the most important and difficult question of all, since it asks for a precise specification of the events, behaviors, or processes in the case that the caseworker will attempt to change. Because of the importance and difficulty of this question, we devote the next chapter to an extended discussion of it. The more precisely the caseworker can answer this question in terms of concrete behavioral events, the easier the task of devising an effective intervention strategy becomes. A few examples may help to make this point clear.

It is easier to "reduce anxiety" than to "increase ego strength" simply because the former objective can be defined in terms of specific behaviors to be modified whereas the latter—the referents of which are abstract functions (e.g., judgment, affect, perceptions, etc.), not specific behaviors—cannot. Intervention consists of specific acts by the caseworker; caseworkers do not "give support," they do specific things, such as reassuring the client that he need not feel guilty about what he did, or reaching out to him by phone or home visit when he is immobilized. And the specific acts of the caseworker have specific effects; the reassurance may evoke a reduction in the sense of guilt, the act of reaching out may instill a belief that the worker is interested and cares. These effects may have more general effects on the client's behavior; his judgement may be more objective now that he feels less guilty, or he may be less suspicious now that he believes the worker cares about him. But the point is that the worker acts upon specific behaviors, not abstract hypothetical entities such as the ego. Moreover, the probable effects of the worker's acts can most reliably be stated in specific behavioral outcomes—one example, among many from the research in behavior modification, is the well-established finding that if the clinician says "uh-huh" every time the client speaks of his mother (or any specific topic) the frequency of his references to mother will rise sharply.[22] (Perhaps a more familiar, if anecdotal, example is the pronounced tendency for the question "why" to evoke rationalized explanations from clients in casework interviews.) Thus, to the extent that desired outcomes or changes can be defined in behavioral terms, the task of identifying actions likely to evoke (or extinguish, if the aim is to eliminate behavior) those behaviors is simplified considerably.

These six questions, then, define the central concerns of diagnosis, since answers to them provide the basis for planning intervention. Some consideration of *all* these questions is essential whatever theory the caseworker holds; he must have some conception of the problem and its seriousness, must understand what the client wants and expects, and must know what he will attempt to change if his interventions are to be purposeful and rational.

THE PROCESS OF DIAGNOSIS

It would be highly desirable, of course, if the steps to be taken in order to answer the above questions were programmed so that the caseworker would know exactly how to go about answering them. This cannot be done, partly because of the limitations of available knowledge, but also —even if more adequate knowledge were available—because of the need for informed professional judgment to meet the special conditions of the individual case.

The guides that the worker can follow in the diagnostic process in addition to (1) the questions he knows he must answer, (2) his understanding of the relationship between these questions and intervention, and (3) his fund of knowledge are (4) the norms and logic of science, which will be considered briefly in this section, and (5) the concept of levels of diagnosis, discussed in the next section of this chapter.

The social worker's commitment to the scientific method, which was discussed at length in chapter 4, entails a responsibility to adhere to the standards of science in the diagnostic process. The importance of this standard can hardly ever be over-emphasized, since it is this possibly above all that distinguishes the caseworker from palmists, astrologers, faith healers, and the like. Essentially, adherence to this standard means that the caseworker will follow the observation-hypothesis formation-experimentation paradigm in his thinking about diagnosis and intervention. His touchstone will be fact garnered from observation rather than from the stars or divine revelation, and he will regard his statements and conclusions as hypotheses to be continually tested against further observations and modified or replaced when they no longer fit the data. This requires of the caseworker the most scrupulous care to avoid confusing observation with inference, and hypothesis with verified knowledge. "Mr. R.'s hands were trembling" describes an observation—a datum—but "Mr. R. was anxious" states an inference, not an observation. If the inference is correct, there is little harm in the summary statement "Mr. R. was anxious." If this seems to be only a semantic quibble, suppose that the correct inference to be drawn from Mr. R's tremulousness is that he has palsy, or that he is weak because he is just recovering from an illness, or that he has just over-exerted himself, or that he is on the verge of a heart attack—if any of these were correct the worker would be on the wrong track. However, the larger problem is not the condensation of observations into inferential statements but rather the failure to distinguish between the two. If the worker who says, "Mr. R. was anxious" recognizes that this is an inference and not an observation he will soon collect additional data, recognize his error, and correct it. But if he thinks he has *observed* anxiety he thereby verifies his inference and precludes any possibility of correcting his error—after all, he *knows* Mr. R. was anxious because he saw his anxiety. If, as is not unlikely, he tries to "help" Mr. R. express his anxiety and is told "but I'm not anxious," the worker is unlikely to doubt that the client is anxious but rather will conclude that the intensity of Mr. R.'s anxiety is such that he needs to deny it.

The problem illustrated in the simple example of Mr. R.'s trembling hands is multiplied greatly when one moves to more complicated diagnostic generalizations. At more complex and therefore more abstract levels of hypothesis-formation there is a strong temptation to reason deductively from theory rather than inductively from observation —to ask how the case fits the theory rather than the reverse. A familiar illustration is the common practice among psychoanalytically oriented caseworkers of asking, *implicitly,* how and to what extent the client mastered the stages of psychosexual development—to ask, for example, how Mr. Y. resolved his wish to kill his father and marry his mother. This is an example of deductive reasoning; the question assumes, on purely theoretical grounds, that Mr. Y. in fact had such wishes; it is equivalent, in more sophisticated form, to asking every husband how he resolved his wish to beat his wife. The question the clinician should ask, *if* the matter is relevant to treatment, is *whether* Mr. Y. had a wish to kill his father and marry his mother, since it has not been established that these wishes are universal.

There are numerous hazards and pitfalls in observation, inference, and hypothesis formation, the processes that enter into clinical judgement.[23] Much has been made in casework of the importance of self-awareness. For the most part, however, this concept has been defined narrowly to refer primarily to the worker's understanding of his feelings and personality patterns. We are suggesting that self-awareness should be expanded to include critical scrutiny by the worker of his thought processes in forming clinical judgments about his cases. To do this, he needs formal training in the logic and methods of science, just as does the professional researcher, for the scientific canons of logic and evidence are no different for the clinician than for the scientist. The caseworker is not free to reach unsupported conclusions simply because he does not call himself a researcher. The responsibility for scientific rationality falls as heavily on the practitioner as on his colleagues engaged in research. It is this responsibility that makes research training an indispensable element of education for social work, and the not infrequent failure of social work students to see the importance of this element for practice reflects, in part, a failure to understand this aspect of their responsibilities as practitioners.

LEVELS OF DIAGNOSIS

Social work has defined its mission in relation to a concern with certain social problems, or with man in relation to society. Consequently, casework diagnosis is inadequate if it is focused only on an individual and his intrapersonal dynamics, no matter how deeply or thoroughly these may be explored. Diagnoses in casework must always attend to the social matrix of behavior; they must always, in short, be psychosocial. This requires that casework diagnosis include the following levels of analysis: (1) the individual, including both intrapersonal factors and his location in a social network, (2) interpersonal systems, or the interaction units (dyads, triads, etc.) implicated in the case situation, (3) the family unit as a social system, and (4) the family unit's interchanges with its social network.

Because no single theory adequately embraces all of these levels of analysis, each level requires use of a different set of concepts and theoretical frameworks. Partly for this reason the more detailed discussion of diagnosis and intervention still ahead of us is organized according to the above levels of diagnosis and intervention.

CHAPTER NINE

GOALS, OBJECTIVES, AND OUTCOME

We have said that casework must have some end in view; that is, some outcome is either implicitly or explicitly desired by both participants in the process. Voluntary casework clients come with needs they can state, if only in nebulous terms; they see themselves as suffering from problems that need resolution. The end result of their encounter with a caseworker is often seen by them as the alleviation of these difficulties. By the same token, the caseworker sees the treatment process as finite; it must end, and its end occurs when certain matters have been accomplished.

What, then, are the ends projected by the caseworker? By what means are they to be determined? How are they related to the ends desired by the client? What outcomes are seen as outside the province of the social caseworker?

GOAL SETTING IN THE FUNCTIONAL SCHOOL
OF SOCIAL CASEWORK

The functional or Rankian school of thought disposes of goals with one magnificent premise: the therapeutic experience is, by itself, the only significant objective. The goal of the functional caseworker is not to relieve symptoms, it is not to transform client behavior from one state to another; it is instead to offer an experience in a relationship within

which the separation-unity dialectic can be played out. That the therapeutic experience may yield concomitants that are, in effect, changes in
behavior is parenthetical to the functional stance. Functionalists set
themselves the goal of providing a relational experience of a certain
order. But this is as far as it goes: symptoms may or may not be relieved; behavior may or may not change—these notions are irrelevan-
cies.[1]

When social caseworkers, of whatever theoretical persuasion, encounter involuntary clients the functional model may well be invoked
as the most reasonable. Involuntary clients do not necessarily see themselves as experiencing difficulties that can be alleviated by the caseworker; hence, they have no positive expectations at all. In this sense, a
client's goals are contingent upon his perceiving that something is
wrong. Lacking such expectations and goals the client may be encouraged to enter into an association with a caseworker just for the sake of
the association. The establishment of a relationship with his unwilling
client thus becomes the objective of the social caseworker in this particular instance, and may well be seen as sufficient in and of itself.

GOALS AND THE VALUE SYSTEM
OF SOCIAL CASEWORK

As we have seen earlier, certain objectives cannot be entertained by the
social caseworker because they conflict with the morality of his profession. There is no need to recapitulate here in any detail the constraints
placed upon the caseworker's goals by the dictates of his professional
ethic. Certainly proposed ends that have as their primary function the ag-
grandizement of the clinician himself are precluded. Thus a caseworker
can never be a Svengali, using the client for his own personal and self-
fulfilling purposes. Some other specific objectives are precluded because
they conflict with the values and even laws of the wider society.

There are, however, a great many possible goals that are on the
fringe of acceptability in regard to both the profession and society. Consider the following hypothetical but not implausible situation. A husband and wife are seen in a social agency for marital counseling. The
wife is immediately responsive to the therapeutic work; she is funda-

mentally a rather sound person; she is in fact a caseworker's delight—
eager, intelligent, and ready to blossom forth into a whole new world
of self-understanding. The needs that propelled her into this marriage
were infantile, if not self-destructive. The husband, on the other hand,
is seen as having only a tenuous hold on his psychic equilibrium and is
thought to be unable to profit by any but the most superficial introspection and insight. The marriage has succeeded in providing a great deal
of stability to his life. The caseworker in this situation is faced with a
dilemma. If he is *too* successful in the treatment of the wife, she may
well renounce the sad events that led to the marriage and seek separation. This would likely have the effect of destroying that modicum of
adjustment thus far obtained by the husband.

Thus, if the caseworker posits a goal for treatment that involves
a maximum of insight for the wife, the end result may well entail the
destruction of the marriage and perhaps harm the husband. If on the
other hand the goal is the alleviation of the marital distress, per se, it is
conceivable that this could be accomplished—but at the expense of
the wife's maximum well-being.

It does little good to argue that the goal is a function of what is defined to be the client unit. That is, if the client is defined to be the wife,
one objective is possible; if the client is defined to be the husband, another objective is viable; if the client is defined to be the marriage itself,
then still a third alternative presents itself. But the problem remains: on
what basis is the definition to be made?

This hypothetical case illustrates something more than the technical intricacies of establishing goals that involve the careful weighing and
balancing of competing and even contradictory ends; it is cited primarily to point to an ethical dilemma: is the disruption of a marriage a
permissible goal for casework in any case situation? Some schools of
thought within psychotherapy seems to assert an affirmative to this
question simply by virtue of absolving themselves of responsibility for
such an eventuality. That is, these schools argue that the business of
psychotherapy is the growth and development of the individual; if such
growth entails divorce, it is not the responsibility of the therapist. Therapy implies release—and let the chips fall where they may.

But it is not only divorce that is involved in such a position; indeed, almost any behavior can follow from the moral neutrality of the

"insight" therapist. As Perry London argues so eloquently, this avowed moral neutrality is not neutral at all; on the contrary, it is the primary article of faith for the libertine.[2] A stance that the free and sincere expression of emotion and instinct is desirable if it does not adversely affect other human beings is an advocation of a morality that is very precise and anything but neutral.

It is not clear that such "libertine" goals and by-products of goals are compatible with society's wishes in regard to psychotherapy. The libertine is not necessarily the end product desired by the community at large. Society may expect a Babbitt and get a Bohemian; it may wish conformity and receive rebellion; it may yearn for marital stability and reap marital discord; it may desire sexual restraint and receive sexual license. The paradox for the clinician involves what may well be an irrevocable conflict between the needs and drives of the individual client and the demands and contraints of the community. That the paradox is insoluble is well argued by the sweeping metaphor of Freud who posits the conflict between id and superego—Eros and Thanatos—as the central dilemma of mankind. And, alas, Freud offers no real resolution to the struggle.

THE RELATIONSHIP OF OBJECTIVES
TO DIAGNOSIS

For the clinician who operates from a more or less deterministic base there is an interdependence between the diagnostic assessment of the client and the ends of treatment. This interdependence is of two forms: first, the objectives can be contingent upon the diagnosis; but, second, the diagnosis can be reached as a function of the anticipated outcome. The first alternative may appear more logical: given a particular state of affairs within the case, certain ends are possible and other ends are improbable. This is a view of the diagnostic school of thought; the clinician observes and gathers data toward the end of constructing a clinical portrait of his client. The portrait, or diagnosis, contains the cues as to what the problem is and the possible outcomes to the problem. Given an assessment of the current situation and an anticipated end, the appropriate therapeutic regimen can be construed. The possible outcomes are seen as necessarily contingent upon the diagnostic assessment. It would be foolhardy to posit a goal of professional education for a mentally deficient youth; commodious or expensive housing for the impoverished; an harmonious daughter-father relationship for the incestuously violated daughter; or the contemplative or intellectual life for the "swinging" hysteric. People *do not* have unlimited possibilities; their becoming is very much a function of what they are. The watchword is *realistic* goals in view of the potentialities of the individual, and the evaluation of what is realistic hinges upon a precise diagnosis.

But in that uncertain world which is psychotherapy, the second alternative intrudes; the diagnosis may very well be a function of preconceived ends. All men should be free and unfettered agents; hence, a permanently crippling psychosis is not a tenable diagnosis. Children are growing organisms; thus, there is no such thing as childhood schizophrenia.[3] There is nothing much that can be done for this patient; hence, he's a schizophrenic or, perhaps worse, he exhibits a character disorder. Strupp has gathered considerable evidence that points to the strong association between the caseworker's appraisal of outcome and his attitude toward the client. A favorable outcome is associated with all that is diagnostically desirable; an unfavorable prognosis yields a halo of diagnostic pessimism.[4]

To the extent, then, that projected ends or goals begin to contaminate diagnoses, the clinician makes an error in temporal logic. But when this serial error is not made, goals may still influence diagnoses. Different schools of psychotherapy stake out different domains of viable outcomes. That is to say, they hope to accomplish different things. And the different objectives lead to particular kinds of diagnostic foci. But these considerations have been raised in the preceding chapter, and we turn now to what is perhaps the central factor in goal setting—the client himself.

THE CLIENT'S ROLE IN
DETERMINING OBJECTIVES

What role can the client play in determining the goals and objectives of treatment? One can respond by stating two contradictory positions: first, the client is the only person who can know what he wants for himself; second, the client is in no position to know what he wants for himself.

The former position is compatible with the principle of self-determination. Ends are *not* to be imposed upon a client by a therapist; the client should determine what the end product shall be. In a case involving marital discord, it is the participants who decide upon the outcome of the marriage; the caseworker does not impose the ultimate result.

But choice of some outcomes must obviously be denied the client. Suicide is not a permissible objective. It can be asserted generally that if the client knew what was best for him, he would not need therapeutic service in the first place. The expert is more equipped to know what is best for the client. Certainly the medical practitioner would be loath to concede to his patient the skills necessary to construct a treatment regimen or a prognosis. And, continuing the medical analogy, the schizophrenic has neither the coherence nor the expertise to posit treatment goals; and the psychoneurotic is similarly handicapped, not so much by a lack of cognitive facility as by a woeful ignorance as to the implications of his disease. But what of the financially handicapped? Does the public assistance applicant know enough about the causes of poverty to insist upon a grant and no more? Does the itinerant laborer have the knowledge to decide whether a handout is his only need?

Social caseworkers by and large have been extremely reluctant to concede these capabilities to their clients. The migrant may get the handout, which may be *all* he sees as his objective, but it may be used by the caseworker merely as a technical wedge. The public welfare agency is not content with providing economic benefits, even when eligibility is established; rehabilitation is seen as a concomitant end. The fact that the recipient may *not want* rehabilitation is irrelevant; the expert knows best.

The dilemma of who determines goals—client or caseworker— grows out of two roots. The first is conflicting theoretical conceptions as to the nature of psychological and social distress. Thus, a model of social welfare problems that is predicated on a psychosocial "germ" theory, that is, a highly complex *disease* model, calls for profound expertise. The client is presumed to lack such professional know-how. On the other hand, a model based on the premise that such problems are essentially *stylistic* and volitional, that is, that they exist mainly because of the client's outlook, renders clients perfectly competent to choose their objectives. The second root is conflicting value conceptions as to what options are legitimately available to people. Thus, suicide is outlawed—people may not choose to do away with themselves. More generally, however, illness is not seen as a permissible alternative; but what of pauperism, or alcoholism, or unhappiness, or sexual deviance, or just plain nastiness? It is a hardy caseworker who can, without flinching, agree with the derelict who says "I want to be a bum," or the welfare client who wants only her check and prefers her squalor untouched.

It seems too simplistic to hold either the client or the caseworker solely responsible for the formulation of goals. Those goals may be best that are mutually arrived at, with the expert and the afflicted arriving at an agreed upon objective after due deliberation. It is probably true that the client knows what is best for him—sometimes; and that the professional knows what is best for his client—sometimes; and that—most times—client and professional together know what is best.

THE SPECIFICITY OF GOALS

Some goals are so attractive and so universally valued that agreement comes easily. No client would reject "personal happiness" as an acceptable end. Social caseworkers are not so naïve as to offer it as an end-product of their services, but technical synonyms are not infrequently used: "adequate social functioning," "restored mental health," "improved ego functioning." The problem with such objectives is that they are as ambiguous and, alas, as unattainable as happiness.

Beyond such considerations, however, the above conceptions of goals of treatment can be criticized as being too gross. Sound ego functioning, for example, embraces all of life, as does "mental health" and "social functioning." Such encompassing objectives are much too grandiose and unspecific for social casework—indeed, for any therapeutic activity. How is "adequate social functioning," for example, to be measured? What are the criteria of "sound ego functioning?" These questions cannot be answered: criteria are not readily arrived at, and measurement problems are almost insurmountable.

Casework requires objectives that are well-defined and measurable. Thus, if a child is suffering from inadequate school performance and is brought to a child guidance clinic for this problem, the end of treatment should be expressed in terms of school performance. Objectives then become contingent upon a precise statement of the case problem.

Delinquent behavior provides a provocative realm within which to consider objectives. The delinquent child probably suffers from a wide range of difficulties, but almost invariably the problem that brings him to the attention of a therapeutic agent is his conflict with the legal system. He is a law-breaker; that is his problem—as defined by society, and, in all likelihood, as defined by himself. He may also be psychopathic, or prepsychotic, or miserable, or he may have a brittle ego, or an inability to control his instinctual impulses. And it may be essential to consider these extra-problematic components in his treatment. But the test of when the treatment has succeeded is met by the child's cessation of delinquent activities. It is fruitless to pose objectives in terms of his "peripheral" problems when one cannot know that these have any direct connection with his delinquency.

Objectives of treatment must ultimately be related to the symptoms of the social work client. It is inconceivable that a case can be seen as successfully treated if the delinquent child remains delinquent, even though his psychodynamic equilibrium is reestablished. And yet, all too frequently, such objectives are seen as the most desirable and fundamental ones. For, it is held, symptoms are only symptoms and it is a superficial treatment indeed that "cures" the symptoms without touching the disease. The problem with this formulation is that we have not yet reached a level of diagnostic sophistication wherein we can separate symptoms from causative agents, and there is nothing inherently dissatisfying about relieving symptoms.

To summarize, the goals and objectives of casework must: (1) be couched in terms of specifics rather than globals, (2) be symptom-oriented rather than disease-oriented, and (3) be posed in such a manner that their attainment be measurable and evident.

THE PROBLEM OF OUTCOME MEASURES [5]

All research, both accomplished and projected, on the efficacy of psychotherapy flounders when it comes to the problem of identifying criteria of success. A good deal of the difficulty is, perhaps, now clear:

traditional psychotherapy has remained indifferent to symptomatology per se and instead has emphasized self-understanding or insight as its end product. Self-knowledge, however, is a perpetual quest; is it to be conceived of as an absolute condition, or is it to be thought of in relative terms, that is, in terms of the potentialities of the client?

To a certain extent, then, there is no end to the pursuit of such objectives, and a treatment that sets itself the task of obtaining them must be interminable. Formal treatment may cease, of course, and the individual may be left to pursue the insight-functioning journey by himself, but the point of cessation must remain fairly arbitrary. The arbitrary end point is well articulated by Freud:

Every analyst of experience will be able to think of a number of cases in which he has taken permanent leave of the patient *rebus bene gestis.* There is a far smaller discrepancy between theory and practice [the theory being that the instincts remain forever troublesome] in cases of so-called character-analysis. Here it is not easy to predict a natural end to the process, even if we do not look for impossibilities or ask too much of analysis. Our object will be not to rub off all the corners of the human character so as to produce "normality" according to schedule, nor yet to demand that the person who has been "thoroughly analyzed" shall never again feel the stirrings of passions in himself or become involved in any internal conflict. The business of analysis is to secure the best possible psychological condition for the functioning of the ego; when this has been done, analysis has accomplished its task.[6]

The "best possible psychological conditions for the functioning of the ego" is apparently to be assessed subjectively, however, and both therapist and client can opt for better and better conditions.

Objectives and goals that are couched in such global terms are, by nature, beyond *measurable* attainment. But such is not the case with more modest ends. We have posited the case of the delinquent youth and argued that a realistic and directly observable end would obtain when the youth ceased committing delinquent acts. There are innumerable examples of this class of case objectives. A youngster who, for whatever reasons, is judged to be a problem because he will not attend school can be thought of as successfully treated when his school attendance becomes reasonably frequent. A child who suffers from enuresis is "cured" when he no longer wets himself. The case of an impotent man can be closed when he experiences erections. An unemployed father is satisfactorily treated when he obtains and holds gainful employment.

The usual objection to a use of such symptomatic indicators was suggested earlier: treating symptoms ignores causes and, following in the logic of any etiological theory, when the cause or motivating element remains untouched other symptoms must follow. Thus, it would be argued, the delinquent youth may cease his delinquent acts but he may suffer acute anxiety; the child may return to school but start biting his nails; the impotent man may become a Don Juan; and the newly employed father may come to beat his children. This objection can be summarized under the parsimonious rubric of "the hypothesis of symptom substitution," an hypothesis that has permeated the field of psychotherapy for several decades. Yet there is little, if any, evidence for it. In the words of Yates, who conducted a thorough review of the hypothesis: "Considering the significant role such a distinction has played in clinical psychology, experimental demonstration of its existence is singularly lacking." *

Notice again the inextricable connection between goals and outcome indicators. If the focus of treatment is on the elimination of specifically defined symptoms, the outcome can be evaluated only within that same context. If one goal is seen as untenable or otherwise outlawed, another goal should be posited and an outcome measured within its frame of reference.

We deal, then, with what can productively be considered as (1) prediction and (2) the criteria for testing the prediction. If the prediction is that a therapy will produce "insight" or "improved social functioning," it is incumbent upon the clinicians using it to propose criteria of such conditions. If the prediction is for "symptom removal," the clinician is obligated to specify indications for that end. We suggest that clinicians will have a much easier task in the latter instance.

* A. J. Yates, "Symptoms and Symptom Substitution," *Psychological Review,* 65 (1957), 371–74. We could also cite Eysenck, who writes: "How about the return of symptoms? I have made a thorough search of the literature dealing with behavior therapy with this particular point in view. Many psychoanalytically trained therapists using these methods have been specially on the outlook for the return of symptoms, or the emergence of alternative ones; yet neither they nor any of the other practitioners have found anything of this kind to happen except in the most rare and unusual cases." H. J. Eysenck, "Learning Theory and Behavioral Theory," *Journal of Mental Science,* 105 (1959), 61–75.

But, of course, the clinician's comfort and ease is not the decisive variable. The central issue is the client's welfare, not the caseworker's. And, within the confines of a perfectly tenable point of view, insight may well be in the ultimate interest of the client. In such a case, the clinician is not relieved of the burden of developing criteria for the attainment of insight; his problem is difficult, vastly more difficult than that of his behaviorist colleagues, but nonetheless obligatory.

The reader should note that the paradigm of prediction and later evaluation of whether the prediction was borne out is the hallmark of scientific endeavor. At first glance it may be difficult to see the close parallel between the process of social casework and the conventional scientific formula of observation, hypothesis, and experiment. And yet, as we suggested much earlier in this volume, the casework procedure of study, diagnosis, and treatment is synonymous with such a formulation. The diagnostic process is simply an exercise in the development of specific and case-centered hypotheses; treatment is the testing of such hypotheses (predictions). What has been sorely lacking, however, in most psychotherapeutic work is the evaluation of the treatment-experiment. It is as though, to stretch the analogy to its extreme, the scientist did everything in his laboratory except record and analyze the outcome of his experiment.

TERMINATION

Upon the evaluation of outcome, however measured, the caseworker is faced with another significant issue. He must prepare his client to go about the business of living without the aid of the caseworker. This may initially appear to be a most presumptuous proposition, since it implies that the casework endeavor has been a central event in the everyday life of the client and that the "business of living" has, in some fundamental respect, been contingent upon the caseworker. In some instances the presumption is totally unwarranted, and termination occasions no special problem. Thus, a caseworker whose contact with a client is focused around the provision of a specific and tangible need—summer camp plans for a child, homemaker service, referral, and the like—may end with his client in a rather matter-of-fact and business-like way. But for many clients and case situations termination is fraught with considerable meaning.

In the first instance, we should recall the circumstances under which casework help is undertaken. Very often it is a time of severe stress for a client; he is by definition in trouble or otherwise in a crisis situation; he is vulnerable; his passions are stirred; and, if the casework enterprise takes hold at all, it is forever colored by the affect of its initial stages. The client had been needy and he found a sympathetic ally. In other words, the caseworker in the above instances has become a meaningful person in the life of his client, simply by virtue of the affect-ridden context of the client's initial need and the succorance attendant upon that need.

And, if we are to accept the psychoanalytic argument of the transference phenomenon, the meaningfulness of the casework relationship to the client is further exacerbated. But transference or not, the relationship of client to caseworker is in the final analysis a human relationship and as such has the potential of being profoundly meaningful. Its severance can generate the same kinds of distressing feelings that any human loss can generate—mourning, helplessness, and grief.

Termination, then, of the meaningful (and sometimes long-standing) association between client and caseworker requires preparation and planning. The client must be weaned, as it were, from a dependent relationship. The typical process involves a gradual reduction of the frequency and intensity of the contact; appointments are scheduled less frequently, affect-laden issues are avoided, and, in some instances, the contacts take on a lighter and more casual tone.

But we cannot close this section on termination without reference to the intrinsic unfairness of it all. The caseworker has encouraged the client to enter into an intense association with him knowing full well that it will end. Moreover, he knows that the end will be painful, and it will be painful in spite of the most careful attention to the process of weaning. Sometimes the manifest injustice implicit in all of this is mitigated by the rationale of "learning." That is to say, the termination of the casework relationship is treated as a prototype for the tribulations the client will experience in all of his encounters. The termination process then becomes an experiment in loss, and apparent injustice is turned into generous instruction.

It can be a painful lesson but, perhaps, an important and unavoidable one.

CHAPTER TEN

STRATEGIES AND TACTICS
OF INTERVENTION

Diagnosis, goal-setting—all the tasks we have discussed thus far—do not constitute intervention (or "treatment"), though they are indispensable in the planning and conduct of it. To provide context for a more specific discussion of treatment at different levels of intervention, we will now discuss: (1) the nature of intervention, (2) the necessary ingredients of intervention theory, and (3) the functions of intervention theory for the practitioner.

THE NATURE OF INTERVENTION

Treatment—*any* form of treatment, including social casework—is an attempt to induce change selectively. This is true even of those therapeutic ideologies that take pains to deny that the therapist attempts to direct the course of treatment toward some specific goal. Even treatment that claims only to "enable the person to help himself" or to "provide an atmosphere to promote self-realization" identify, by these very claims, specified goals (i.e., "helping oneself," "self-realization") and imply a set of procedures designed to achieve these aims. They differ from other goals only in being more general. Change sought in treatment is distinguished from change that occurs naturally—as in the course of growth and development—or accidentally—such as the changes that follow disasters or crises—in that the change sought in treatment has a specified end in view and is to be induced through the interventions of a "change agent." It is the difference between asking in what ways will Mr. Smith change in the next year and how can Mr. Smith be induced to be, say, less rigid by one year from now?

When intervention is defined so broadly it becomes apparent that a wide range of persons engage in this activity, including teachers, and ministers, and lawyers as well as social workers, psychiatrists, and psychologists. In fact, it is unfortunate that caseworkers have almost uniformly used the word "treatment" to refer to what they do, since through common usage this term has come to connote the medical "disease" model in which intervention is seen as a *curative* process, thereby excluding other models, such as the educative model, in which "treatment" is viewed as a *learning* process, the *counseling model* used in law, guidance work, and, to some extent, in Perlman's conception of casework as problem-solving, or the broker-advocate model advanced in recent years. The definition of "treatment" offered here is not meant to imply such restrictions, and that should be understood whenever the term is used in this book, even though we recognize that the medical connotations are strong.

When treatment is defined as an attempt to induce change selectively, it follows that the development of treatment theory requires study of the conditions under which specific changes can be brought about. Thus, the sources of knowledge that should be drawn upon in the construction of casework treatment theory are not only the experiences of caseworkers and clinicians in other disciplines but a broad range of studies bearing on the problems of induced change, from laboratory experiments on learning to studies of brain washing, religious conversion, and social change. Recently, there have been some efforts [1] to systematize the diverse bodies of knowledge relevant to the problems of inducing change; such efforts may help correct the failure of social work education to acquaint students with more than a small segment of these bodies of knowledge.[2]

TYPES OF INDUCED CHANGE

It may be useful to begin our attempt to formulate a broader conception of treatment by identifying four general approaches to the inducement of behavioral change.[3] The first type is change induced by *altering the responding mechanism*. Familiar examples of this approach are the use of drugs or surgery (e.g., lobotomy) to induce behavioral change. These techniques alter, physiologically, responding mechanisms in the organism and thereby effect changes in overt behavior. It might be noted that these techniques, as well as those associated with the other types of change identified below, are often used by persons to induce change in their own behavior. A familiar example is the use of alcohol to change one's mood and behavior.

A second type is change induced by *altering the individual's response repertoire through learning*. A delinquent youth learns how to apply for a job. A person, perhaps through catharsis and cognitive restructuring or "insight" into past events, converts hate for his mother into love or perhaps changes his self-image.

The third type is change induced by *alteration of the situational events* that elicit particular behaviors. The sensation of hunger can be ended by eating. A child's angry behavior often can be dissolved by introducing an interesting toy. A similar, if more complex example is the attempt by the psychiatric social worker to change factors in the family that are presumed to evoke and perpetuate pathological behavior in the nominal patient.

These first three types of change have in common the assumption that the client is the object or target of change, that his behavior needs to be modified in some specified way. The fourth type, on the other hand, is *change in some sector of the client's social world*. In order to change unemployment to employment it may be necessary to find a job for the client (it may, of course, also require changes in the client). In other words, the client's problem may be indicative of an inadequacy in the social system and not in the client, in which case the appropriate *target* for change is the specific defect in the social system.

The helping professions have developed preferences, amounting virtually to biases, regarding these different types of change. The traditional psychotherapists, for example, exhibit a clear preference for changes of the second type, that is, change in the patient's response repertoire; reliance on other types of change tends to be regarded as a compromise. Caseworkers have favored change in situational events as well as modification of the client's response repertoire, with some controversy regarding their relative value and importance. Both disciplines have tended to actively devalue change of the first type; that is, the use of drugs in outpatient treatment tends to be viewed with disfavor by psychotherapeutically oriented practitioners. Caseworkers generally have avoided change of this type altogether, for reasons that can only partly be attributed to the fact that most of the techniques required to induce changes in responding mechanisms can by law be administered only by physicians.

Change of the fourth type, in which some part of the client's social world rather than the client himself is the target of change, also is devalued by many psychotherapists and caseworkers. In fact, the client who believes that his problem is "out there" typically is considered to have a poor prognosis, because his externalization of the problem is construed as a projection, or a denial, of his contribution to and responsibility for his problems. While it is true that casework has reserved a place for "environmental manipulation" in its treatment armamentarium, this treatment modality has received little attention and virtually no systematic theoretical development. Moreover, environmental manipulation has been conceived as consisting largely of providing tangible services and helping clients with "practical" problems. Recent suggestions that caseworkers should perform social broker and advocacy functions indicate that the long neglect of this type of intervention may be coming to an end.[4]

The preferences that have developed among psychotherapists and caseworkers for one type of change over another do not seem to represent choices based on evidence about their relative effectiveness. Rather, the types of change preferred appear to reflect the heavy emphasis in western societies on individual responsibility, self-help, and self-reliance, coupled with the penchant among many intellectuals for introspection and a cognitive approach to problem-solving. The above combination of values predisposes clinicians in our society to favor changes in the individual's response repertoire in dealing with social and psychological problems. This preference pervades American society. A preferred approach to most social problems, from delinquency to discrimination and poverty, is education designed to modify the behavior of certain groups in the population. Institutional or structural change in the society as an approach to these problems is devalued as "tinkering," and those who advocate it are sometimes regarded as dangerous. Modifications in the responding mechanism also sometimes are considered dangerous, even immoral, as exemplified in the fear of drugs (e.g., fluoridation). And even change in the situational factors that evoke the problem is devalued—until quite recently, efforts to reduce automobile casualties have been directed primarily toward the behavior of drivers and not the hazards in the automobile.

Moral values are not irrelevant to the selection of intervention modalities. On the contrary, moral issues are highly relevant to the choice of methods of inducing change, but the moral basis of these choices should be carefully examined, and moral judgments ought to be informed and influenced by the known consequences of intervention alternatives. For example, we may, on moral grounds, generally prefer solutions that do not involve the use of drugs, but fluoridation is shown by considerable evidence to be effective and harmless. It may be desirable for the poor to have more training and education, but poverty simply cannot be eliminated by training and education alone. And while we might prefer to reduce automobile casualties through driver education, we should *know,* when resources are to be allocated to the problems, that safer automobiles can be made. Of course, it is equally undesirable to choose among intervention alternatives solely on the basis of their objective consequences without analysis of their moral implications— enforced sterilization conceivably would be an effective approach to some social problems, but its use raises grave moral issues.

INTERVENTION THEORY

The point of the preceding for the caseworker is that he needs to be aware of the types of change that are possible and of their probable effects, and he needs to develop an awareness of his own moral preferences so that his moral judgments are deliberate and not capricious or simplistic. In short, his interventions should spring from a systematic set of assumptions and values regarding induced change and consideration of what is possible and within his means to affect.

Of course, all casework practitioners do base their actions on some theory or set of assumptions about treatment—where they vary is in the extent to which these assumptions are explicit and systematic. In fact, some practitioners argue that caseworkers should not become too systematic about what they do, since this would destroy some essential though nebulous quality at the heart of treatment. For example, Gordon Hamilton, who generally favored a systematic, scientific approach to social casework, cautioned: "While the social worker who relies on intuition to understand another person may become lost in mysticism, it is possible also to overestimate the intellectual approach—as yielding real meaning." [5] Fear is widespread in the field that the rational, scientific attitude will dehumanize the caseworker's therapeutic endeavors. In his penetrating analysis of the contradiction between caseworkers' express commitment to make their practice "scientific" and their extreme reluctance to subject the "core of the counseling experience" to scientific scrutiny, Paul Halmos observed:

Some counsellors try to escape from the dilemma by pleading rather thoughtlessly that they practice an art, forgetting that, were it so, no generalization about their practice would have more than either an aesthetic, and, therefore a morally ambiguous, or even only trivial, significance. The theoreticians of counselling who resign from the scientist's role put an end to the expectation that eventually the process of counselling could be broken up into minute and discrete stages of engineered learning, or rather unlearning and relearning, and that the techniques of managing this process in counselling, that is prompting it, sustaining it, and concluding it, could be similarly broken up into discrete and learnable elements. . . . The plain fact for all to see is that, at least until now, the counselling literature has everywhere included observations and admissions about the unbreakable total front of the personality's holistic function, and about the unanalysable nature of the counsellor's love for his patient.[6]

Halmos concludes that the caseworker's reluctance to submit the heart of his therapeutic endeavors to scientific analysis is an attempt to defend his faith in the healing power of love, out of a fear that this faith would evaporate if exposed to the cold glare of science. Halmos—somewhat pensively, one feels—shares this fear, largely on semantic grounds. The atomistic, dispassionate language and imagery of science will dissolve the "molar and personalistic images of love" and lead to the dissolution of "naive and spontaneous affection." [7] " 'Love,' 'compassion,' and 'fellowship,' " Halmos continues, "still carry the accumulated reverence of past ages, and the complex notions still act as powerful stimuli to socially necessary performances." [8] Thus, curiously, does Halmos invoke the jargon of science to argue for the exclusion from scientific dissection of love and faith in the healing power of love.

We do not share Halmos' fears. If love or "unconditional positive regard" for the client is a necessary and sufficient condition to help the client, then we should know it, so that caseworkers can act accordingly —so that, for example, the caseworker continues with a case *only* if he can feel unconditional positive regard for the client, and transfers the case to someone else if he cannot.

Halmos also raises another issue: the possibility that the scientific attitude is inherently dehumanizing and, of special concern to Halmos, undermines faith and hope. There *is* a debatable issue here, and the apprehensions Halmos expresses have been sounded in many quarters, most notably by the existentialists. In response it can be said that such a claim rests on an inadequate conception of science. Science is an attempt to satisfy certain human desires and concerns for which men have constructed other faiths in the past, namely the desire to penetrate the mysteries of existence and to improve the human condition. Science, in short, can be thought of as another faith, not a polarity to faith. In common with other faiths, science has a creed, an ethic, and a ritual. While it may suffer aesthetically by comparison with other faiths, its virtues include a stringent, self-correcting pragmatism and a firm, if idealized, belief in man's capacity to discover truth and thereby to improve his condition. Thus, the scientist's doubts, like the doubts of Job, do not spring from a profound cynicism but represent an affirmation of his faith that it is possible to know with greater certainty and to use that knowledge to act more effectively. Unfortunately, science is no more immune to bastardization than the faiths that have gone before it—it too has its hypocrites and charlatans.

The advantages for the caseworker of following a systematic, explicit, scientifically oriented theory of treatment in his practice are considerable. A systematic intervention theory provides a means of classifying events so as to differentiate the relevant from the irrelevant. Classification is necessary for generalization. Generalization, in turn, makes possible prediction. And prediction is important because it is implied whenever a caseworker intervenes—namely the prediction that what he is about to do is more likely to benefit the client than anything else he could do at that moment; there is, in fact, no other justification for his interventions. He says to himself, in effect, "I will reassure Mrs. Brown because that will reduce her guilt and anxiety, which, in turn, will make her better able to cope with her problems." In this example the caseworker is making two predictions: that reassurance will, better than anything else he could do, reduce the client's guilt and anxiety; and that the client will cope with her problems more effectively with less rather than more guilt and anxiety.

Finally, adherence to an explicit, systematic theory provides specific guides to action; it tells the practitioner what to do, *as if* the theory were valid. This is an important advantage, given the present state of knowledge, since if practitioners were to act only in those instances where fully tested knowledge is available they could rarely act at all. Theory is the caseworker's tool for coping with the uncertainty that inescapably surrounds him. A particular theory may not be appropriately applicable, but if this becomes apparent, since the theory is explicit the caseworker can retrace his steps, discover where he took a wrong step, and thereby learn from his experience. The caseworker who undertakes his practice without a theory courts chaos, since he has no guide to tell him which events are relevant for his purposes and cannot generalize from his experiences. Without a set of principles to guide him, his interventions are likely to be haphazard and capricious.

Unfortunately, it is easier to see the advantages of using a theory of treatment than it is to select one, for several reasons. If the caseworker adopts one treatment theory for all cases, such as psychoanalytic theory or Perlman's problem-solving model, he runs the risk of forcing some of his clients into a mold that does not fit them. Evidence is considerable that caseworkers sometimes have committed this error in the past.[9] On the other hand, the caseworker who would avoid this risk, as the existentialists and phenomenologists have attempted to do, by adopting the client's subjective view of his situation and problems may be taking a viewpoint that will serve him no better than it has the client. Many clients come to the worker *because* their view of their situation has not provided them with satisfactory solutions to their predicaments. And if the caseworker adopts a more eclectic stance, as we advocate, he must avoid the possible risk of confusing himself and his client by making sure that he understands the theories he is using and what he is doing with them.

The more general problem, common to all these approaches, is that if the practitioner applies an inaccurate or inappropiate set of concepts and assumptions to the situation before him, he and the client may fail in their attempt to work together on the client's problems. Thus it may be, as we have suggested elsewhere, that the various clients with which different schools of treatment have had their greatest successes are different types of persons or problems, that the range of applicability of any specific school of thought is limited. If this is so—and it is a plausible hypothesis—it suggests that different types of cases require not simply differential treatment within one theory of treatment but different *theories* of change. After all, there is no logical reason to assume a priori that a theory of change valid for delinquents will also be applicable to adolescents with other problems.

In view of these dilemmas, how can a practitioner select an intervention theory to follow in his practice? He might attempt to build his own "theory" through his own practice, drawing upon what seemed to work in the past as his guide for intervention in future cases. But this is a limited approach in that it does not take advantage of knowledge accumulated elsewhere, including the experience of colleagues. Another possibility is to follow whatever is the prevailing consensus among recognized experts; after all, if psychoanalytic theory, for example, is widely used in the field it must be valid. The problem with this basis for selecting a theory is that the experts may be wrong—if Copernicus had accepted the prevailing consensus to form his conceptions of the cosmos we still might believe that the earth is the center of the universe. Similar problems arise if the caseworker commits himself to the ideas of some particularly prestigious practitioner, such as a Gordon Hamilton or a Helen Harris Perlman. Moreover, masters and schools breed disciples, and discipleship tends to induce conformity to the "school" and to inhibit innovation, which is apt to be regarded as deviation from the central ideas of the master. Innovation is reserved for the master—as someone once observed, Freud was not a Freudian and Sullivan not a Sullivanian.

The only scientific basis for selecting a theory of intervention—

assuming that it is consistent with our professional values—is its empirical validity and effectiveness. If a theory of casework were devised that, if followed, would produce successful results in 80 percent of the cases, caseworkers would be ethically obligated to use the theory whether or not they found it personally appealing. At present, because of limited knowledge, the practitioner can choose among available treatment theories on the basis of their relative empirical validity only for a limited number of problems. For example, the practitioner who encounters a phobic reaction should always consider use of systematic desensitization because of its demonstrated effectiveness. The fact that there are more such examples today than there were ten years ago provides hope that increasingly the social caseworker will be able to base his practice on more certain knowledge. Ultimately, if the promise of science can be delivered, there should be only one system of intervention for a specific problem. There is no virtue, in the long run, in the present multiplicity of treatment theories, although in the short run, in a period of uncertainty, it may be desirable to follow all possible roads to Rome in order to discover which ones actually lead there.

At present, then, the choice of intervention theory must be made by the practitioner himself. Consequently, some will be doctrinaire disciples of a "school," others will develop an amalgam of their own, and still others will systematically experiment with different theories of intervention. Which pathway is followed should be of less concern than that no theory be unshakably adopted; a theory should be regarded as a tool to be replaced if and when another is found to be more useful or effective.

As more adequate evidence is found for choosing among alternative approaches to intervention, the choice of a particular theory will become less what it has been, namely a matter of preference, subject to all the influences that affect preferences. But even in the absence of evidence the choice need not be whimsical. For one thing, the practitioner may, as we have suggested, systematically experiment with different intervention theories; unfortunately, few practitioners have followed this course, partly because casework supervisors have not encouraged it. Second, there are requirements that any adequate theory of intervention should satisfy, and these requirements provide a measure for evaluating the theories currently available.

First, an adequate theory must be explicit about the question of *goals*. It should be clear what is to be changed so that the practitioner will know whether he is to be concerned with changing attitudes or overt behavior or feelings or problem-solving patterns. And the desired outcomes of change should be clear. Many theories are exceedingly vague about the latter, relying on concepts that defy precise definition, such as "self-realization" and "ego strength." Generally, the task of devising an effective intervention strategy is simplified considerably if the outcomes desired can be stated in specific behavioral terms. And an adequate theory must deal with the issue of who sets the goals of intervention and how this is to be done. Many theories do not satisfy this requirement and thereby intensify some of the moral dilemmas we discussed in chapter 2.

Second, an intervention theory can be evaluated according to its assumptions about what *can* be changed. Some theories could be called pessimistic, such as those in which it is assumed that life styles and character are set early in life and can afterward be changed only slightly, in contrast to other theories that assume that persons can change radically and fundamentally at any time in their lives. The available evidence supports neither of these positions consistently.[10] While it appears to be true that persons develop behavior patterns that are highly persistent over time, nevertheless persons have been known to undergo radical transformations at all stages of life. The optimistic view has the practical virtue of orienting the practitioner to potentials for change and to searching for more effective and powerful ways of bringing it about.

Third, it should be clear what effective application of the theory would require of the client. For example, does appropriate use of the theory mean that the client will be expected to examine his personality in intensive interviews with the caseworker over an extended period of time? If the caseworker considers that advocacy is an appropriate approach, is there a risk that the client will be treated punitively by the agency for challenging its decisions? Some approaches to family treatment, for example, depend upon completely frank, even blunt, expression of feelings among members of the family, a requirement that some families find difficult if not impossible to satisfy. Explicit statements about what is required of the client are absent in many theories, with the result that practitioners sometimes attempt to apply theories to persons for whom they are inappropriate. These requirements should be separated from assessment of the client, to avoid the problem of labeling him an unmotivated person with a poor prognosis simply because the intervention theory being used imposes requirements unsuited to that client. Perhaps more important, it is essential for the practitioner to know what application of the intervention theory requires of the client if he is to make it possible for the client to be helped.

Fourth, an adequate theory should specify, in behavioral terms, what the practitioner needs to do in order to bring about the desired changes. Injunctions to "give support to the client" or to "clarify the client's feelings," are of little use unless the theory specifies, in terms of behaviors to be performed by the practitioner, how support may be given or how feelings may be clarified. Often, as the examples just given illustrate, intervention theories describe what the practitioner is to do in terms of the effects his activities should produce. "Support" and "clarification" describe effects, not the actions to be taken to produce them. Such prescriptions amount to telling the practitioner to "make the client feel better," or "improve the client's social functioning." The prescription "praise the client whenever he is more assertive and urge him to continue to assert himself" is informative to the practitioner in a way that "support the client's efforts to assert himself" is not. Theories that fail to provide such precise behavioral prescriptions not only leave to the practitioner the difficult task of translating the theory into action but preclude anything more than gross tests of the effectiveness of the theory.*

Fifth, since treatment typically is conducted in a special setting and not in the client's customary surroundings, an intervention theory should indicate what the practitioner needs to do in order to make sure that changes that occur within the treatment situation are carried over

* This failing of treatment theories is sometimes used, curiously, to defend them. For example, Mary McDonald's critique of *Girls at Vocation High* relies heavily on the notion that the study failed to distinguish between appropriate and inappropriate applications of "casework theory." Since casework theories have tended to rely on abstract rather than behaviorally specific intervention prescriptions, it is difficult to deduce concrete guides to action that cannot be challenged as inappropriate by another interpreter of the theory. Mary McDonald, "Reunion at Vocational High, An Analysis of *Girls at Vocational High*," *Social Service Review*, 40 (June, 1966), 175–89.

into the client's real life. Every practitioner knows or has heard of cases in which the client appeared to progress in interviews but showed no change in his life outside of treatment—he may be a better client, but the problems that brought him for help remain unchanged. Behavior therapists, who give considerable attention to this problem, have developed methods for dealing with it, such as giving specific assignments to the client to test behavioral changes in natural situations. This problem also is lessened in some modes of intervention, such as family group treatment, where the treatment situation is less isolated from the client's living situation.

Finally, the theory should tell the practitioner how to assess the outcome of his intervention efforts. How is he to know when treatment should end and whether it was successful? Without such guides, treatment may continue indefinitely and the practitioner will have difficulty obtaining a clear sense of the most important thing he needs to know about his professional performance, namely his effectiveness. And it is important that he have a clear way of distinguishing between failures attributable to the theory versus those arising from his application of it.

Intervention theories vary in the adequacy with which they answer the above questions. The one theory that comes closer to satisfying them than any other is the behavior modification approach. In part this is due to the insistence in this theory on describing objectives, outcomes, and intervention methods in terms of observable behaviors. Thus, for example, case reports by behavior therapists tend to be highly practical since the behavioral description of the methods used is sufficiently specific that other practitioners can replicate them quite precisely. The greater adequacy of behavior modification theory in relation to the above criteria explains in part the fact that although this approach was virtually unknown in social work until a few years ago, it already has generated more empirical practice-related research than any of the longer-established treatment theories.

LEVELS AND MODES OF INTERVENTION

The social caseworker is not concerned only with the problems of individual persons but also with problems that arise in the relationships be-

tween persons and in family units. Nor can the caseworker afford to
hold fixed preconceptions regarding whether the locus of the problem in
a case will be a person, interpersonal relationships, the family unit, or
the social context. This judgment must be made anew in each case.
Consequently, the caseworker requires intervention theories that make
it possible for him to operate at three levels of intervention: (1) the
family as a unit, (2) interpersonal relationships, and (3) the individual.
His interventions may be directed at any one or any combination of
these levels. Thus the caseworker's client can be an individual, a relationship (such as a marriage), or a family group. And, as we have suggested elsewhere, the *target* of intervention may be not the person but
some part of his social world.

Subsequent chapters on the tactics of intervention are organized
according to the levels of intervention scheme outlined above. Moreover, we have indicated that the function required of the caseworker is
not always that of a therapist; sometimes the case requires that he perform other functions, such as of counselor, problem solver, social broker, advocate, or reformer. We turn to these other functions in chapter
13, where we discuss current developments and trends in social casework.

CHAPTER ELEVEN

CASEWORK WITH THE FAMILY

Mary Richmond's belief that the family ought to be a central concern of the caseworker has been echoed throughout the history of social casework. Experts and laymen alike are inclined to attribute to the family enormous power to influence the lives of persons and, through them, the social order. Families are blamed for all manner of problems, from delinquency and crime to mental illness, and at the same time they are given credit for instilling in the nation's leaders those qualities that made them successful. The greatest joys and the deepest sorrows of existence are said by many to be found in the family circle.

To be sure, such beliefs exaggerate reality. Nevertheless, there can be no doubt that the family is one of the most important institutions in societies, that the family is implicated in many of the problems of concern to social workers, and that many of the problems that come to the attention of caseworkers are patently family problems.

Anyone who reads the original documents that make up the history of social casework will see that caseworkers always recognized, however dimly and implicitly, the importance of the family to their work.[1] It seems equally clear, however, that until recently caseworkers never quite knew how to implement their recognition that, in many cases at least, their practice ought to be family centered. But the case-

This chapter draws heavily upon Scott Briar, "The Family as an Organization: An Approach to Family Diagnosis and Treatment," *Social Service Review*, 38 (September, 1964), 247–55.

worker cannot be faulted for his inability to practice family-centered casework. He, like any practitioner, is limited in his practice by the tools available to him. Just as no physician could prescribe penicillin before it was discovered, nor an architect rely on prestressed concrete before it was developed, caseworkers could not analyze and treat the dynamics of family groups before they had the conceptual and methodological tools to do so. To be sure, the tools currently available still are crude and far from adequate, but they are sufficient to generate forms of practice that are more clearly family oriented in ways that earlier practices were not.

In fact, methods of family treatment have developed so rapidly in recent years that one needs a chart and lexicon to avoid confusing the ten or so identifiable schools of "family therapy" that have emerged, for the differences among them are substantial.[2] We believe, however, that the various schools of family treatment can be subsumed within five distinguishable perspectives for the analysis and treatment of families and their problems. Thus, rather than examine the schools as such, we will discuss the five perspectives and evaluate their usefulness for the problems and tasks confronting the caseworker. These five perspectives are: (1) the family as a collection of individuals, (2) the family as a network of interpersonal relations, (3) the family as a small group, (4) the family as a social organization, and (5) the family as a social institution.

THE FAMILY AS A COLLECTION
OF INDIVIDUALS

From this perspective the family is viewed as a collection of individual persons. To understand a family and its problems, it is necessary and sufficient to understand the psychodynamics of the persons in it. A diagnosis of a family is essentially a set of diagnoses of all members of the family, and treatment of the family consists of individual treatment of some or all family members. The concepts for discussing family problems and their treatment are drawn from the language of individual pathology. Thus, there are "neurotic" families and marriages, "schizophrenogenic" families, and "sado-masochistic" families. The successful resolution of family problems is achieved by resolving the psychosocial problems of individuals in the family.

This is the perspective on the family held by such practitioners as Florence Hollis,[3] Emily Mudd,[4] and Irene Josslyn,[5] whose early attempts to focus on family problems mark the beginnings of efforts to develop family-centered clinical methods.

Important as it is in working with families to understand the members of the family as individuals, it is now recognized that this perspective alone is not adequate either to explain or effectively modify many family problems. The characteristics of the individuals in a family simply are not the sole determinants of the behavior and problems of the family. Families with members whose personal characteristics are very similar may behave quite differently *as families,* and families composed of persons with quite different personalities may behave similarly as families. Moreover, there are families that have serious family problems even though the persons in the family are "normal" as individuals; conversely, there are families that function adequately even though individuals in the family are disturbed. A particularly conspicuous example of the limitations of this perspective are the data indicating the relationship between certain family problems, such as desertion and separation, and social variables, such as social class and ethnicity.[6] It would be exceedingly difficult to explain these systematic variations as functions of the personalities of family members.

The limitations of this perspective led other family-oriented practitioners to search for different perspectives that could more adequately comprehend familial rather than only individual dynamics.

THE FAMILY AS A NETWORK
OF INTERPERSONAL RELATIONS

A second perspective that emerged quite early in the family treatment movement is one that focuses on interpersonal relationships in the family. This viewpoint was foreshadowed in the individual perspective with its emphasis on the affective tone of relationships and on the symbiotic character of some family relationships. To these notions, Ackerman,

Winch and others [7] added the concepts of reciprocity and complementarity, which directed attention to the degree of "fit" between the affective needs and role expectations of the different parties in a relationship. The hypothesis is that there is a direct relationship between the degree of reciprocity or complementarity in family relationships and satisfying, effective family functioning. For example, if a man who needs a wife who depends upon him is married to a woman who needs to depend upon her husband, they will have a more successful and satisfying marriage than a couple whose needs for each other do not mesh that well.

More recently, the preoccupation of clinicians working within this perspective has shifted to communication. Probably the best known example of this emphasis is found in the work of Virginia Satir, Don Jackson, and their coworkers [8] on the "double-bind" and other disturbances in family communicative patterns. The double-bind refers to the communication of two simultaneous and conflicting messages from one person to another, which puts the receiver in a bind because he does not know to which of the two messages to respond. For example, a mother may tell her child she loves him and yet at the same time reject him by her actions; the child does not know whether to respond to the protestations of love or the experiences of rejection. Another essential condition for the "bind" is the existence of constraints that prevent the receiver from commenting upon the conflict in messages. The developers of this concept believe that the "double-bind" is a crucial factor in the etiology of schizophrenia and a source of other problems, but solid evidence for this hypothesis is lacking. The treatment approach developed by Satir, Jackson, and their followers focuses almost entirely on encouraging the open expression of feelings and thoughts among family members so that there are no longer any "hidden messages." While communication has tended in recent years to be the dominant dimension of family interaction attended to by family practitioners, some work has continued on other dimensions of family interaction, as in the work of Wynn and his coworkers,[9] whose notions of pseudomutuality carry forward some of the earlier work done on complementarity and reciprocity. Pseudomutuality, as the term implies, refers to relationships that have the appearance but not the substance of mutuality and complementarity. A couple acts

as if they satisfy each other's needs but it is only an act, though not necessarily a deliberate one. Some "double-bind" relationships, for example, may have the surface appearance of mutuality.

The work of Jackson and Satir clearly illustrate both the virtues
and limitations of this perspective on family behavior. It is obvious that
communication is important in the family, as it is in any network of interpersonal relationships, from lovers to sport teams to complex organizations. More specifically, it seems equally evident that the clearer the
communication the better for the participants in the relationship, and
that "double level," "double-bind" communication, in which contradictory messages are sent about basic needs in the relationship (e.g., "I
love you" but "stay away from me"), probably have negative effects on
participants.

Nevertheless, it would be difficult to marshal evidence to support
an argument that communication is the most important dimension of interaction to consider in clinical work. For example, the research that
has emanated from the ideas of Jackson and Satir has not yet provided
strong support for their speculations regarding the potency in family
and individual pathology of the communication disturbances and distor-
tions they have identified and described. The absence of such support
perhaps is not surprising. Examination of common experience provides
ready examples of situations in which clear and unambiguous communication exacerbated rather than reduced conflict, as in instances where
increased clarity and precision of communication served to expose differences between the interactants of which they previously were unaware. While in many instances exposure of such differences might be
useful and beneficial, only a person who puts absolute clarity of communication above all other considerations could maintain that such exposure is desirable and beneficial in *all* situations. In political and diplomatic negotiations, deliberate vagueness and ambiguity in some
communications are useful because they serve to minimize rather than
amplify conflict, without either denying or ignoring it. While families
are not essentially political or diplomatic entities, nevertheless situations arise in all families that perhaps can best be described as political
or diplomatic in character. In any event, it remains to be demonstrated
whether the sort of unrelenting, absolute, and, if necessary, brutal hon-

esty in the family advocated by some clinicians who emphasize communication is (1) an effective tool for problem-solving, and (2) a viable norm for family interaction.

A more important and more general limitation of this perspective is the tendency of those who work within it to focus their attention on processes occurring within the nuclear family to the exclusion of interactions between the nuclear family and its environment. Thus, to return to the example used earlier, Satir emphasizes clinically the *patterns* of communication occurring between persons rather than the *content* of their communications.* Moreover, without a perspective that takes into account a broader range of influences on life within the nuclear family, the significance of particular interactions and specific patterns may be misunderstood. One dramatic example of this point is the study by Jules Henry in which he shows the effect of formal and informal processes in the high school on the most intimate aspects of family interaction and the effects of the mass media on interaction styles and contents in both the school and the family.† Another more recent example is Eliot Liebow's study of interaction between fathers and the families from which they are separated in Washington's Black ghetto.[10] This study illustrates the impossibility of acquiring an adequate understanding of family life without careful attention to the social matrix in which it occurs. Thus, for example, Liebow describes the marked contrast between the inadequate, stunted relations of the fathers being studied to their own children, in comparison to the warmth and spontaneity of their relationship with the children in families they had informally "adopted." One set of observations without the other would have generated inaccurate inferences about the relationship capacities of these fathers, and the differ-

---

* Carried to the extreme, an emphasis on form over content is a type of communication disturbance, as in the case of the husband who usually responds to the *manner* in which his wife says something and only rarely to *what* she says, making it nearly impossible, of course, for the wife to transmit messages to her husband.

† Particularly pertinent to our preceding discussion of communication patterns is Jules Henry's suggestion that the logic of television commercials is becoming the logic of everyday discourse. If this hypothesis has any validity it suggests a somewhat different interpretation for some of the communication disturbances described by Satir and others. Jules Henry, *Culture Against Man* (New York, Random House, 1963), pp. 45–99.

ences between the two sets of observations are explicable only by reference to the larger socioeconomic context in which these men and their families live. In this family situation, the relationship tendencies and communication patterns that are central for so many family therapists appear, in part, the outcomes of social and economic forces that seem unlikely to be changed by any reconstruction of intrafamily dynamics, no matter how extensive.

Thus, a weakness of this perspective, as with the first perspective, is its too-limited view of the factors affecting life in families. At the same time, however, this interpersonal perspective is indispensable in order to identify aspects of life within the family unit that are important for the clinician to notice and understand.

THE FAMILY AS A SMALL GROUP

It would seem logical to expect that efforts to develop a perspective for work with families that could encompass a larger array of the significant variables in family interaction would lead to efforts to apply to this work the body of social science theory and research on the small group, for much of what is known about small groups ought to be applicable to the family; such knowledge should be useful to practitioners working with family groups. Yet the convergence of small group and family theory has not occurred, at least not to the extent one might expect. Efforts have been made to bring about an interpenetration of the two fields, but they have been few.[11] Among the reasons for the failure to use small group theory and methods in clinical work with families is a factor that has to do with the characteristics of the family itself.

The family is a small group, but it is a very unusual and, in some respects, unique one. The research on small groups that informs small group theory and, increasingly, social group work was done largely on nonfamily groups. The groups studied have varied greatly in composition, function, and in other ways; yet compared to them, nuclear families typically are (1) smaller, (2) more heterogeneous, and (3) have a much longer duration as a group.

In addition to such quantitative differences, families also differ from other small groups in qualitative ways that may be of more fundamental importance. For example, family groups (1) are bound by laws written explicitly to regulate them (i.e., the body of family law), (2) are the object of less formal but no less explicit or potent sets of norms pertaining to even the most intimate aspects of interaction in the group,[12] and (3) are expected to perform crucial functions for the social order, such as reproduction and socialization of the young. In families, the influence of these factors may be fundamental, but while some small group theory incorporates variables that could reflect these factors, they are not central to most small group theories. Such theories are more apt to reflect, in their ordering of variables, the properties of small, short-lived, homogeneous groups in which either interpersonal attraction or the group task are the focal factors. Thus, it may be that while small group theory and research do apply to family groups, they simply do not go far enough to grapple with certain variables more important in families than in other small groups. A similar observation could be made about the literature and experience of social group work. Group work methodology, like small group theory, reflects the properties of the kinds of groups with which it was developed and tested, and by and large these groups were not families but rather social, activity, or therapy groups. The same could be said of group therapy, an activity to which group workers have turned increasingly in recent years, for group therapy is designed for groups *formed* for the purpose of therapy, in which the commitment of group members to the group and to therapy is not at all comparable to the commitments of family members when the family unit becomes the object of intervention. Some group workers have attempted to bridge these gaps, but the efforts thus far attempted have been limited.

It is unfortunate that to date this perspective has had so little to offer practitioners working with families. The small group perspective, with its social-psychological orientation to behavior, seems, on the face of it, to be well-suited for clinical work with individual families. The development of the potential of this perspective will require the systematic efforts of social workers working with families who also know the small group field. Glasser, Feldman, and others have shown the directions that some of this work may take.[13] The danger that must be avoided is that of over-weighting intragroup variables (which may be appropriate for the ad hoc short-lived groups studied in much of the research on small groups) at the expense of extragroup variables that seem more important in an institutionalized group that is expected to perform crucial functions for the society.

THE FAMILY AS A SOCIAL ORGANIZATION

Just as the family is a small group, it also is a social organization, in the sense that it is a group of people who are expected to coordinate their efforts in order to achieve certain goals. Thus, the concepts and propositions of organization theory can be applied to families, provided allowances are made for the differences between families and other types of organizations. Some beginning efforts have been made to develop an organizational approach to work with families, as seen in the work of John Bell,[14] Scott Briar,[15] and Robert MacGregor and his co-workers.[16]

While Briar is most explicit in developing the application of organization theory to the analysis of families, Bell and MacGregor have demonstrated the advantages that can follow from employing an organizational perspective in which the family is viewed as a goal-oriented, structured system. Bell's work, for example, emphasizes the significance for parent-child problems of the distribution of power in the family. The unconventional and, it appears, effective methods developed by MacGregor and his associates illustrate, among other things, that shifts in the patterns by which a family organizes itself or deals with problems can be set into motion within a remarkably brief period of intervention and that, once started, these shifts tend to continue over time with positive effects on the problems the changes were intended to alleviate. For example, MacGregor and his colleagues worked with each family for only two days. Yet follow-up interviews conducted eighteen months later revealed that only one of the sixty families studied had found it necessary to seek further professional help.

The organizational view appears to be a particularly useful perspective from which to begin an analysis of the dynamics and problems of a particular family, because the perspective forces the practitioner to begin by asking himself what the goals of a particular family are and how the family members have attempted to organize themselves in order to realize their aspirations for the family. Families are more inclined to see themselves as goal-oriented entities than as sensitivity or therapy groups, the group model implied in those family therapies that emphasize communication processes. Family members can talk about what they want and hope their family will do and how adequately it has realized their aspirations for it. Such knowledge of "where the family is" and where members hope it is headed is important in order to understand family behavior—for example, how it has allocated its resources—that might otherwise be incomprehensible or, at best, improperly understood if interpreted in light of goals and standards other than those of the individual family itself. While it is true that some of the goals of every family are set for it by the society, families differ in the order of importance they assign to those socially prescribed goals, and families adopt additional, self-defined objectives. In other words, one important reference point against which to comprehend and evaluate the behavior of a family is the family's own aims and standards of achievement, to the extent that one can ascertain them. And the organizational perspective, more than the others, specifically directs the practitioners to pursue those questions.

This perspective also directs attention to the transactions between the family unit and its social matrix, and to the influence of the latter on the family. MacGregor and his associates, for example, often included persons from the family's social network (e.g., the minister, a probation officer, a family physician, etc.) in the treatment team.

The major limitation of this perspective is that it does not focus on the detailed emotional and psychological nuances of interpersonal processes within the family group. While this can be a virtue in the sense that it reduces the risk of interpreting some aspect of intervention as idiosyncratic or pathological when in fact it is socially patterned (e.g., characteristic of the subcultural matrix of which the family is a part) or instrumental to the family's aspirations, this tendency to misinterpret needs to be corrected by the use of the interpersonal perspective described earlier.

THE FAMILY AS A SOCIAL INSTITUTION

Finally, there is the perspective that focuses not on individual families but on the family as an institutional arrangement in the society. While this perspective is particularly pertinent to social workers concerned with social policy issues affecting the family, it is an essential ground for the clinical practitioner as well.

No matter how much he may wish to avoid it, the practitioner working with individual families cannot avoid taking normative positions regarding what is desirable for families. He ought to take those positions consciously and in light of knowledge about the institutional character of the family, its historical evolution, the pressures to which it is currently subjected, and its possible future evolution. That the clinician probably rarely looks at his client-families in this context is evident in Hope Leichter's research, which indicates that caseworkers give little attention to extended kin relations and, when they do take notice of relationships between the nuclear family and extended kin, tend to discourage these relationships.[17] Leichter's findings suggest that caseworkers are relatively uninformed about kinship patterns and their function in the family institution. Apart from the fact that relationships with extended kin have remained much stronger and more developed in contemporary society than many have believed,[18] whether nuclear families should be encouraged to have stronger or weaker ties with extended kin *is* an issue of family policy, even when the position is taken only on a case-by-case basis, as Leichter's research indicates. Whatever position the clinician takes on this issue he should take deliberately; in other words, he should have a family policy within which he makes decisions in individual cases.

For many years clinicians tried to maintain that such normative judgments were not their business—they would help their clients make these judgments for themselves. The empirical impossibility of that position has been established for some time,[19] but clinicians have yet to articulate a systematic methodology for dealing with the fact that they inevitably make normative and moral judgments. The development of an institutional view of the family provides a means for at least making those judgments in a consistent manner.

WHICH PERSPECTIVE?

The clinician may be disappointed because we have not found a perspective that, by our standards at least, is the one he should use, the one that offers what he needs in order to assess and help the families who come to him. Instead, we conclude, once again, that family diagnosis and treatment, like so many other aspects of the caseworker's activities, is a complex and, given the present state of knowledge, an indeterminate affair. For the caseworker that conclusion will be comforting or discomforting, depending on his capacity to practice in the face of uncertainty. But for his client families this state of affairs can only be disquieting, for uncertainty and complexity, no matter how unavoidable, are of no immediate help to them, and it is help they seek, expect, and should receive.

But the plight of our clients, no matter how understandable, cannot change in the slightest what we know and what we do not know. It will help no one, least of all ourselves, to pretend that we can offer more than we can deliver. And yet it seems that at times we have done just that. The physician who would claim for cancer therapy what has been claimed, at least implicitly, for family therapy, and with no more evidence than has been accrued for the effectiveness of family therapy, undoubtedly would be subjected to severe criticism, and worse. To be sure, the problems most families bring to family therapists are not matters of life and death, but that should not reduce the practitioner's moral responsibility to be reasonably scientific about his claims.

If the above sounds harsh and overdrawn, perhaps one example will indicate that it is not. The family treatment methods developed by Virginia Satir and Don Jackson have attracted wide attention from practitioners, and their effect on clinical work with families continues to expand.[20] The practice of caseworkers from Atlanta to Seattle and from San Diego to Boston have been influenced by their methods. Yet in all the years that Satir and Jackson have developed and perfected their techniques, with the support of research grants, not one report has been published assessing the effectiveness of the methods they have successfully advocated. It could be argued that such an expectation is inappropriate and unfair: their task, which they have performed well, is exploratory and developmental; testing and evaluation is for a later stage. And, one could also argue, has anyone done more? The answer to the latter question is yes, some have done more. In 1964, a small group of clinicians, working in Galveston, Texas, reported the results of their work with families.[21] From the beginning of their efforts, they decided to follow up each of their cases by home visits at six *and* eighteen month intervals, because they considered it essential to be able to say something about the effectiveness of their methods. Their results were remarkably effective, all the more so in view of the fact that the period of treatment lasted only two days! But with the published report, the Galveston project ended, and, as far as we know, no one is using the methods developed and tested by MacGregor and his coworkers. Meanwhile, the untested methods of Satir and Jackson continue to gain adherents.

One theme that runs throughout this book is the need for innovation and experimentation in casework practice to discover more effective methods. An equally important theme, which the above example underscores, is that experimentation must be joined with reasonably rigorous evaluation from the start to determine not only whether the new methods are effective but whether they move in a promising direction at all. Only in this way can tradition and faith be replaced by demonstrated effectiveness and not simply by other traditions and other faiths. Only if they do this, and guide their practice by the results of these evaluations, can caseworkers honor their public commitment to their clients to make use of the best available knowledge in their helping efforts.

For the above reasons, we have chosen not to review in any detail *methods* of healing families. Only a handful of effectiveness studies have been reported, and only two of those have been done with sufficient care to yield meaningful, usable results. One, the Chemung County study,[22] indicates rather convincingly that the casework methods developed for and widely applied in work with multiproblem families are not effective—if some practitioners using these methods think otherwise, it is for them to demonstrate their effectiveness in view of the Chemung County results. The second is the multiple impact therapy project in Galveston described earlier. The methods developed in that project, which were remarkably effective, are not now in use.

THE MULTIPLE IMPACT THERAPY PROJECT

In view of the successful results reported by MacGregor and his colleagues, a brief description of their methods is in order. (However, anyone interested in using these methods should study the book by MacGregor et al. in which their methods and techniques are described in considerable detail.) Each family (all members of the family unit were included) spent two full days at the clinic, following a brief intake interview conducted some weeks before. MacGregor and his colleagues worked together as a team, which varied in size from four to as many as nine or ten persons, including MacGregor (a psychologist), one or more social workers, one or more psychiatrists, and often, as mentioned earlier, someone from the family's social network. The first day typically began with a brief team conference in which members of the team tentatively planned how they would proceed during the first morning with the family. This was followed by a longer conference attended by the family and all members of the team. This conference focused primarily on discussion of the nature of the presenting problem as perceived by different family members. At the end of the conference, each member of the family began an individual interview with one or more members of the team; in other words, in this step, all members of the family were engaged, in different offices, in individual interviews. After forty-five minutes to an hour the members of the team exchanged places with each other and the individual interviews continued, but with different team members assigned to family members. By lunch time, then, each member of the team had participated in a conference with the whole family and had participated in individual interviews with at least two members of the family.

At lunch the team would meet to review what had been learned during the morning and to develop hypotheses concerning primarily (1) family interaction practices that tended to maintain and perpetuate the problem and (2) changes in family practices that might reduce the problem. An example of such hypotheses might be the following: The team observes that the father is distant and tends not to be involved in important aspects of family life, for example, decision-making, discipline, etc.

They hypothesize that this contributes to the problems seen in the oldest son, so that if the father were to become more involved, these problems would subside. In the afternoon, separate interviews were resumed with individual family members or subgroups of the family (e.g., husband and wife, or father and son, or the children together, etc.). In these sessions, team members would begin to share their findings and hypotheses with family members, partly as a way of beginning to test and refine them—for example, do they agree that the father is distant; do they think this contributes to the problem; do they believe that if the father were more involved the family's problems would decrease? At this stage, interviewing arrangements become increasingly spontaneous. For example, the team member interviewing the father might telephone his colleague interviewing the mother to say that he has been discussing the father's distance with him, something important about that subject came up in the discussion, and he and the father would like to discuss it with the mother and the team member interviewing her. Thus, the team members continued their discussion of their hypotheses (including their disagreements) in the presence and with the active participation of the family. In this manner, by the end of the first day, the team typically had reached a consensus about the changes in family practices they would attempt to induce.

The second day was devoted to helping the family begin to effect the desired changes in their interaction patterns. It should be emphasized that by this time the changes desired were no mystery to family members, since these changes, along with possible others, had been openly discussed, in a tentative manner, the afternoon before. Work with the family toward this end was carried out in a combination of individual, joint, and group sessions with family members, following no particular pattern, but determined according to (1) what needed to be done with different members and subgroups of the family in order to bring about the desired changes and (2) which team members were in the best position to work with specific family members. While the interviewing arrangements sound confusing, one of the authors participated as a member of the team in the treatment of one case and found initial confusion soon disappeared as the team developed its hypotheses and planned its approach.

What accounts for the reported success (75 percent of the sixty families studied showed substantial improvement in follow-up interviews)? While this question cannot be answered with certainty, behavior modification research suggests that the high rate of success may be attributable, in part, to the modesty and behavioral specificity of the treatment goals typically adopted. MacGregor and his coworkers did not attempt to solve all the family's problems but only to set into motion change in specific behavior patterns in the family. And their approach to bringing about these changes was direct and straightforward: they made clear to the family what changes they were attempting, showed them (sometimes through role playing) how to effect the changes, gave the family specific directives to follow, rewarded them for following the directions, and corrected their errors in attempting the desired changes. The use of multiple therapists obtaining information about the same matters from the perspective of different members of the family appeared to contribute to the formulation of hypotheses about what needed to be changed that were useful to the whole family, and it provided each member of the family access to a team member who represented that family member's interests. Hopefully, some practitioners will attempt to replicate and test these methods elsewhere.

Some more recent methods (e.g., advocacy) and techniques (e.g., behavioral techniques) that we will describe in chapter 13 are applicable to work with families as well as individuals.

Caseworkers have long had a legitimate concern with the family and its problems, but the development of a methodology that adequately honors that concern remains a task for the future of casework.

CHAPTER TWELVE

CASEWORK WITH SUBSYSTEMS
OF THE FAMILY

Whereas the view of the family as an organic whole may be relatively new to psychotherapeutic thought, collectivities within the family have been a focus of concern for quite some time. Certainly, within social casework, the marital pair and parent-child systems have been the focus of attention and thought. Concern with these traditional familial subsystems, however, has been severely constrained by available theory. Although marital problems are old hat for social workers, they have for the most part been treated in terms of the individuals who comprise the marriage. That is to say, personality theories have been used to diagnose and treat these collectivities, and, by definition, personality theories concern themselves with individual personalities.

A husband and wife comprise a marriage. A therapist can approach this marriage from one of two vantage points: he can concentrate on the husband and the wife as two distinct personalities in a particular kind of interactive situation, or he can focus on the interactive situation itself as his primary emphasis. The first alternative has been the more viable simply because personality theories are available: the therapist has ways to think about individuals. The second alternative presents enormous problems. If the individuals, as individuals, are conceptually removed from the marriage, what is left but a name? How does one diagnose and treat a marriage as distinct from the individuals who make up the marriage?

It should not be assumed that the second alternative is, on the face of it, inferior or somehow strained and unreal. There are many ways to look at events that occur in the physical and behavioral world, and any given way becomes comfortable and "sensible" only as a result of arbitrary choices. The physicist may look upon the functioning of the human anatomy from the vantage point of the individual atoms making up the system; but it is possible to invoke a model that incorporates collectivities of atoms—the molecular structure of organic compounds within the body—or, from a still larger perspective, the functioning of bodily organs. It would be naïve and incorrect to argue that the *better* perspective is that of the physicist, and that somehow he has the theoretical position that is fundamental and most true. The biophysicist, biochemist, and physiologist, however, are in the happy situation of being able to choose from among an array of theoretical perspectives, and the choice is dictated by the particular problem they face. Unhappily, the social caseworker has only personality theory available to him, and so his choice is forced. But the fact remains that other choices are theoretically viable, and the individual perspective need not be claimed as the most fruitful one.

It is the intent of this chapter to discuss various subsystems of the family and to examine some theoretical constructions available that cast light on the diagnosis and treatment of these subsystems. But a word of caution is in order lest the reader be disappointed: once the level of individual personality is left behind, there remains nothing but tentative and fragmentary theoretical conceptions. We can do no more than tease the reader with these fragments. Complete satisfaction is something only the future can provide.

TYPES OF FAMILIAL SUBSYSTEMS

As was suggested, certain types of subsystems within the family have long been identified. There is of course, *the marriage*—sometimes, depending upon the whimsy of the author, called the marital relationship, the marital pair, the spouse system, etc. Whether these different identifying labels represent subtle differences in meaning is not always clear. Another type familiar to all clinicians in and out of child guidance is the *mother-child* system. This troublesome familial dyad has given rise to a large variety of theoretical speculation bearing on personality development. Less familiar to social caseworkers in spite of its central position in psychoanalytic theory is the *father-son* system. Thus, subsystems that, in one variant or another, encompass a parent and a child are more or less known to clinicians. *Sib-sib* systems, however, are almost void of attention in the clinical literature.

We will return to these better-known collectivities within the family, but we must note here that they by no means exhaust the combinations of possible groupings within the family. Consider, for a moment, a simple family of four comprising father (F), mother (M), son (S), and daughter (D). There are four sets of triads within this simple structure, namely:

1. FMS		3. FSD	
2. FMD		4. MSD	

and six dyads:

5. FM		8. MS	
6. FS		9. MD	
7. FD		10. SD	

But this does not begin to exhaust the possibilities. Both dyads and triads within this family impinge upon other subsystems. We have four triads impinging upon individuals:

11. FMS : D		13. FSD : M	
12. FMD: S		14. MSD: F	

and twelve possible sets of dyads impinging upon individuals:

15. FM : S		21. MS : D	
16. FM : D		22. MD : F	
17. FS : M		23. MS : F	
18. FS : D		24. MD : S	
19. FD : M		25. SD : M	
20. FD : S		26. SD : F	

Finally, there are three dyadic systems that impinge on other dyads:

27. FM :SD
28. FS :MD
29. MS :FD

Thus, we have a total of twenty-nine theoretically meaningful subsystems within a simple family of four, not counting the family unit as such (FMSD) or the four individuals within the family (F, M, S, D). In larger families the number of subsystems becomes overwhelming. In a family of five, for example, there are ten triadic systems, ten dyads, twenty triads impinging upon individuals, thirty dyads impinging upon individuals, and thirty dyads impinging upon other dyads. But the five-member family generates new possibilities: quadrads. Thus, there are five quadratic systems and five such systems impinging upon individuals. Finally, we find ten triads impinging upon dyads. This yields a total of 120 *different* subsystems within a family of five. In families of six or seven or more, these possibilities become completely unmanageable and serve to obfuscate rather than simplify an already sufficiently complex problem.

What is the clinician to do with these possibilities? Is it at all realistic to imagine that he can deal with all the subsystems simultaneously? If not, how is he to pick and choose among them? And after making his selection of the particular subsystem(s) for attention, what theoretical guidelines does he have for proceeding?

There are clusters of entities within the above list of possibilities that have received some attention in the theoretical literature. As was suggested earlier, the dyadic systems of father-son, mother-child, and child-child have been explored by Freud, Rank, and Adler. The spouse system, of course, is *the* central focus of the literature bearing on marriage counseling. The dyads that impinge upon individuals have also received some attention; Freud's postulation of the family romance—father, mother, and son—is well known to clinicians. The situation of three family members juxtaposed against a fourth is exactly the condition inherent in family scapegoating—a situation likewise familiar to family counselors. Finally, dyadic systems that impinge upon other such systems are not unfamiliar: father and son against mother and daughter (the original battle of the sexes); father and mother pitted against children (the struggle of generations); father and daughter versus mother and son (the conflict of "incestuous couples"). But apart from these beginning and tentative analyses, the central theoretical problem awaits solution.

THEORETICAL CONSIDERATIONS THAT
BEAR ON THE TRIAD

One would expect that theory and research stemming from the field of group dynamics would throw some light on the larger subsystems of the family. There is every reason to believe that such subsystems are just special instances of a small group and that whatever lawful principles underlie the structure and functioning of a small group would be applicable to triads within the family. Alas, "small group theory" is a misnomer; it deals with small groups, but it stretches a point to use the appellation "theory" to describe what is nothing more than a collection of disjointed concepts. Most of the empirical research on group dynamics concerns itself with rather small and isolated fragments of a larger problem. This research is increasing both in quantity and in methodological sophistication, however, and it is hoped that before too long there will evolve a more comprehensive and encompassing theory of small groups.[1]

A good deal of small group research concerns itself with the effect of group processes on individual behavior. The tradition of this research is well exemplified by the classic studies of Asch,[2] and it culminates in the recent work of Milgram.[3] But, by and large, this research is still within the confines of personality research; the questions posed concern themselves with individual behavior as a function of independent variables located within a group situation.

Another segment of small group research concerns itself more directly with the issues that comprise this chapter, the small group as an entity in and of itself—hence, research on communication processes and networks, problem solving, power alignments, and leadership. It is impossible to summarize these empirical and theoretical endeavors for the reason mentioned earlier: they are fragmented and disjointed. But the clinician would be well advised to acquaint himself with these fragments for, if nothing else, they throw light on the enormous complexities inherent in small aggregates of individuals.*

* See note 1 for sources in this regard.

Otto Pollak, in an attempt to speak directly to the problem of familial subsystems, looks at these collectivities in terms of their temporal
developments and their relationships to each other.[4] If one considers the
life stages of a family group, various patterns of association among subsystems become apparent. The marital pair, at the beginning, will draw
closer together; interdependency and the mutual satisfaction of needs
are most important. With the arrival of children the balance shifts.
Affective investment resides within the parent-child system; the parents
grow somewhat apart. As the children mature and develop, the intense
association of parent and child becomes diluted and the parents, once
again, turn to each other for emotional nurturance. These proclivities
within the chronology of family life are subsumed by Pollak under the
concept of "relationship tendencies." Aberrations from the norm result
in various forms of pathological states. Thus, Pollak suggests that "relationship tendency reversal" occurs when parents do "not separate" with
the arrival of children, but rather grow closer together—at the expense
of the children. "Relationship tendency arrest" occurs when the ebb and
flow of such patterns does not occur. These relationship tendencies, and
their vicissitudes, can be further confounded by specific neurotic or psy-
chopathological characteristics of individual family members.

In further work, Pollak posits models of healthy subsystems within
the family.[5] There is, first, the ideal spouse system, characterized by
health in the "give and take" or independence-interdependence balance
and in which "positive ambivalence outweighs negative ambivalence."
The parent-child system is characterized by balance in the union; eman-
cipation problems take place throughout the development of the child.
Finally, the sib-sib system provides objects for identification on a peer
level with rivalry and positive feelings accepted by the parents.

Pollak pursues his notion of healthy relationship tendencies:

From this conceptual point of view, the family model can be visualized as a
relatively constant interrelationship of role performers with individually and
socially satisfactory results. Pervading the three sub-systems is a functioning
of the total system which provides the family members with a consciousness
of group identity apart from all other groupings which they claim and which
society accords to them.[6]

Pollak's discussion of family subsystems is predicated on a model
middle-class American family with both spouses living in the home, and

two children—preferably a boy and a girl—fairly close in age. Indeed, fraternal twins, one male and one female, would fit it ideally. A large proportion of clients would not conform to such a model, and hence the theoretical structure concocted by Pollak may, in the long run, have little relevance for clinical practice. But with his contributions we begin to get a glimmer of scholarly insight into the complexities of triadic relationships within the family.

THEORETICAL CONCEPTIONS THAT
BEAR ON THE DYAD

When we consider the dyadic system, the reservoir of theoretical work and empirical research is larger, but again we have little unified, systematic theory. The two largest segments come from "role theory," spawned by the social psychologists, and "communication theory," coming, by and large, from clinical practitioners.

ROLE THEORY

The concept of "role" has been used by sociologists and social psychologists for many, many years. Unfortunately, it has been used in different ways by different writers, sometimes without specified definition. Neiman and Hughes have made a study of the literature around this very question and have concluded that the term is defined in three ways: (1) definitions in terms of society as a whole, (2) definitions in terms of personality development, and (3) functional definitions in terms of specific groups.[7]

"Role" carries connotations of expected or anticipated behavior. Pollak puts it this way: "The concept of social role has been defined as a pattern, or type of behavior which one person builds up in terms of what others demand or expect of him." [8] The converse of this is also true, that is, "For every role expectation of other there is a reciprocal role expectation of self." [9] Role expectations have particular significance in the discussion of familial role patterns.

One other facet of "role" should be mentioned before we leave the subject of definitions: the use of social role in the sense of social or cultural norms of behavior. For example: there are certain social expectations of the role of "mother"; that is, there is a broad continuum of behaviors that encompass the role of mother that is more or less well known to all in a society. In other words, individual A has certain expectations of his mother that are unique to her and his relationship to her, but he also has general role expectations of "mother" in the generic sense. Newcomb speaks of this aspect of role:

When we study human behavior in terms of roles, we are looking at its public or shared aspects. Whether we like it or not, we are all assigned to various positions, and we are perceived by others as occupants of those positions. And whether we ourselves know it or not, we think and feel and act as occupants of positions—whether lifelong ones, as in taking sex roles, or momentary ones, as in taking the role of a bride. Thus both our behavior and others' perceptions of our behaviors—which, together, constitute the two-way process of communication—are determined by our role assignments.[10]

Newcomb's use of the word "position" is equivalent to the sociological concept of "status."

Given this two-dimensional definition of role, that is, role as the adaptational unit of personality to other personalities, and role as the unit of normative behavior, it becomes more clear how this theoretical construct is of value in looking at the family. The family is made up of individual personalities *joined* together. The cement, so to speak, is role. The nature of the bond should be explainable by a "role theory." The various family roles, mother-child, father-child, parent-parent, child-child, etc., are reciprocal and interdependent. Meyer, who is interested in the complementarity of the marital couple, sees role theory as helping ". . . to define the marital relationship in terms of role expectations, failure and success, [and] adherence and deviance of the individual in his appropriate social role." [11] The emotional well-being or equilibrium of the family unit, according to Slavson, demands ". . . that each member of it has a specific role which he discharges adequately and that the result is emotional harmony rather than the discord of conflicting interests and drives." [12] Ackerman also sees "role" as a key to understanding the inner dynamisms of the family:

The stabilizing mechanisms of a family pair or group is a function of the pattern of reciprocal family role relations. Such stability may be promoted on the basis of a relatively static or rigid pattern of role reciprocity, or on the basis of a more flexible capacity to accommodate to change and achieve a new improved level of reciprocity.[13]

Ackerman, as well as Meyer, is interested in the concept of complementarity and also sees the concept of "role" as a means of describing this phenomenon:

Of special importance in this connection is the ability to achieve patterns of family role complementarity. The term, complementarity, refers to a specific patterning of family role relations which provide satisfactions, avenues of solution of conflict, support for a needed self-image, and the buttressing of crucial forms of defense against anxiety.[14]

The reason we have quoted from the above sources (Ackerman, Meyer, Slavson) is to illustrate the fact that a theory of role has been thought of by various authors on the subject of family interaction as a fruitful if not indispensable way to approach the problem. It may be well to point out, however, that there is difficulty sometimes in understanding how the terms of role, role patterns, role behavior, etc., are defined by some of these authors. On occasion it seems as though the term "role" is used synonymously with the term "behavior."

It should be noted that the phenomenon of social role is not restricted solely to the family, even though that is the focus of this chapter. Obviously, there are many categories of role other than familial roles (father, mother, brother, etc.)—there are economic roles (wage earner, employer, etc.), occupational roles (doctor, lawyer, etc.), recreational roles, and so on. The important point is that role, in the sense of its being the "adaptational unit of personality" is applicable to every phase of society and to every aspect of social interaction.

We would like to address ourselves now to the problem of role conflict and its effect on individual and family pathology. If the premise is accepted that an individual carries within him the potential for enacting more than one role, the possibility for conflict between these roles becomes apparent. Moreover, the dichotomy of "individual" and "social" roles also suggest potential for conflict, as do the conceptions of role acquisition and role learning. On the basis of these three sources of role conflict, then, the following kinds of role conflict can be envisaged:

1. Role conflict may be based on the incompatibility of roles, (a) within the personality itself (being both a father and husband toward

the same object), (b) between the personality and the society (a child's role as truant is incompatible with the community's expectations, but it may be completely compatible within the internal economy of the child), or (c) within the society itself (preacher and playboy within one person). Cottrell suggests the following proposition: "The greater the number of incompatible roles and the more overlapping the situations are which evoke them, the greater the amount of conflict in the personality." [15]

2. Role conflict may be based on unclear, ill-defined, or nebulous roles: in a sense, the individual becomes paralyzed through lack of social direction. The concept of "Anomie" may be synonymous with this idea.

3. Role conflict may be based on conflicting role expectations, as Parsons points out:

The exposure of the actor to conflicting sets of legitimized role expectations such that complete fulfillment of both is realistically impossible. It is necessary to compromise, that is, to sacrifice some at least of both sets of expectations, or to choose one alternative and sacrifice the other. In any case the actor is exposed to negative sanctions and so far as both sets of values are internalized, to internal conflict. There may, of course, be limited possibilities of transcending the conflict by redefining the situation, as well as evasion, as, for example, through secrecy, and segregation of occasions.[16]

Sarbin has this to say about the issue:

A person must move cautiously and uncertainly when role expectations of others are partly known or entirely unknown or unknowable. Role-role and self-role conflicts are likely to follow from ambiguous role expectations. The persisting need for solution of such conflicts may lead to socially invalid role enactments.[17]

4. Role conflict may be based on lack of role continuity: Benedict suggests that some cultures have an harmonious, continuous pattern of roles for an individual during his or her passage through various age levels.[18] She further suggests that this is not so in the American middle-class culture, as is attested to by the no-man's land of adolescence.

5. Role conflict may be based on fluctuating, variable, unstable roles, such as transitory or migratory occupational groups, unique familial roles as a result of family catastrophe, etc.

The above kinds of role conflict primarily manifest themselves in pathology within the individual. However, insofar as "role" is a concept that by definition includes at least one other interacting organism, these conflicts must have meaning in terms of the complementary partner or other pair, triad, etc. within the family. For example, the uncertain, hesitant mother without adequate sense of a mother role, through lack of role acquiring experiences or whatever, is going to have a child who reflects this ill-defined mother role in a reciprocal manner.

Spiegal has taken these conceptions of role theory and applied them to the functioning of dyads within the family.[19] Postulating a principle of homeostasis within families, Spiegel considers both the mechanisms of disequilibrium and those of re-equilibrium that occur within family dyads. He suggests five ways in which role equilibrium can break down and proposes means whereby the equilibrium can be restored.

The clinical usefulness of Spiegel's conceptions depends on whether or not these types of role conflict and conflict resolution are applicable to most family dyadic systems. To the extent that they are generalizable across many different types of role situations, and to the extent that they accurately describe what is happening among role participants, Spiegel's typology affords considerable therapeutic opportunity to the enterprising clinician.

On the other hand, the application of role theory by Ackerman in his work on Family Diagnosis and Treatment is rather pedestrian and straight-forward.[20] In spite of a rather elaborate discussion of the use of the concept of "role" by sociologists and social psychologists, Ackerman invariably uses the term as a synonym for behavior. This, of course, is not to say that Ackerman has nothing to contribute to the theory and practice of family treatment. It is only to say that his nod to role theory is peripheral to the main thrust of his argument.

COMMUNICATIONS THEORY

Considerable research is accumulating that falls under the rubric of communications theory. This research comes from sources as disparate as electronics engineering and the clinical treatment of schizophrenia. Intermediate on this continuum of disparity comes theory and study from the areas of psychophysics and perception. Like "small group theory" and "role theory," communications theory is not expressible in a single formulation but is instead an aggregate of ideas and conceptions that bear on a wide range of human events. We restrict our attention to work that focuses on aberrant communications that affect human development.

The school of therapeutic thought most noted for this particular focus is the Palo Alto group of Jackson, Bateson, Weakland, Haley, Satir, et al.[21] In chapter 7 the skeletal outlines of this group's theoretical position were presented: in essence, human development depends on the communicative process, and human behavior can be understood in terms of the structure and regulations that govern communication processes. The Palo Alto school emphasizes the concept of the double bind. The double bind, as we mentioned in the previous chapter, occurs when two people are in an interactive situation and: (1) a primary negative injunction is transmitted from A to B, in the form of either "Do not do X or I will punish you," or "If you do not do X I will punish you"; and (2) a secondary injunction is simultaneously transmitted from A to B that directly conflicts with the first—this second order communication may take the form of "Do not submit to my prohibitions," or "Do not see this as a punishing act."

The double bind, in effect, puts B in an impossible situation: he receives two powerful messages from A that are antithetical and from which there is no escape, as when B is an infant and A is the mother or another significant nurturing figure.

The Palo Alto school proposes that pathological behavior is in part a consequence of such paradoxical communications. Indeed, when the double bind is the characteristic mode of communicative interaction during the developmental years of an individual, schizophrenic processes may be the outcome, and the universe is perceived in double-bind patterns. Less problematic outcomes are more frequent, however, especially where the double bind is a less chronic pattern of communication. The primary or secondary injunctive messages need not, of course, be verbal. Gestures, tone of voice, and other nonverbal transmissions succeed in creating the paradoxical situation.

The Palo Alto school further posits the importance of rules and regulations governing the communicative process within families. There are topics that are approved and others that are disapproved for discussion among family members. Perhaps more importantly, the particular affect surrounding the substance of communication is subject to regulation; anger may or may not be permissible; but so, too, warmth and affection may be "legislated" in or out of familial interactions.

The therapeutic procedures that follow from the above conceptions have not been fully explicated. In gross terms, the therapist seeks to understand the regulations developed by a particular family or family subsystem to govern communication. The task of the therapist is then to bring the family to understand these patterns, for, it is assumed, they may be so complex and so "natural" to the family members that their nature may be unrecognized. With the explication of the communicative regulations, conscious efforts can be employed by the family to amend rules thought to be undesirable. Satir uses the structured interview as a means of clarifying the rules governing family communication patterns.[22] The structured interview revolves around specific tasks to which the family members, in varied combinations, address themselves. The therapist observes the interactions surrounding the accomplishment of the task and, from these data, draws inferences about the rules that govern family communication.

THE CLASSIC SUBSYSTEMS

We now turn to a series of conceptualizations that are more familiar to social caseworkers and that have a more metaphoric ring.

FREUD'S FAMILY ROMANCE [23]

Oedipus, the King of Thebes, unwittingly slew his father and married his mother, Queen Jocasta. This tragic drama encapsulates the heart and soul of the family romance. The central struggle, of course, is between father and son; as the drama unfolds and these two males engage in their eternal struggle, mother waits in the wings—a passive trophy for the victor. The outcome of this drama is as certain as was the Delphic prophecy, the child cannot possibly win. He is, after all, only a child. But if he cannot win he makes the best of a bad bargain: rather than replacing the hated old man he becomes *like* his rival. The heir to this struggle and to the ferocious passions of mutilation, murder, and incest is the superego, a rather beneficent outcome to what is, at heart, a nasty romantic affair.

In spite of the Elektra parallel, the family romance of Freud centers primarily on the man-child. Freud, evidently, neither understood nor cared for the feminine equivalent of what the little boy experiences in the parental fold. His followers, elaborating on the original psychoanalytic conceptions, paid considerably more attention to the romantic struggles of little girls.

The dyad of father and mother impinging on the son, then, is essentially a masculine struggle, and a harsh and brutal one at that. The fantasied consequences of the enterprise are not at all pretty— castration is forever in the air, and when it is eclipsed, murder takes its place. Freud's metaphoric love story is a vicious struggle for a woman —tenderness and warmth have little place in the developing tragedy.

It is as a result of deviations in the classical plot that neurotic problems arise. Hence, the therapist who is confronted with a patient suffering from psychoneurotic illness must pay close attention to what occurred in the early developmental years. The therapy, in the tradition of psychoanalytic thought, is simple: lay bare the unconscious memories of the aberrant script; with awareness the neurosis will vanish.

RANK'S MOTHER-CHILD DIALECTIC [24]

The family romance relegated the mother to the role of prize. Rank's theoretical constructions installed the mother as a central antagonist of the child (of either sex) and played down the influence of fathers upon children. Rank's theory of human development invoked broad dualistic ideas: life-death, separation-unity, engulfment-liberation, and will-counterwill. The child, suggested Rank, begins life in a state of blissful harmony with his all-nurturing mother. The trauma of birth— sudden, painful, and cruelly rejecting—puts an end to this paradise and serves as a prototype for all future anxiety. But separation is not only necessary and inevitable, it is life giving and growth producing. The dialectic between mother and child continues. By the very fact of physical immaturity the infant is bound to the mother—and the mother is bound to the child by the fact of her motherhood. But separation continues inexorably; the child moves away, comes close, moves away still further, and returns again. The closeness is a delight, but it is also engulfment and, ultimately, death; the moving away is life itself, but it is also terror and aloneness. Life and death, separation and unity—such dialectic is *the* characteristic of human experience, and the modalities of the human interchange are learned in the mother-child system of the family.

The Rankian therapist has his task clearly spelled out for him. Since human suffering is a function of an unhappy experience in the separation-unity dialectic, its cure resides in a new experience—one will pitted against another with the struggle played out against the panoply of the life and death fear.

The poetic metaphor of Rank reaches the heights of Freud's Greek tragedy—and is worthy of equal attention.

ADLER'S SIBLING RIVALRY [25]

Adler perceives mankind as forever social and interpersonal. The individual, argues Adler, lives within a community, a group, and the stylistic characteristics of his functioning within this social milieu are determined by his experiences as a child within the prototype of all groups—the family. But families consist of more than parents; siblings are a crucial component of this developmental environment, and it is here that Adler makes his most significant contribution. The personalities of individuals, according to Adler, differ as a function of order of birth. The oldest, middle, and youngest children are quite different. The first born is king, the center of all attention, until he is rudely dethroned by the second born. This leads to what Adler suggests is a more or less permanent feeling of insecurity in the oldest—a "Weltanschauung" of impending and sudden disaster. The middle child (or children), on the other hand, is of necessity ambitious. It is not easy to dethrone a king, especially when the monarch is older and wiser. Hence rebelliousness and envy become the characteristic of the second born. The youngest child is, of course, the spoiled pet, the darling of the family group. If the oldest is the king, and the middle child the unsurper, then the youngest child becomes the court fool or jester—beloved by all, respected by no one.

Adler's theoretical emphasis on siblings and their interactions has led to a considerable amount of empirical research on the effects of birth order on personality development. To indicate the flavor of this research we cite a study on birth order and primogeniture by Altus, who found that the first born is over-represented among college students. This finding is interpreted within Adlerian conceptions. Altus concludes: ". . . the most significant aspects of birth-order linkage to college attendance are the loss to society from the untrained, though presumptively educable, later borns." [26]

Adler's ideas offer more in the way of diagnostic insight than direct treatment implications. He does conclude however, that the personality effects of birth order are not irrevocable, and "proper" planning by the parents, as successive children are born into a family, can mitigate such ordering effects.

THE MARITAL PAIR [27]

Marital counseling is big business. And it is everybody's business. There is incessant concern in the United States over what is alleged to be an ever-rising and perilous divorce rate, a breakdown of moral values among marital partners, and a generally pervasive malaise and silent misery within marriages. The roots of these alleged marriage problems are thought to reside in the urbanization of American society and its consequent mobility, or in the economic system, or in the secularization of society, or in the cold war, or in a decay of moral values, or in combinations of these. American marriage is in bad shape, saith the public, and marriage counseling is thought by many to be an institutional device that can provide a partial remedy.

It is not clear that the charge as to the decay of modern marriage is correct. Divorce rates are ambiguous; in some states the rate of divorce appears to be dropping, and the marriage rate itself continues to increase, which suggests that it is still in style. Indeed, the most important *empirical* investigation of modern American marriage that addresses itself to the charge concludes:

Most wives are satisfied with the love, the understanding and the standard of living provided by their husbands . . . [and] there seems to be little evidence, from the 909 wives interviewed, that American marriage as an institution is on the verge of collapse. On the contrary, as long as men and women continue to have important needs satisfied by their partners, marriage is "here to stay." [28]

But whether the charge is true or not, marriage counselors see people who are having problems, and, on the surface at least, these problems are marital ones. The clinician who is confronted with these difficulties is faced with enormous problems.

There is, first, the ethical question of whether termination of a marriage is a possible objective of treatment. By adopting a neutral position on this issue, the clinician takes a stand, and the stand is quite clear: divorce is an acceptable outcome.

Very often, the hapless clinician is seen by the applicant as a last stop before the attorney. The marriage is usually in an acutely precarious state when the husband and/or wife comes for help. One of the partners may already have decided to end the marriage, and the visit may be simply an attempt to have such a decision blessed by the counselor; the couple may have been referred by an attorney; one or both parties may see the visit as a device to accrue credits for the forthcoming legal struggle; a spouse may come at the behest of the other partner to "at least do this much for me."

It is very important, then, that the motivation for marital counseling be thoroughly explored and quickly addressed. The central question that the clinician must pose to his clients is "What do you want from marital counseling?" Often the latent answer is "Nothing, I just want out." When ambivalence is strong, however, and when the marital partners are truly concerned with salvaging their marriage, the clinician has, in fact, something to grapple with—namely a conflict.

The therapeutic task then becomes one of explicating the conflict. One of the more remarkable characteristics of marital conflict is that the two parties are often not aware of what is bothering the other. One spouse may be quite clear about the nature of his own dissatisfaction but have only the fuzziest notion of the other's malcontent. And, surprisingly enough, just the articulation of both parties' "gripes" can have an immediate and lasting beneficial effect.

Such therapeutic endeavors can be subsumed under homey rubrics such as "clearing the air," or "laying the cards on the table." They are essentially treatment tactics that serve to open avenues of communication between the spouses. The joint interview is often the most productive setting for this kind of interchange, *providing that the uncommunicated desires and needs are not too devastating to the other party.* An unexpressed complaint that "my husband doesn't love me" is perfectly safe when the husband does in fact love his wife. He can express surprise that she could possibly feel this way and quickly reassure her. When he does not love her, however, such an explication will scarcely reunite them.

If the partners can't stand each other there may be little the clinician can do. In the first instance, opening up avenues of communication through joint interviews is very often quite successful. In the second instance, the clinician may serve no other function but that of giving his blessings to the official disruption of the marriage. In this latter situation, the caseworker may serve to clarify certain specific alternatives for the people involved. Ending a marriage of many years duration is a profound act, and its implications may not be immediately apparent to the dissident partner. Alternatives can be brought into the client's field of view, and certain adaptive procedures can be considered. But, like other clinical problems, the basically healthy marriage is the one most amenable to therapeutic aid.

THE MOTHER-CHILD PAIR [29]

This final "classical" subsystem of the family provides the clientele for the child guidance clinic. This dyadic unit, however, differs markedly from that of the marital couple by virtue of the unique character of one of its members, the child. Children are, by nature and definition, dependent people; they need a parent. Whereas husband and wife are assumed to be equals in that they are autonomous and rational beings, children are not and cannot be autonomous, and their ability to make rational choices is presumably limited. A child cannot divorce his mother—although he can behave in a manner that will insure his removal from the home. Such behavior, which is the only alternative for some children, may have serious consequences, however; the child can become very disturbed and, hence, labeled psychotic, or he can become asocial and be called delinquent. The dissatisfied wife is merely a divorcee—the dissatisfied child is "sick."

Although the separation of mother and child, a last resort, is considered in some cases, by and large the child guidance worker seeks an accommodation within the dyadic unit. The younger the child, the more essential is it that the mother be favorably disposed to make certain changes in her behavior. The very young child, of course, has almost no opportunity to develop independently of his mother; as he increases in age, he gains more autonomy and hence can be more responsible for putting into play adaptive mechanisms of his own. We have, in effect, a continuum on which at one extreme the child guidance problem becomes a task of treating mothers—through treating mothers and children—and that culminates in the opposite extreme of treating latent adults independently of their mothers.

But the dependent position of the child client vis-à-vis the mother is only one unique attribute of the child guidance situation. The adult client is a being who is presumed, at least in the Freudian tradition, able to cope with a rationalistic treatment endeavor. That is to say, an intellectual and cognitive management of life is both the means and the end of treatment. But the child is presumed to be ill-equipped for rational discussion—in the language of contemporary psychoanalytic theory, his ego lacks sufficient development to labor consistently within an intellectual framework. Accordingly, a new discourse needs to be developed, and child guidance councelors have devised "play therapy" as the new vehicle.

The mother-child system receives the main attention of the child guidance clinic, but this family subsystem is treated as two independent units—mother and child. The dyad in itself has not been addressed for the reason that there is a woeful lack of theory geared to the system as such.

THE PLACE OF THE THERAPIST IN THE
STRUCTURE OF THE SUBSYSTEM

Thus far we have talked of familial subsystems, whether of the triad or dyad. It is essential to emphasize that in the treatment situation the therapist himself is incorporated into the system. In essence, then, even in the traditional modality of one-to-one treatment, the irreducible conceptual unit is *not* the individual but the dyad of therapist and patient. That clinician and client interact with each other has always been known and recognized, as is evidenced by such concepts as "the therapeutic relationship," "transference," "counter-transference," and "will-counter will." Concepts from small group theory, role theory, and communications theory are as applicable to the therapist-client system as they are to collectivities of the family. In this sense, personality theory is always inadequate to explain the therapeutic process. When we hold joint interviews, as with a husband and wife or mother and child, our unit of attention is more than the dyad—it is the triad of husband-wife-*therapist*. The clinician becomes, of necessity, a part of the trans-actional field, and diagnostic and treatment considerations must bear this inevitable fact in mind.

SUMMARY COMMENTS

In spite of beginning formulations stemming from the scholarly endeav-ors of social psychology, there is a dearth of theory in casework to guide the clinician as he treats subsystems of the family. But, as we have seen in our discussion of role theory and communication theory, the clinician does not have to wait for the academic disciplines to generate such theory for him. The clinician is in an ideal and crucial position to de-velop needed theory. Therapeutic attention focused on these subsystems, as units of treatment, will eventually lead to the construction of theory.

One final note: treatment of familial subsystems does not neces-sarily have as a consequence joint or multiple interviewing. In current psychotherapy a rationale is developing that holds that family diagnosis and treatment means interviewing everybody simultaneously. We argue, however, that the *concept* of family subsystems as units of therapeutic attention is important—not simply how many people are in the office. Ideas as well as form make for therapeutic innovation.

CHAPTER THIRTEEN

CURRENT DEVELOPMENTS
AND TRENDS

The issues and controversies concerning psychotherapy and social case-work that we have reviewed in this book are rooted in variations in three sets of assumptions: (1) assumptions about the nature of human behavior, (2) assumptions about the nature and causes of human problems, and (3) assumptions about how behavior can be changed.

Variations in these assumptions have given rise to a proliferation of schools of thought. Thus, the history of casework—and of psychotherapy, with which it has long been associated—is in part a history of emerging theories—psychoanalytic theory, Rankian theory, Sullivanian theory, learning theory, etc.—formulated from shifting assumptions about the nature of man and the causes of his problems.

These theories were developed partly in response to man's need to explain himself, to account for why he behaves as he does. And, indeed, these theories have provided a varied and, in some instances, exotic array of explanations for the behavior of man. Still, certain hard, persistent, pragmatic realities generate doubt that this search for explanations —for answers to the question "Why?"—has contributed significantly to the efficacy of the therapeutic enterprises that sprang up in response to these theories. Even though much of the research to date is tentative, what has been done suggests that practitioners operating within these different theories of behavior do not differ in their effectiveness and that none of these schools of thought have achieved a dramatic level of therapeutic effectiveness, with the probable exception of the behaviorists.

One possible reason for this unhappy state of affairs is that the explanations offered by the theories are in error, and this interpretation finds some support in the attempts that have been made to test hypotheses derived from some of these theories. More important, we have argued that even if an explanatory theory is valid, it is not a sufficient guide for changing behavior, which necessarily involves variables not contained in an explanation of a problem. And, in many instances at least, such an explanation is not even necessary in order to correct the problem. For example, behavior modification techniques reliably and effectively extinguish phobias in the absence of a complete explanation of their causes, and in so doing they rely on variables (e.g., relaxation) not contained in any of the theoretical explanations for phobias that have been proposed.

Thus, the connections between these explanations and the intervention principles that are supposed to follow from them have been speculative and loose, or even nonexistent. Such theories seek to explain how a problem came about, not how it can be changed, and these are quite different, sometimes even independent, questions. It is not surprising, then, that many casework students have failed to see in intricate psychological diagnoses the utility for practice that their teachers sometimes have claimed for them. The translation of an explanation of a client's problem into a treatment plan is inevitably speculative, and the clinician who impresses his peers often is the one who can artfully and plausibly connect the explanation with the course of intervention he proposes.

This state of affairs is bound to continue until theories of intervention are available, that is, theories centrally concerned with the question "How can this problem (or behavior) be changed?" Only then can systematic analysis of that question be substituted for speculations and inferences drawn from theories that never were designed to answer it.

When that time arrives—and it is beginning to arrive now—we would expect to see more variation and much greater specificity in the delineation of intervention methods and techniques. In some instances, these variations may be subtle and undramatic, but the subtle differences may be crucial insofar as outcome is concerned. For example, operant conditioning rests on the assumption that behavior is determined by its consequences: behavior that is followed by reinforcement is repeated; unrewarded behavior terminates. When this principle is stated at that level of generality, it is possible to infer, as many have, that operant conditioning is nothing more than another label for what any good practitioner of supportive psychotherapy and casework has been doing for years, that is, supporting the client's strengths. When the operant learning principle is specified in detail, however, the superficial similarity to supportive intervention evaporates. For it turns out that questions such as the timing of the reinforcement, how it is given, what is used as a reinforcer, and the precise selection of behavior to be reinforced, are decisive, in the sense that on these questions hangs the success or failure of the change effort. More important in the context of this discussion, the answers to these questions do not depend on clinical intuition and inference but can be determined systematically and empirically.

We are suggesting, then, that the school of practice based on social learning principles offers a paradigm for the kind of intervention theory —and therefore the kind of theory—that caseworker practitioners need most of all. That is not to say that the principles and methods of behavior modification are correct in all instances; the theory still is too undeveloped to draw such a conclusion. Rather, underlying the logic of this approach to the *task* of intervention is the logic that an adequate *theory* of intervention should follow, which cannot be said to the same extent for any of the theories that preceded it. For these reasons, we will discuss the behavior modification approach in detail in this chapter in an attempt to make clear the importance that should be attached to it.

Before beginning that discussion, however, another direction for the future development of casework theory should be mentioned. We have repeatedly emphasized that in the development of theories of intervention, casework needs to formulate more sophisticated theories for that broad spectrum of activities that have been called "environmental manipulation." Although environmental manipulation has been integral to casework practice throughout its history, theoretical and methodological development of this dimension of practice has been neglected at the expense of elaboration of more psychological approaches. Now that the social aspects of casework practice have been firmly and visibly reemphasized, it is time to remedy these theoretical and methodological deficiencies. Fortunately, here too important beginnings have been made, to which we will turn later in this chapter.

TOWARD INTERVENTION THEORIES
FOR SOCIAL CASEWORK

BEHAVIOR MODIFICATION

The principles that inform behavior modification were developed from theoretical and empirical attempts to answer the question of how the behaviors of persons are acquired and modified or, more generally but less exactly, how persons learn. As we have repeatedly emphasized, that is precisely the question most central and urgent for the practitioner, namely, how can the behaviors that his client wants to change be modified in the desired direction? This convergence between the questions of concern to theoreticians, researchers, and practitioners accounts for the rapid development of this approach once practitioners began to apply social learning principles in clinical work.*

While the behaviorists were not the only ones concerned with the question of learning, they made an early strategic decision that distinguishes their work from that of most other students of learning. The decision was that in pursuing the question of how persons learn, the answers are to be sought only in terms of variables that can be observed. Unobservable internal states, prevalent in the psychological theories that have dominated casework and psychotherapy, were eschewed in favor of overt behavior and observable environmental events. The behaviorists argued that only in this way could a scientific, empirical account of learning be developed, while their critics complained that in not attending to internal states, the behaviorists were denying a crucial dimension of human experience. Philosophical considerations aside, however, the issue can be resolved into an empirical question: Can the

---

* Many of the principles used in behavior modification had been established long before any important efforts were made to apply them to clinical work. While all the reasons for this lag are not clear, one is the response that "behaviorism" has evoked in many clinicians who believe it to be mechanistic and somehow dehumanizing.

behaviorists deliver on their claims? Thus far, at least for the effort to apply social learning principles to the modification of behavior, the answer appears to be a qualified yes; and some of the results are impressive.

The insistence on observable behavior forced practitioners using behavioral principles to focus their attention on molecular rather than molar units, on specific behaviors rather than, say, identity or ego states. This had the advantage of simplifying the intervention task, in the sense that it probably is easier to devise a plan for changing a person's lack of assertive behavior, for example, than to alter his "identity," and this characteristic of behavior modification may account for part of its success.

Respondent conditioning. Possibly because of the focus on molecular units of behavior, much of the early work of practitioners applying behavioral principles centered on work with phobic reactions, since these provide specific, visible, delimited behavioral targets for intervention. The methods used appear deceptively simple and rest on the principle that a person cannot be anxious and relaxed simultaneously.[1] In general, the procedure, called desensitization, is (1) to establish a hierarchy of situations that elicit the phobic response, ranging from the mildest to the most severe (e.g., from a gymnasium to a phone booth in the case of claustrophobia), (2) to train the client to relax, and (3) to present the hierarchy of situations while the client is in a relaxed state until he can imagine himself in the most severe situation without experiencing anxiety. The relaxation training must be effectively done, the hierarchy must be carefully constructed, and the anxiety response at each step in the hierarchy must be extinguished before moving to the next one. But if these procedures are followed carefully and properly, they are highly effective and reliable, so much so that it would seem to be unethical not to offer these methods to persons seeking help with a phobic problem. And no positive evidence has been reported that symptom substitution occurs, as critics of the method have predicted, even though a number of careful follow-up studies have been conducted in an effort to test this prediction.

Behaviorists view phobias as one instance of anxiety responses, and similar procedures have been used successfully to eliminate other anxiety responses. For example, Gordon Paul used a similar procedure in desensitizing students suffering from public speaking anxiety, as reported in his careful evaluative study comparing the effectiveness of these procedures with conventional psychotherapy.[2] Desensitization achieved a success rate of 100 percent, while the results of more conventional psychotherapy did not differ from those obtained with placebo and no-treatment control groups. Other examples suggest that desensitization is applicable and effective for a broad array of anxiety responses.[3]

There also is evidence indicating that desensitization is effective for other emotional responses not ordinarily called anxiety. For example, one of the authors successfully used desensitization techniques to reduce impulsive outbursts of anger. The client, a forty-five-year-old truck driver, came for help in his marriage, which, after several separations, was near dissolution. He wanted to save the marriage, as did his wife, but the latter complained that she no longer could tolerate his sudden outbursts of anger in which he abused her verbally, though not physically. From a careful analysis of the situations that aroused these outbursts, a hierarchy of anger-rousing situations was constructed, the husband was trained in relaxation techniques,[4] and then he was desensitized to each situation in the anger-arousing hierarchy. Diminution of his outbursts with his wife began while desensitization was still in process. After desensitization was completed, the client's outbursts at home ceased and had not reappeared six months later. He was still capable of anger, but the explosive, uncontrolled outbursts ceased, and he also reported that he did not have any sense of being constricted or of expending energy to "keep the lid on" his anger. Applications of learning principles to similar problems have been reported by others.[5]

Desensitization is one of a class of procedures for what is called *respondent conditioning,* which refers to modifying behaviors assumed to be controlled by classical or Pavlovian conditioning.[6] Anxiety, fear, anger, and other responses that occur *automatically* and *involuntarily* following presentation of certain stimuli fall into this class of behavior. Pavlov's dog was presented with food and a ringing bell simultaneously. The food (the unconditioned stimulus) evoked a salivation response from the dog; the bell (the conditioned stimulus) did not. Eventually, however, after repeated presentations the bell became linked to food and the dog salivated upon presentation of the bell alone. A common human experience illustrates the same principle. A person is driving on the freeway and suddenly and unexpectedly finds himself in a situation in which he narrowly escapes a serious accident. He is frightened, shaken, and anxious. The next time he drives on that section of the freeway he becomes tense, slows down, and is aware of feeling anxious. In some instances he may avoid that section of the freeway entirely.

Respondent conditioning seeks, in effect, to de-condition the conditioned stimulus so that it no longer elicits the undesired response. This can be done in a variety of ways, including repeated presentation of the conditioned stimulus in the absence of the unconditioned stimulus (after the dog has learned to salivate to the bell, if the bell is repeatedly presented in the absence of food, the bell will eventually fail to elicit the salivation response), punishment or aversive conditioning, and eliciting incompatible responses simultaneously, as in the desensitization procedures described above. Choice of technique depends on the nature of the stimulus and response, the possibilities in the intervention situation, the durability and persistence of the response, and ethical considerations; for example, punishment of the response might be highly effective (though generally it is not) but ethically unacceptable. And in some instances, operant conditioning techniques, which are discussed below, may be used to modify respondent behaviors.

Social caseworkers ought to be trained in the use of these techniques, since they often are called upon by their clients to modify the class of behaviors for which these techniques have been developed. And such training would be eminently useful; these techniques have been shown to be effective, and therefore should be substituted, in training and practice, for the less effective techniques caseworkers have been using to modify such behaviors.

Operant conditioning. Only a portion of the behaviors that practitioners attempt to modify fall into the respondent class discussed above. Numerically greater, and probably more important in the work of caseworkers, are what behaviorists sometimes call *operants,* or behaviors controlled by operant conditioning. Operant conditioning is based on the "law of effect," which holds that behavior is controlled by its consequences. Generally, if a behavior is rewarded or reinforced, the frequency of that behavior will increase; if it is not reinforced, the behavior will appear less frequently. An example is the lay belief that children have tantrums in order to get attention. Many clinicians long ago dropped that explanation for tantrums, but recent evidence indicates that the lay view was correct, in many instances at least. A number of reports have appeared describing rapid and reliable extinction of tantrums simply by withholding reinforcement of them.[7] *

Operant techniques are quite varied and are undergoing constant development out of the work of inventive practitioners.[8] Theoretically, operant principles are applicable to an enormous array of behaviors (in principle, to all except respondent behaviors, and even to those in some instances), and clinical applications thus far have ranged from autism [9] to delinquency,[10] and from anorexia nervosa [11] and alcoholism [12] to stuttering.[13]

Although the results reported thus far are uneven, in some instances they are dramatic, and of course serious and widespread effort to apply these techniques in clinical work began only a few years ago.

Recent work has shown that operant principles lend themselves to application in (1) groups, where use of modeling techniques to elicit and shape certain behaviors (e.g., assertive behavior) is facilitated [14] and (2) institutional and organizational settings, such as the development of token economies that make possible immediate reinforcement of a great variety of behaviors.[15] Moreover, once a behavioral analysis has been done and a conditioning program designed by a trained professional, many of the techniques can be learned and applied by subprofessionals.[16] This latter characteristic has made it possible to modify the behavior of children by training their parents in behavior analysis and behavior modification principles,[17] thus opening many possibilities for the application of these principles in family treatment. In view of the flexibility possible in the application of behavior modification principles, it is far too early to say what the limits of applicability may be. In theory there are none, but in spite of the remarkable promise behavior modification already has shown, we remain skeptical about any claim to unlimited potentialities.

* Any effort to review the behavior modification approach runs the risk of oversimplification because of the parsimony of the principles involved. Not all tantrums are so easily extinguished, particularly in children whose repertoire includes few behaviors that elicit positive responses from the environment, whether because of behavior deficits in the child or the lack of positive reinforcers in the child's environment, or both.

One of the most important characteristics of the behavior modification approach, as a paradigm for intervention theory, has little to do with the principles of the approach. The insistence that change targets and outcomes be precisely specified in terms of observable behaviors means that effectiveness is not ambiguous. Either the behavior to be modified changed in the desired direction (extinguished, decreased, or increased in frequency) or it did not. This feature of the approach, together with the conviction that failure is a reflection on method and technique and not on the client provides a powerful dynamic for methodological improvement. Probably any intervention theory subjected to this sort of feedback would over time show an increase in effectiveness, but the difficulty with previous approaches has been that outcomes are indeterminate because the change objectives have not been stated in terms that are easily observed and assessed.

Process. Practitioners working within the behavioral approach begin with a process analogous to diagnosis but which they often prefer to call "assessment" or "behavioral analysis." [18] Beginning with the client's complaint and his statement of what he wants to change, the worker makes a careful analysis of the behaviors of concern to the client, their frequency, and the precise circumstances under which they occur (or fail to occur in those cases where the client wants to acquire new behaviors). Behaviorists assume that behaviors that the client wants to eliminate persist because they are reinforced, and they seek to discover the reinforcers that maintain such behaviors.

It also is important, in assessment, to discover what is reinforcing to the client. Events, situations, or behaviors that are reinforcing to one person are not necessarily equally so to another. And that is even the case with such generalized reinforcers as money, food, or sex. If possible, the practitioner should try to construct a hierarchy of reinforcers for each client, from least to most potent. The importance of identifying the reinforcing agent is that in planning an intervention program for the client the practitioner can seek to use the reinforcers most potent for that client and so work toward behavior modification. Not all the reinforcers will be supplied by the practitioner; in many instances, the changes induced in the client's behavior will elicit an increase in positive reinforcement from his environment. For example, in the case of the man with impulsive temper outbursts described earlier, when his outbursts subsided this change elicited positive responses from his wife and other relatives. And it is important to plan the intervention program so as to maximize an increase in positive reinforcement in the environment, since this will serve to maintain the changes in the client's behavior and not make their continuance contingent on reinforcers supplied by the practitioner.

Thus, the assessment process has two aims. The first is to identify the behaviors that are to be modified. Essentially, the practitioner of behavior modification is concerned with three basic types of behavior change: (1) decreasing the frequency or intensity of certain behaviors, as in reducing the frequency of anxiety responses, (2) increasing the frequency of certain behaviors, such as assertive behavior, and (3) the acquisition of new behaviors not currently in the person's repertoire, such as the shaping of speech in autistic children. The task of determining which behaviors are to be modified or acquired is complicated by the fact that only in limiting cases, such as phobias, is only one set of behaviors involved. More commonly, certainly in casework practice, several sets of behaviors are to be changed. Thus, for example, for a client who seeks help because he is immobilized in social situations, it may be necessary to desensitize his anxiety responses to social situations and also to increase the frequency of assertive behavior.

The second aim of behavior analysis is to plan a behavior modification program designed to bring about these changes. This program must specify: (1) the order in which the different sets of behavior are to be modified (in the above example, should desensitization of anxiety responses to social situations precede or follow training to increase the frequency of assertive behavior?), (2) the methods and techniques to be used in modifying each set of behavior, (3) a plan for maintaining the changes once they are achieved and for insuring that they carry over into the client's life situation, and (4) procedures for monitoring progress to determine whether the methods are successful.

Throughout the assessment process, the client's participation is crucial, since the practitioner seeks to bring about the changes the client wants; practitioners of behavior modification tend to be scrupulous about limiting their efforts to changes the client desires. (This is complicated in the case of captive or involuntary clients, such as children, offenders, and institutionalized clients, but that dilemma is not unique to practitioners of behavior modification.) If, in order to achieve the client's objective, it is necessary to change behaviors in addition to those he identifies, this must be explicitly and carefully explained to the client. Once there is agreement about the changes to be sought, the practitioner of behavior modification tends to assume more of an expert role than has been customary in conventional casework and psychotherapy. He describes the program of behavior modification that he prescribes and, typically, explains the rationale for it to the client. One of the benefits of the latter is that many clients can acquire the ability to modify their own behavior on the basis of the principles they learn in their work with the practitioner.[19]

Comprehensive catalogues of behavior modification methods and techniques are not yet available, although some books provide descriptions of a wide array of them.[20] But rapid developments in this field make it essential that the practitioner who wishes to apply these principles keep abreast of the reports that appear in several journals.[21] Many of these reports describe work with one or a few cases and therefore must be evaluated with the caution appropriate to any conclusions drawn from case reports. However, the practitioner is apt to find these case reports unusually useful because (1) the methods and techniques typically are described in such concrete detail that the reader could duplicate them if he wants to and (2) the behaviors of the client that were the target of change also are described in such detail that the practitioner can easily tell whether they match those he is seeking to modify in his own clients. The advantage of such concreteness for the practitioner who reads case reports in order to discover methods and techniques he can use seems obvious.

The range of this body of literature is wide; it describes methods and techniques that have been applied to the problems encountered in many of the agencies in which caseworkers practice, including family agencies, mental hygiene clinics and community mental health centers, child guidance clinics, and institutions. However, many of the problems encountered in some other agencies, such as correctional agencies, public welfare departments, and child placement services, have yet to receive sufficient attention from behaviorally oriented practitioners. But the clear message of the work done thus far is that the principles of behavior modification lend themselves to flexible application to a large array of problems in a variety of settings, and there is reason to believe that these principles will prove useful in casework practice generally.

There is no intent to imply that behavior modification is the answer to the caseworker's prayers. At present, however, among all the various intervention approaches available, it appears to be the most effective, and that is a strong point in its favor. Moreover, adaptions of this approach carry with it few of the hazards for the profession that attended other theories adapted in the past because of an important characteristic of behavior modification. The insistence that methods and techniques be describable and that outcomes be measurable means that replication is inevitable and that any erroneous claims to effectiveness cannot long stand. Thus, doctrinaire adherence to any particular theory probably cannot long survive the pragmatic test of effectiveness, and that can only benefit the profession and its clients. And the rapid changes in methods and changes that have already occurred in this field lend support to that prediction. For example, imagery, a phenomenon long anathema to "pure" behaviorists, who avoided anything that suggested mentalistic inner states, has recently become an important dimension of behavior modification, suitably reconceptualized within a behavioral perspective.

Issues. Behavior modification has attracted a host of critics.[22] Of the variety of criticisms that have been raised about it, two in particular seem to be of greatest concern to social work critics.[23] One is that the behavioral perspective omits important aspects of human nature. Behaviorists typically make no mention of identity, ego strength, defenses, unconscious conflict, transference, and other concepts familiar and important to many caseworkers.* Consequently, some of the social workers who would give a place to behavior modification in the caseworker's repertoire suggest this approach should supplement and augment the established concepts and methods of dynamic casework, not replace them. This criticism contains both a fallacy and an important truth. The fallacy is the conclusion that because a theory does not find a place for unconscious conflict—or any other concept—the theory therefore is

---

* It should be noted that behaviorists have attempted to show that learning principles can be applied generally to human development and behavior. See for example: Arthur W. Staats and Carolyn K. Staats, *Complex Human Behavior* (New York, Holt, Rinehart and Winston, 1964).

incomplete. Unconscious conflict is an hypothesis, not an indisputable characteristic of human behavior, but through repeated usage some caseworkers have reified this and other concepts so that they are regarded as realities rather than constructs. If a theory of behavior is developed that empirically succeeds without such concepts then it indeed has no need of them. The important truth in the criticism is that caseworkers cannot afford to be doctrinaire adherents to any *one* theory. Their mission is to help people, and to this end they should use whatever methods are most helpful, regardless of the theories on which they are based.

A second criticism of special concern to social workers is the suggestion that behavior modification is morally objectionable.[24] In part, at least, this concern is a response to the language of behavior modification. In a way, it is unfortunate that behavior modification relies on words such as conditioning, reinforcement, shaping, punishment, and other terms that for some carry connotations that somehow are less human and warm than words such as support, ego strength, clarification, and insight. Halmos, for example, is concerned that the objectification and atomization of human experience that is part of the behavioral approach may destroy certain ideas that might be essential to the success of social-psychological helping efforts.[25] As we have indicated earlier in this book, this argument seems strained—not that the connotations of the terms of a theory are of no consequence, but that the consequences are less serious than Halmos fears and they are, in any event, modifiable over time as the behavior modification approach demonstrates its usefulness and as the mystery and misconceptions attached to the approach are dispelled by greater familiarity with it.

But the moral objections to behavior modification go beyond language to the complaint that it is manipulative, treats persons as objects, and makes little allowance for self-determination. These are serious matters to social workers, as they should be. Yet it is difficult to see precisely in what sense the behaviorist is more manipulative than the practitioner who follows any other approach. If a person asks for help to relieve his distress, is the practitioner who applies behavior modification principles more manipulative than another practitioner who applies different methods to help the person? Both have offered, implicitly at least, to endeavor to change the behaviors that the client wants changed, which is no more and no less than what all caseworkers claim to do. It may be that the behaviorist is more directive than other practitioners in the sense that he explicitly assumes the responsibility for planning and guiding the program of intervention, but that hardly seems objectionable if he makes clear to the client what is to be done, what will be expected of him, and allows the client to decide if he wants to follow that course of action.

Perhaps the moral objections arise because the behaviorists so blatantly proclaim that they seek to modify behavior, whereas many other practitioners mask their identical intent by claiming only to promote health or to facilitate self-realization, implying that whatever changes follow their efforts are ones that would have occurred naturally anyway if the client's life situation had been more favorable. And the naïve statements made by some behavior therapists about involuntary clients —criminals, delinquents, etc.—to the effect that "society" sets the goals of behavior changes for such persons, have not helped to reduce the moral concerns about their methods.

We would suggest that any approach that makes it possible for one person successfully to modify the behavior of others in specified directions raises for all of us the spectre of a society in which a few can control the many. Since the fields of social casework and psychotherapy have been seeking just such approaches for decades, it was perhaps inevitable that some would be found. When highly successful methods of changing behavior are found, no matter how benign they may otherwise appear to be, they will evoke the legitimate fear that they may be used to immoral ends. It is this larger issue that behavior modification urgently poses for us, and to which we ought to direct our attention in anticipation of the probability that highly effective methods for behavioral change will be developed. At the same time, we must continue the search for more effective ways of helping the persons who seek our services. With reference to the latter objectives, the evidence indicates that behavior modification probably is the most promising of the various approaches currently available for application by social caseworkers.

Finally, efforts currently are being made to apply social learning principles to the analysis and change of social systems.[26] The results of such efforts may yield applications that caseworkers can use in their work in the environment, a subject to which we turn our attention in the next subsection of this chapter.

SOCIAL INTERVENTION

In the heart of San Francisco's skid row, every Wednesday afternoon at 1 P.M., a van of the type used by campers pulls to the curb and parks in front of a dilapidated but still popular flop house. Taped to the sides of the van are small posters on which are printed, in large letters, the words "HELP CENTER." A petite, pretty young woman steps down from the driver's cab, circles the van, and opens the double side doors. Inside are a small sofa, a table, a swivel chair, a cabinet with sink, file drawers, a record player, and a mobile telephone. Within a few minutes, music is pouring out on the street from the loudspeakers mounted on top of the van, coffee is brewing in a pot on the cabinet inside, and the young woman and her assistant, a tall muscular young Black man, begin to receive a steady stream of visitors.

All afternoon they come, men and women, all ages, colors, and nationalities, to seek what the van claims to offer: help. Sometimes five, six, or more persons are waiting their turn to get inside the van and tell of their need. At 4:30 P.M. the van must close its doors and move on to avoid being towed away. Later that evening it will reappear, this time at a location in the heart of another Mission slum district. The next day, and every day of the week, the same routine is followed, each day at a different location in San Francisco's central poverty area.

The problems brought to the van by its visitors represent the range of problems experienced by residents of low-income urban areas, from a young man who needed bus tokens to take his wife to the hospital to a tearful, sick old woman about to be evicted from a nearby flop house. A middle-aged man just released from prison was seeking a job, any job; a bearded nineteen-year-old youth urgently asked for hospitalization because of excessive drinking that began when he recently stopped taking drugs; and a twenty-seven-year-old, neatly dressed Chicano youth with a spine deformed by tuberculosis described his vain efforts to obtain an office job, despite business training, because of his handicap. Others asked for nothing more than a donut and a cup of coffee, or a chance to pass the time of day with someone who listened and seemed interested.

And some, as the young lady in the van acknowledged, simply enjoy a chance to talk to a pretty girl. All the visitors appear to trust and respect the young lady and her assistant. Perhaps because they are there, where their clients live? Or perhaps because they ask nothing? Or because their efforts to help are immediate and highly visible?

Inside the van, the young lady and her assistant use an extensive set of information files and the mobile telephone in their efforts to connect the request for help with the service delivery system, such as it is —but more of that later. Thus, the van offers a social broker service, a function that goes back to the beginnings of social work but has only recently been rediscovered and labeled. The young woman who coordinates the work of the help center was graduated just a year before from a school of social work where her particular course and field work experience centered on casework in psychiatric agencies. When she completed her graduate social work education, however, she decided she wanted something that would be, in her own words, "broader and less limited" than the work she had done in a psychiatric clinic during her last year in school. Watching her standing on the sidewalk in conversation with a skid-row resident evokes the image of the lady bountiful and friendly visitor of social work's early years, but without the patronizing moral overtones that characterized the work of her early predecessors. With the latter element removed, what remains is a genuine, professionally disciplined effort to help the person find what is needed to relieve his distress, or to realize his tender aspirations, or simply to listen.

After an afternoon working in the help center, one conclusion that seems strikingly obvious is the rationality of the concept. If social welfare services exist primarily to serve persons who have need of them, shouldn't there be a single point of entry to the otherwise bewildering maze of services, one place where a person can go to ask for whatever help he needs, and a place that is close by and highly visible? If that logic is sound, it should follow that the characteristics of the service system would be influenced by the demands made upon it by persons at the point of entry. To note that this is not presently true of the social service system is not to make a new or surprising observation. But the second conclusion that clearly emerges from the experience of such centers is the incredible irrationality of the social service system, at least for important segments of the population.

For these groups, such as the skid-row residents described above, many of the services most needed are either nonexistent or ineffective, and other services that are available are not needed or wanted. Which agencies help the man without special skills who wants a job, *any* job, and who has been to the employment office daily for weeks without success? The obvious answer, a service that creates and provides jobs, does not exist. And what of a man of fifty who worked for over twenty years in the freight business before he went to the prison from which he was just released a few days before, when a call to his former union hiring hall evokes from the hiring supervisor the comment, "tell him to go on welfare like everyone else these days"? Where does the social broker turn to help the Chicano youth with the deformed spine when twice before he underwent extensive work training with the Vocational Rehabilitation Agency only to discover, in the end, that they could not overcome the resistance of prospective employers?

These questions point to one of the most important functions of an undifferentiated, accessible, social broker service: namely it provides a sensitive index to the condition of the social service system. If that system were rationally organized, the information gathered in such help centers could be an important determinant of the structure of the system and of the allocation of resources within it. As it stands now, however, exactly the opposite sometimes seems to be true: such help centers exert no appreciable influence on the service system but, on the contrary, are utterly dependent on it and on the agencies that, from the vantage point of such centers, appear to be pursuing their own definitions of what the population wants and needs. Because of their strategic position at the interface between persons and the service system, line staff in such centers are confronted not only with persons in need but with social policy issues of the most fundamental sort. If such centers become more influential in the social service system, the information they collect would be useful in shaping social welfare policy, which is one of the reasons why some of the line staff need to be professionals with the training to identify and analyze the policy implications of the information the center accumulates through its experiences with persons seeking help.[27] Moreover, the enormous range of problems, some extremely difficult, that are brought to such centers requires the presence of skilled professionals to make the complex judgments required if the best possible help is to be provided. And for some, the brief services given at the center itself can be of benefit if skillfully done.

Few centers of the sort described above exist in the United States, although elements of the concept can be seen in some of the multifunction service centers spawned by the war on poverty, some funded by CAP agencies, others by state departments of social welfare and other agencies. An especially interesting variant are the switchboards that have sprung up in urban areas across the country modeled after the first one established in San Francisco's Haight-Ashbury district. Although subsequent switchboards often have been more limited in scope, the one in San Francisco extends its services twenty-four hours a day to the whole community and will accept any request, from locating missing persons to locating the manager of a rock group, and from how to arrange an abortion in Mexico to how to file an appeal against the welfare department. Manned almost entirely by volunteers, the switchboards have not yet received much attention from the social work profession.

The fate of such social broker services remains in doubt, despite their obvious rationality and utility. Funding for them is limited and uncertain, for they have not yet become institutionalized in the social service system. Moreover, the work done in these facilities, and the knowledge and skills required to operate them effectively, have yet to be described and codified so that they can be incorporated in educational programs.

The same can be said for another social work function that also has been recently rediscovered, namely advocacy.[28] Whereas the social broker's function is to help the person connect successfully with the place in the service system most likely to meet his need, the advocate's essential function is to make sure that the system is responsive to the persons it is supposed to serve and that persons receive all the benefits to which they are entitled. However well intentioned they may be, social welfare agencies are subject, as are all bureaucracies, to tendencies toward displacement of goals and means, and often other needs of the organization take precedence over service to clients. For example, toward the close of the fiscal year, public welfare agencies may interpret assistance regulations more stringently because of budget limitations, or public psychiatric services may subtly screen intake to satisfy the interests of the staff. As Joel Handler has observed, service agencies need external gadflies to correct these tendencies and to keep before the agency its central commitment to service.[29]

Except for a few field training units for social work students,* we know of no social work agencies that have been established solely or even primarily to offer advocacy services. Welfare rights organizations, as they originally developed, devoted much of their energies to the provision of advocacy services to welfare recipients, and the agencies established in recent years to extend legal services to the poor offer specialized advocacy services in those instances where recourse to formal legal processes is involved.

But unlike the social broker function, the practice of advocacy does not necessarily require specialized agencies. It should be one of a range of functions that social workers, and social caseworkers particularly, can perform in any agency, depending on the needs of the client, although the development of specialized agencies to provide advocacy services in especially complicated situations may be desirable.† As Piliavin and others have emphasized,[30] effective advocacy may entail risks for social workers in existing agencies, since they may find it necessary to press demands in the interest of their clients that run counter to the interest of administrators, or at least conflict with other interests that administrators must consider. If the social worker-advocate is making such demands of his own agency, he may even risk his job. It has been suggested, therefore, that the National Association of Social Workers should establish machinery to protect social workers who suffer punitive action as a result of their efforts to serve as advocates on behalf of their clients.[31]

Since the self-conscious practice of advocacy by social caseworkers has reappeared only recently, the experience accumulated thus far is neither extensive nor easily studied, and the meager literature on the subject is largely exhortative. Until recently, at least, much of this work

---

* Such units have been established by the School of Social Welfare, University of California, Berkeley. And the School of Social Work at Wayne State University has involved its students in advocacy activities. David Wineman and Adrienne James, "The Advocacy Challenge to Schools of Social Work," *Social Work,* 14 (April, 1969), 22–32.

† One way to accomplish this may be to add social workers and other nonlegal personnel to the staffs of legal assistance agencies.

has been done on behalf of welfare recipients in relation to welfare agencies. In this area, the activities of the caseworker-advocate range from intercession on behalf of the recipient, as in making a telephone call to the welfare department to ask why the agency interpreted its rules as it did (e.g., why a seemingly legitimate request for special needs was not granted; or why the client's application for aid was denied), to representing the recipient in a formal hearing to appeal a decision made by the agency. But welfare recipients are not the only persons who may become victims of agency unresponsiveness or of the misuse of discretion by agency officials, and it can be expected that advocacy services will be extended to other groups in relation to other sectors of the social welfare system, such as corrections, mental health, rehabilitation, and family services.

As indicated earlier, a comprehensive codification and description of the methods and techniques used and of the knowledge needed to apply them in performing broker and advocate functions is not yet possible. Nevertheless, from the limited experience thus far gathered, some general principles can be identified. First, since caseworkers performing social broker and advocacy functions often are contending with social agencies at the level of administrative regulations and policies, they need a more sophisticated knowledge of organizational dynamics and administrative processes than do caseworkers performing only a therapeutic function. Second, the broker and the advocate need to acquire an intimate familiarity with the policies, regulations, and appeal machinery of the agencies with which they deal and of how these can be used in the interests of their clients. Not that caseworkers performing these functions should be walking encyclopedias about the regulations of the local agencies, but they must know how to find the relevant regulations and how to interpret and use them. Third, particularly for the advocate, familiarity with law and legal process is important; attorneys have emphasized that social work advocates should keep in mind that the case before them may eventually require formal legal intervention, a possibility that has important consequences for how the social worker-advocate should go about his work. Fourth, these functions sometimes require of caseworkers a more aggressive style of work than that to which they have been accustomed in the past. The cooperative style that has tended to characterize the caseworker's relation with staff in other agencies in an effort to accomplish the therapeutic function may be insufficient when the problem for the client has to do with administrative regulations in the other agency that may not be easily modified by a friendly conference between two caseworkers. Finally, the change principles of the behavior modification approach, discussed in the first section of this chapter, are compatible with broker and advocacy practice, since both emphasize the importance of environmental events.

The outcomes of advocacy tend to be concrete and visible: the client either gains the benefit or the right to which he believes he is entitled or he does not. The limited evidence available indicates that advocate services can be quite effective. Research reported by Briar and Kalmanoff revealed that welfare recipients represented at fair hearings by advocates had nearly double the chance of winning their appeals as unrepresented recipients.[32]

But the results of effective advocacy often go beyond the tangible benefit won or lost by the client. The psychological benefit to the client can be profound. For some clients, the experience of presenting their case to agency authorities and having it heard can counteract feelings of powerlessness and impotence in the face of what is experienced as an impersonal and arbitrary bureaucracy. Some clients who have failed to get the benefit they sought nevertheless have reported that what they gained in self-respect and self-confidence was more important.[33] In this sense, advocacy can have therapeutic as well as concrete benefits. Finally, advocacy efforts on behalf of one client may affect many others. For example, a caseworker in a California probation and parole agency, in the process of seeking to have one of his parolees accepted into a job training program, brought about a statewide policy change regarding eligibility for admission to these programs, to the benefit not only of his client but of many other parolees. As another example, it appears to be only a matter of time before lawyers in legal assistance agencies succeed in changing the status of decisions reached in public welfare hearings from their current ad hoc standing to that of cumulative decisions that in effect become state policy. This would mean that a decision reached in one case could be extended to all similar cases in the state, thereby making the appeal hearing a powerful tool not only for assisting recipients but also for changing welfare policy.

The recent reappearance of broker and advocate functions in the practice of social caseworker—this time conducted with greater professional sophistication and without moral condescension—suggests that at last casework may be on the verge of fulfilling its commitment to a concern for the "total situation" of its clients. While the methods and techniques appropriate to these functions have yet to be elaborated before they can be fully incorporated into the training of all caseworkers and thereby become part of every caseworker's repertoire, the rationality, utility, and relevance of these functions offer hope for their future development.

CONCLUSION

One thing that seems clear from the current trends in casework is that the scope of the caseworker's functions is being broadened; it is moving away from the narrow confinement of a therapeutic role that persisted for many decades. This expansion of scope by no means diminishes the importance of the therapeutic function; in spite of the changes represented by the reappearance of the broker and advocate functions, a major change taking place in the caseworker's therapeutic work, namely the development of the behavior modification approach, is equally significant, since it may considerably increase the effectiveness of caseworkers as change agents. What is most important and most promising, when all these trends are taken together, is that caseworkers are developing a sophisticated array of functions, methods, and techniques more appropriate to the complex life situations of their clients, who sometimes come for help because something about themselves needs to be modified, but who also come because something in their life situation is missing or needs to be changed. If he learns from past experience, the caseworker of the future will be less likely to promise more than he can deliver, but he also will not be so willing to settle for less than might be possible.

NOTES

CHAPTER ONE

THE DEVELOPMENT OF CASEWORK TREATMENT

1. Bertha Reynolds, "Rethinking Social Case Work," *Social Work Today* (1936), pp. 3–4.

2. Frank Bruno, *Trends in Social Work* (New York, Columbia University Press, 1957).

3. Virginia P. Robinson, *A Changing Psychology in Social Casework* (Chapel Hill, University of North Carolina Press, 1930), pp. 48–49.

4. Florence Hollis, "Social Case Work," in *Social Work Year Book* (New York, Russell Sage Foundation, 1943), p. 491.

5. Robinson, *Changing Psychology in Social Case Work*.

6. Jessie Taft, "The Relation of Psychiatry to Social Work," *The Family*, 7 (November, 1926), 199.

7. Gordon Hamilton, "A Theory of Personality: Freud's Contribution to Social Work," in Howard Parad, ed., *Ego Psychology and Dynamic Casework* (New York, Family Service Association of America, 1958).

8. Grace Marcus, "The Status of Social Case Work Today," *Proceedings of the National Conference of Social Work, 1935* (Chicago, University of Chicago Press, 1935), p. 129.

9. Mary W. Glenn, "The Growth of Social Case Work in the United States," in Fern Lowry, ed., *Readings in Social Casework* (New York, Columbia University Press, 1939), p. 76.

10. Robinson, *Changing Psychology in Social Case Work*.

11. Mary Jarrett, "The Psychiatric Thread Running Through All Social Casework," *Proceedings of the National Conference of Social Work, 1919* (New York, Columbia University Press, 1919).

12. Taft, "Relation of Psychiatry to Social Work," p. 201.

13. Robinson, *Changing Psychology in Social Case Work,* pp. 54–55.

14. *Bulletin,* New York School of Social Welfare, 1923, p. 25.

15. Jessie Taft, "Problems of Social Case Work with Children," *The Family,* 1 (July, 1920), 1.

16. Gordon Hamilton, "A Social Worker," *The Family,* 3 (December, 1922), 195.

17. Helen Myrick, "The Mental Hygiene Element in Social Case Work," *The Family,* 4 (February, 1924), 246.

18. Marcus, "The State of Social Case Work Today," p. 136.

19. Reynolds, "Rethinking Social Case Work," p. 12.

20. American Association of Social Workers, *Social Case Work: Generic and Specific* (New York, American Association of Social Workers, 1929), p. 11.

21. Hamilton, "A Theory of Personality: Freud's Contribution to Social Work."

22. Hollis, "Social Case Work."

23. Reynolds, "Rethinking Social Case Work."

24. Taft, "The Relation of Psychiatry to Social Work."

25. Grace Marcus, "Changes in The Theory of Relief Giving," *Social Work Today,* Vol. 8 (June–July, 1941).

26. Robinson, *Changing Psychology in Social Case Work.*

27. Phillip Klein, "Social Work," in Edwin R. A. Seligman, ed., *Encyclopedia of the Social Sciences* (New York, MacMillan, November, 1934), XIV, 165–83.

28. Hollis, "Social Case Work," p. 492.

29. Robinson, *Changing Psychology in Social Case Work,* p. 165.

30. Jessie Taft, ed., *Family Casework and Counselling: A Functional Approach* (Philadelphia, University of Pennsylvania Press, 1948), pp. 7–8.

31. Florence Day, "Changing Practices in Casework Treatment," in Fern Lowry, ed., *Readings in Social Casework* (New York, Columbia University Press, 1939), pp. 332–33.

32. Hollis, "Social Case Work," p. 49.

33. Michael Harrington, *The Other America* (Baltimore, Penguin Books, 1962).

34. Abraham Flexner, *Is Social Work a Profession?* Conference of Charities and Correction (Chicago, Heldman Printing Co., 1915), pp. 576–90.

35. Florence Hollis, "The Techniques of Casework," in Cora Casius, ed., *Principles and Techniques in Social Casework: Selected Articles 1940–1950* (New York, Family Service Association of America, 1950); Gordon Hamilton, *Theory and Practice of Social Casework* (2d ed.; New York, Columbia University Press, 1951); Lucille Austin, "Trends in Differential Treatment in Social Casework," in Cora Casius, ed., *Principles and Techniques in Social Casework: Selected Articles 1940–1950.*

36. Family Service Association of America, *Scope and Methods of the Family Service Agency* (New York, Family Service Association of America, 1953).

37. Hans Eysenck, "The Effects of Psychotherapy," *International Journal of Psychiatry,* 1 (January, 1965), 97–143.

38. Richard Cloward and Irwin Epstein, "The Case of Family Adjustment Agencies," in Mayer N. Zald, ed., *Social Welfare Institutions: A Sociological Reader* (New York, Wiley, 1965), pp. 623–43.

39. Helen Perlman, *Social Casework: A Problem-Solving Process* (Chicago, University of Chicago Press, 1957).

CHAPTER TWO

VALUES IN SOCIAL CASEWORK

1. See, for example, National Association of Social Workers, *Goals of Public Policy* (New York, National Association of Social Workers, 1959) and *Code of Ethics* (1960).

2. William J. Goode, *The Family* (Englewood Cliffs, N.J., Prentice-Hall, 1964).

3. As an example, see E. Westermarck's reference to the Nardi in his *History of Human Marriage* (New York, Macmillan, 1925).

4. David Soyer, "The Right to Fail," *Social Work,* 8 (July, 1963), 72–78.

5. For a further discussion of these issues, see Henry Miller, "Value Dilemmas in Social Casework," *Social Work,* 13 (January, 1968), 27–33.

6. For a fictionalized treatment of other models, see B. F. Skinner, *Walden II* (New York, Macmillan, 1948) or Anthony Burgess, *A Clockwork Orange* (New York, Ballantine Books, 1963).

7. For a further discussion of the value of self-determination, see Miller, "Value Dilemmas in Social Casework," Saul Bernstein, "Self-Determination: King or Citizen in the Realm of Values," *Social Work,* 5 (January, 1960), 3–8; and Alan Keith-Lucas, "A Critique of the Principle of Self-Determination," *Social Work,* 8 (July, 1963), 66–71.

8. For a more extended enunciation of the canons of confidentiality, within social work, see "Principles of Confidentiality in Social Work," Committee on Records of the Columbia Chapter American Association of Social Workers, 1946, or "Confidentiality in Social Services to Individuals," Ad Hoc Committee of Confidentiality of National Social Welfare Assembly, Inc., 1958.

9. Hobart Mowrer, *The Crisis in Psychiatry and Religion* (Princeton, Van Nostrand, 1961) and *The New Group Therapy* (Princeton, Van Nostrand, 1964).

10. Perry London, *The Modes and Models of Psychotherapy* (New York, Holt, Rinehart and Winston, 1964).

CHAPTER THREE
VIEWS OF MAN IN SOCIAL WORK PRACTICE

1. Jerome Bruner and Renata Taguiri, "The Perception of People," in Gardner
Lindzey, ed., *Handbook of Social Psychology* (Cambridge, Mass., Addison-Wes-
ley, 1954), II, 634–54.

2. Beatrice Simcox Reiner and Irving Kaufman, *Character Disorders in Parents of
Delinquents* (New York, Family Service Association of America, 1959), p. 171.

3. Bettye M. Caldwell, "The Effects of Infant Care," in Martin L. Hoffman and
Lois W. Hoffman, eds., *Review of Child Development Research* (New York,
Russell Sage Foundation, 1964), I, 9–87.

4. E. M. Hetherington and Y. Brockbill, "Etiology and Covariation of Obstinacy, Orderliness, and Parsimony in Young Children," *Child Development,* Vol.
34 (December, 1963), p. 939.

5. Caldwell, "The Effects of Infant Care," p. 55.

6. *Ibid.*

7. George A. Kelley, *The Psychology of Personal Constructs* (2 vols.; New
York: Norton, 1955).

8. Saul Bernstein, "Self-Determination: King or Citizen in the Realm of Values?"
Social Work, 5 (January, 1960), 3–8; and Alan Keith-Lucas, "A Critique of the
Principle of Client Self-Determination," *Social Work,* 8 (July, 1963), 66–71.

9. Gordon Hamilton, *Theory and Practice of Social Case Work* (New York, Columbia University Press, 1951), pp. 22–23, 43–46.

10. *Ibid.,* p. 13; and Helen H. Perlman, *Social Casework: A Problem Solving
Process* (Chicago, University of Chicago Press, 1957), p. 60.

11. Perlman, *Social Casework: A Problem Solving Process,* pp. 7–19, 126–29.

12. Ernest Nagel, *The Structure of Science* (New York, Harcourt, Brace and
World, 1961), pp. 599–606.

13. Adolph Meyer, *Collected Papers of Adolph Meyer,* E. E. Winters, ed. (3
vols.; Baltimore, Johns Hopkins Press, 1951).

14. Mary E. Richmond, *Social Diagnosis* (New York, Russell Sage Foundation,
1917).

15. Maurice R. Friend, "The Historical Development of Family Diagnosis," *Social Service Review,* 34 (March, 1960), 2–15.

16. Helen H. Perlman, "Freud's Contribution to Social Welfare," *Social Service
Review,* 31 (June, 1957), 192–202.

17. Sigmund Freud, *Collected Papers of Sigmund Freud,* Vol. I, Ernest Jones, ed.
(London, Hogarth Press, 1924).

18. Marion E. Kenworthy, "Psychoanalytic Concepts in Mental Hygiene," *The
Family,* 7 (November, 1926), 213–23.

19. Lester Luborsky and Jean Schimek, "Psychoanalytic Theories of Therapeutic and Developmental Change: Implications for Assessment," in Philip Worchel and Donn Byrne, eds., *Personality Change* (New York, Wiley, 1964), p. 85.

20. E. E. Southard, "The Kingdom of Evils, Advantages of an Orderly Approach in Social Case Analysis," *Proceedings of the National Conference of Social Work, 1918* (New York, Columbia University Press, 1918), pp. 334–40; and Mary C. Jarrett, "The Psychiatric Thread Running Through All Social Case Work," *ibid.,* pp. 587–93.

21. Jarrett, "The Psychiatric Thread . . . ," p. 589.

22. Jessie Taft, "Problems of Social Case Work with Children," *Proceedings of the National Conference of Social Work, 1920* (New York, Columbia University Press, 1920), p. 378.

23. Sigmund Freud, *The Future of an Illusion* (New York, Liveright, 1949), p. 93.

24. Erich Kahler, *Man the Measure* (New York, Braziller, 1956), p. 485.

25. Heinz Kohut, "Discussion of Paper by Miss Annette Garrett: 'Modern Casework, the Contribution of Ego Psychology,' " Chicago, April, 1956, unpublished.

26. Karl Menninger, *Theory of Psychoanalytic Technique* (New York, Basic Books, 1958).

27. K. R. Eissler, "The Chicago Institute of Psychoanalysis and the Sixth Period of the Development of Psychoanalytic Technique," *Journal of General Psychology,* 42 (January, 1950), 103–57.

28. Lucille N. Austin, "Trends in Different Treatment in Social Casework," in Cora Casius, ed., *Principles and Techniques in Social Casework* (New York, Family Service Association of America, 1950), pp. 324–38; and Florence Hollis, "The Techniques of Casework," in Casius, *Principles and Techniques in Social Casework,* pp. 412–26.

29. Cora Casius, ed., *A Comparison of Diagnostic and Functional Casework Concepts* (New York, Family Service Association of America, 1950); Virginia Robinson, ed., *Jessie Taft: Therapist and Social Work Educator, a Professional Biography* (Philadelphia, University of Pennsylvania Press, 1962); and Jessie Taft, *A Functional Approach to Family Case Work* (Philadelphia, University of Pennsylvania Press, 1944).

30. Herbert Aptekar, *Basic Concepts in Social Case Work* (Chapel Hill, University of North Carolina Press, 1941).

31. For example, see Charlotte Towle, "Basic Concepts in Social Casework (book review)," *Social Service Review,* 16 (September, 1942), 563–66.

32. Anna Freud, *The Ego and the Mechanisms of Defense* (New York, International Universities Press, 1954).

33. Merton Gill, ed., *The Collected Papers of David Rapaport* (New York, Basic Books, 1967); H. Hartmann, *Ego Psychology and the Problem of Adaptation* (New York, International Universities Press, 1958); and H. Hartmann, E. Kris, and R. M. Loewenstein, "Comments on the Formation of Psychic Structure," in

The Psychoanalytic Study of the Child (New York, International Universities Press, 1946), II, 11–38.

34. Howard J. Parad, ed., *Ego Psychology and Dyanamic Casework* (New York, Family Service Association of America, 1958); and Howard J. Parad and Roger Miller, eds., *Ego-Oriented Casework* (New York, Family Service Association of America, 1963).

35. Mary Sarvis, Sally Dewees, and Ruth F. Johnson, "A Concept of Ego-Oriented Psychotherapy," *Psychiatry,* 22 (August, 1959), 277–87.

36. Gerald Caplan, "An Approach to the Study of Family Mental Health," *Public Health Reports,* 81 (October, 1956), 1027–30.

37. David M. Kaplan, "A Concept of Acute Situation Disorders," *Social Work,* 7 (April, 1962), 15–23.

38. Howard J. Parad, ed., *Crisis Intervention* (New York, Family Service Association of America, 1965).

39. Lydia Rapoport, "The State of Crisis: Some Theoretical Considerations," *Social Service Review,* 36 (June, 1962), 211–17.

40. David Rapaport, *Organization and Pathology of Thought* (New York, Columbia University Press, 1951).

41. Alfred Kadushin, "The Knowledge Base of Social Work," in Alfred J. Kahn, ed., *Issues in American Social Work* (New York, Columbia University Press, 1959), pp. 39–79.

42. Alex Inkeles, "Personality and Social Structure," in R. Merton, L. Broom, and L. Cottrell, eds., *Sociology Today: Problems and Prospects* (New York, Basic Books, 1959), pp. 249–76.

43. Bruce Biddle and Edwin J. Thomas, eds., *Role Theory: Concepts and Research* (New York, Wiley, 1966).

44. Nathan Ackerman, *The Psychodynamics of Family Life* (New York, Basic Books, 1958).

45. Francis Purcell and Harry Specht, "The House on Sixth Street," *Social Work,* 10 (October, 1965), 69–76.

46. Perlman, *Social Casework: A Problem Solving Process.* In later writings, Perlman attempted to elaborate her use of role concepts. See Helen H. Perlman, "The Role Concept and Social Casework," Parts I and II, *Social Service Review,* 35, 36 (December, 1961 and March, 1962), 370–81, 17–31.

47. Florence Hollis, *Casework: A Psychosocial Therapy* (New York, Random House, 1964).

48. Ad Hoc Committee on Advocacy, "The Social Worker as Advocate: Champion of Social Victims," *Social Work,* 14 (April, 1969), 17–22; George A. Brager, "Advocacy and Political Behavior," *Social Work,* 13 (April, 1968), 5–15; Scott Briar, "The Casework Predicament," *Social Work,* 13 (January, 1968), 5–11; and David Wineman and Adrienne James, "The Advocacy Challenge to Schools of Social Work," *Social Work,* 14 (April, 1969), 23–32.

49. Medard Boss, *Psychoanalysis and Daseinanalysis* (New York, Basic Books, 1963).

50. Rollo May, ed., *Existential Psychotherapy* (New York, Random House, 1961).

51. Carl Rogers, *Client Centered Therapy: Its Current Practice, Implications, and Theory* (Boston, Houghton, 1951).

52. Perry London, *The Modes and Morals of Psychotherapy* (New York, Holt, Rinehart and Winston, 1964).

53. Donald Krill, "Existential Psychotherapy and the Problem of Anomie," *Social Work,* 14 (April, 1969), 33–49; and John J. Stretch, "Existentialism: A Proposed Philosophical Orientation for Social Work," *Social Work,* 12 (October, 1967), 97–102.

54. Albert Bandura, *Principles of Behavior Modification* (New York, Holt, Rinehart and Winston, 1969); Robert L. Burgess and Don Bushell, eds., *Behavioral Sociology: The Experimental Analysis of Social Process* (New York, Columbia University Press, 1969); Cyril M. Franks, ed., *Behavior Therapy: Appraisal and Status* (New York, McGraw-Hill, 1969); L. Krasner and L. P. Ullman, eds., *Research in Behavior Modification* (New York, Holt, Rinehart and Winston, 1965); Richard H. Rubin, ed., *Advances in Behavior Modification—1969* (New York, Academic Press, 1970); L. P. Ullman and L. Krasner, eds., *Case Studies in Behavior Modification* (New York, Holt, Rinehart and Winston, 1965); and Aubrey J. Yates, *Principles and Practice of Behavior Therapy* (New York, Wiley, 1970).

55. As an introduction to behavior modification for social workers, we can recommend Edwin J. Thomas, ed., *The Socio-Behavioral Approach and Applications to Social Work* (New York, Council on Social Work Education, 1967), where the central ideas of behavior modification are presented, together with examples of their application to practice problems in social work.

CHAPTER FOUR

THE SCIENTIFIC METHOD IN CASEWORK PRACTICE

1. Harold A. Larrabee, *Reliable Knowledge* (Boston, Houghton-Mifflin, 1945).

2. Jerome Frank, *Persuasion and Healing* (New York, Schochen Books, 1961), presents a brilliant overview of such "off-beat" practitioners of healing.

3. The classic reference in this regard is Morris R. Cohen and Ernest Nagel, *An Introduction to Logic and Scientific Method* (New York, Harcourt, Brace and World, 1934).

4. Margaret Blenkner, "Obstacles to Evaluative Research in Casework," Part I, *Social Casework,* 31 (February, 1950), 54–60, and Part II, *ibid.,* 31 (March, 1950), 97–105.

5. Hans J. Eysenck, "The Effects of Psychotherapy," *International Journal of Psychiatry,* 1 (January, 1965), 97–143.

6. As one example, see Leonard Krasner and Leonard Ullman, eds., *Research in Behavior Modification* (New York, Holt, Rinehart and Winston, 1965).

7. See chapter 2.

8. Examples of this "agonizing reappraisal" are endless. As a start, the reader is urged to examine any recent volume of the *Proceedings* of the National Conference on Social Welfare.

9. See chapter 9.

10. The central thrust of the problem is well stated by Joseph Eaton, "Science, Art and Uncertainty," *Social Work,* 3 (July, 1958), 3–10.

11. Jessie Taft, *The Dynamics of Therapy in a Controlled Relationship* (New York, Dover, 1962), pp. 118–19.

12. *Ibid.,* p. 283.

CHAPTER FIVE

REALITIES AND EMERGENT TASKS IN CASEWORK PRACTICE

1. David M. Austin, "Broadening the Membership Base—Where Next?" *Social Work,* 13 (January, 1968), 113–16.

2. Carol H. Meyer, *Staff Development in Public Welfare Agencies* (New York, Columbia University Press, 1966).

3. Jane K. Thompson and Donald Riley, "Use of Professionals in Public Welfare: A Dilemma and a Proposal," *Social Work,* 11 (January, 1966), 22–27.

4. Arthur Blum, "Differential Use of Manpower in Public Welfare," *Social Work,* 11, (January, 1966), 16–21; John C. Kidneigh, "Restructuring Practice for Better Manpower Use," *Social Work,* 13 (April, 1968), 109–20; Frank M. Lowenberg, "Social Workers and Indigenous Nonprofessionals: Some Structural Dilemmas," *Social Work,* 13 (July, 1968), 65–71.

5. Francis Purcell and Harry Specht, "The House on Sixth Street," *Social Work,* 10 (October, 1965), 69–76.

6. Jona M. Rosenfeld, "Strangeness Between Helper and Client: A Possible Explanation of Non-Use of Available Professional Help," *Social Service Review,* 38 (March, 1964), 17–25.

7. Scott Briar, "Welfare from Below: Recipients' Views of the Public Welfare System," *California Law Review,* 54 (May, 1966), 370–85.

8. Dorothy Fahs Beck, *Patterns in Use of Family Agency Service* (New York, Family Service Association of America, 1962).

9. L. Bellak and L. Small, *Emergency Psychotherapy and Brief Psychotherapy* (New York, Grune and Stratton, 1965); Anita Gilbert, "An Experiment in Brief Treatment of Parent," *Social Work,* 5 (October, 1960), 91–97; Lydia Rapoport, "Crisis-Oriented Short-Term Treatment," *Social Service Review,* 41 (March, 1967), 31–43; L. R. Wolberg, ed., *Short-Term Psychotherapy* (New York, Grune and Stratton, 1965).

10. Leonard S. Kogan, J. McVicker Hunt, and Phyllis F. Bartelme, *A Follow-up Study of the Results of Social Casework* (New York, Family Association of America, 1953).

11. Robert MacGregor, Agnes M. Ritchie, Alberto Serrano, and Franklin Schuster, *Multiple Impact Therapy with Families* (New York, McGraw-Hill, 1964); and William J. Reid and Ann W. Shyne, *Brief and Extended Casework* (New York, Columbia University Press, 1969).

12. Hollis, *Casework: A Psychosocial Therapy,* p. 169.

13. *Ibid.,* p. 168.

14. *Ibid.,* p. 169.

15. Richard Cloward and Irwin Epstein, "Private Social Welfare's Disengagement from the Poor: The Case of Family Adjustment Agencies," in Mayer W. Zald, ed., *Social Welfare Institutions: A Sociological Reader* (New York, Wiley, 1965), pp. 623–43.

16. Alfred H. Stanton and Morris S. Schwartz, *The Mental Hospital* (New York, Basic Books, 1954); Irving Goffman, *Asylums* (Chicago, Aldine, 1961).

17. Irving Piliavin, "Restructuring the Provision of Social Services," *Social Work,* 13 (January, 1968), 34–41.

18. Richard A. Mackey, "Professionalism and the Poor," *Social Work,* 9 (October, 1964), 108–10; Davis McEntire and Joanne Haworth, "The Two Functions of Public Welfare: Income Maintenance and Social Services," *Social Work,* 12 (January, 1967), 22–31; William B. Tollen, "Why Social Workers Resign: A Study of Personnel Turnover," *Social Work Education,* 7 (February, 1959), 13–15.

19. A more detailed discussion of the ways in which this strain influences practitioners' diagnostic judgments can be found in James Bieri et al., *Social and Clinical Judgment* (New York, Wiley, 1966), ch. 8.

20. An example is the institutionalization of the treatment classification in some family agencies described in *Range and Emphases of a Family Service Program* (New York, Family Service Association of America, 1962).

21. Dorothy Miller et al., "Effectiveness of Social Services to AFDC Recipients," in *California Welfare: A Legislative Program for Reform,* Staff report to the Assembly Committee on Social Welfare (Sacramento, California Legislature, February, 1969), Appendix I.

CHAPTER SIX

WHO IS THE CLIENT?

1. Eliot Studt, "Worker-Client Authority Relationships in Social Work," *Social Work,* 4 (January, 1959), 18–28.

2. Bernard Davitto, personal communication based on research near completion.

3. Amitai Etzioni, *Modern Organizations* (Englewood Cliffs, N.J., Prentice-Hall, 1964), p. 77.

4. Andrew Billingsly, "The Role of the Social Worker in a Child Protective Agency," *Child Welfare,* 43 (November, 1964), 472–79.

5. Jona M. Rosenfeld, "Strangeness Between Helper and Client: A Possible Explanation of Non-Use of Available Professional Help," *Social Service Review,* 38 (March, 1964), 17–25.

6. Helen Harris Perlman, *Social Casework: A Problem-Solving Process* (Chicago, University of Chicago Press, 1957), pp. 183–206.

7. Florence Hollis, *Casework: A Psychosocial Therapy* (New York, Random House, 1964), p. 209.

8. Amitai Etzioni, *A Comparative Analysis of Complex Organizations* (New York, Free Press, 1961).

9. Glenn Oscar Haworth, *Social Work Students' Theoretical Orientation Toward Human Behavior,* unpublished doctoral dissertation, University of California at Berkeley, School of Social Welfare, 1967.

10. Hans H. Strupp, *Psychotherapists in Action: Explorations of the Therapist's Contribution to the Treatment Process,* (New York, Grune and Stratton, 1960).

11. Donald M. Sundland and Edwin N. Barker, "The Orientation of Psychotherapists," *Journal of Consulting Psychology,* 26 (June, 1962), 201–12.

CHAPTER SEVEN

COMMUNICATION AND THE WORKER-CLIENT RELATIONSHIP

1. Mary Ellen Richmond, *Social Diagnosis* (New York, Russell Sage Foundation, 1917).

2. Mary Ellen Richmond, *What is Social Case Work? An Introductory Description* (New York, Russell Sage Foundation, 1922).

3. *Ibid.,* pp. 98–99.

4. *Ibid.,* p. 102.

5. *Ibid.,* p. 108.

6. For a discussion of this period of Freud's life see Ernest Jones, *The Life and Work of Sigmund Freud* (New York, Basic Books, 1953), I, 207–19.

7. Anna Freud, *The Ego and the Mechanisms of Defense,* translated by Cecil Baines (New York, International Universities Press, 1954 [c.1946]).

8. Virginia Pollard Robinson, *A Changing Psychology in Social Casework* (Chapel Hill, University of North Carolina Press, 1930).

9. *Ibid.,* p. 136.

10. Lucille Austin, "Trends in Differential Treatment in Social Casework," *Journal of Social Casework,* 29 (June, 1948), 203–11.

11. Florence Hollis, "The Techniques of Casework," *Journal of Social Casework,* 30 (June, 1949), 235–44.

12. Family Service Association of America, *Scope and Methods of the Family Service Agency* (New York, Family Service Association of America, 1953).

13. Annette Garrett, "The Worker-Client Relationship," in Howard J. Parad, ed., *Ego Psychology and Dynamic Casework* (New York, Family Service Association of America, 1958), pp. 53–72.

14. Felix Paul Biestek, *The Casework Relationship* (Chicago, Loyola University Press, 1957), p. 12.

15. Alfred Adler, *The Practice and Theory of Individual Psychology,* translated by P. Radin (New York, Humanities Press; London, Routledge and Kegan Paul, 1951).

16. George Alexander Kelly, *The Psychology of Personal Constructs* (New York, Norton, 1955), Vol. I.

17. Carl G. Jung, *Psychological Types or the Psychology of Individuation,* translated by H. Goodwin Baynes (London, Kegan Paul, Trench, Trubner; New York, Harcourt, Brace, 1938).

18. For a good summation of Rogerian thought, see Carl Rogers, *Client-Centered Therapy* (Boston, Houghton-Mifflin, 1951).

19. Kelly, *The Psychology of Personal Constructs.*

20. *Ibid.*

21. Joel Greenspoon, "The Reinforcing Effect of Two Spoken Sounds on the Frequency of Two Responses," *American Journal of Psychology,* 58 (1955) 409–16.

22. Selma Fraiberg, "Some Aspects of Casework with Children," Parts I and II, *Social Casework,* 33 (November–December, 1952), 1.

23. The technical literature on play therapy is most extensive. The reader is referred, as a start, to the following: Virginia Axline, *Play Therapy: The Inner Dynamics of Childhood* (Boston, Houghton-Mifflin, 1947); Cuthbert Hamy Rogerson, *Play Therapy in Childhood* (London, Oxford University Press, 1939); Mary Haworth, *Child Psychotherapy, Practice and Theory* (New York, Basic Books, 1964); Frederick Alan, *Psychotherapy with Children* (New York, W. W. Norton, 1942); Melanie Klein, "The Psychoanalytic Play Technique," *American Journal of Orthopsychiatry,* 25 (April, 1955), 223–37.

24. William Haase, "The Role of Socioeconomic Class in Examinee Bias," in Frank Riessman, Jerome Cohen, and Arthur Pearl, eds., *Mental Health of the Poor* (London, Free Press of Glencoe, Collier-Macmillan, 1964), pp. 241–47; Betty Overall and H. Aronson, "Expectations of Psychotherapy in Patients of Lower Socioeconomic Class," *ibid.,* pp. 76–87.

25. Silvano Arieti, *Interpretation of Schizophrenia* (New York, Robert Brunner, 1955), pp. 183–273.

26. As an example, see John N. Rosen, *Selected Papers on Direct Psychoanalysis* (New York and London, Grune and Stratton, 1953), Vol. I.

27. Jerome D. Frank, *Persuasion and Healing: A Comparative Study of Psychotherapy* (Baltimore, Johns Hopkins University Press, 1961), p. 62.

28. Jay Haley, *Strategies of Psychotherapy* (New York, Grune and Stratton, 1963).

29. *Ibid.*, pp. 8–9.

30. *Ibid.*, p. 9.

CHAPTER EIGHT

DIAGNOSIS

1. Gordon Hamilton, *Theory and Practice of Social Case Work* (2d ed.; New York, Columbia University Press, 1951), p. 219–36; and Florence Hollis, *Casework: A Psychosocial Therapy* (New York, Random House, 1964), pp. 178–99.

2. Ernest Greenwood, "Social Science and Social Work: A Theory of their Relationship," *Social Service Review,* 29 (March, 1955), 20–33.

3. Emil Kraepelin, *Clinical Psychiatry* (2d ed.; New York, Macmillan, 1907).

4. Sigmund Freud, *The New Introductory Lectures on Psychoanalysis* (New York, Norton, 1964).

5. American Psychiatric Association, *Diagnostic and Statistical Manual, Mental Disorders* (Washington D.C., American Psychiatric Association, 1952).

6. Benjamin Mehlman, "The Reliability of Psychiatric Diagnosis," *Journal of Abnormal and Social Psychology,* 47 (April, 1952), 577–78.

7. For some examples, see Lucille N. Austin, "Trends in Differential Treatment in Social Casework," *Journal of Social Casework,* 29 (June, 1948), 203–11; Community Service Society of New York, *Method and Process in Social Casework* (New York, Family Service Association of America, 1958); Florence Hollis, "Explorations in the Development of a Typology of Casework Treatment," *Social Casework,* 48 (June, 1967), 335–41; Mary Richmond, *Social Diagnosis* (New York, Russell Sage Foundation, 1917); Ada Eliot Sheffield, *Case Study Possibilities* (Boston, Research Bureau of Social Casework, 1922); Jessie Taft, *Family Casework and Counseling: A Functional Approach* (Philadelphia, University of Pennsylvania Press, 1948).

8. Donald B. Glabe, Leo J. Feider, and Harry O. Page, "Reorientation for Treatment and Control," *Public Welfare,* Vol. 16 (April, 1958), Special Supplement.

9. Marguerite Warren et al., *The Community Treatment Project* (Sacramento, California Youth Authority, 1967).

10. Lillian Ripple and Ernestina Alexander, "Motivation, Capacity, and Opportunity as Related to the Use of Casework Service: Nature of the Client's Problem," *Social Service Review,* 30 (March, 1956), 38–54.

11. William J. Reid and Ann W. Shyne, *Brief and Extended Casework,* (New York, Columbia University Press, 1969).

12. Dorothy Miller et al., "Effectiveness of Social Services to AFDC Recipients," in *California Welfare: A Legislative Program for Reform,* Staff report to the Assembly Committee on Social Welfare (Sacramento, California Legislature, February, 1969), Appendix I.

13. Scott Briar and Alvin Kalmanoff, *Fair Hearings in California,* University of California at Berkeley, School of Social Welfare, unpublished mimeographed, 1968.

14. A. A. Lazarus, "Group Therapy of Phobic Disorders by Systematic Desensitization," *Journal of Abnormal and Social Psychology,* 63 (November, 1961), 504–10.

15. Gordon L. Paul, *Insight Versus Desensitization in Psychotherapy* (Stanford, Stanford University Press, 1966).

16. T. L. Rosenthal, "Severe Stuttering and Maladjustment Treated by Desensitization and Social Influence," *Behavior Research and Therapy,* 6 (February, 1968), 125–30.

17. R. Hawkins, F. Peterson, E. Schwad, and S. Bijou, "Behavior Theory in the Home: Amelioration of Problem Parent-Child Relations with the Parent in a Therapeutic Role," *Journal of Experimental Child Psychology,* 4 (September, 1966), 99–107; and Robert G. Wahler and Marie Erickson, "Child Behavior Therapy: A Community Program in Appalachia," *Behavior Research and Therapy,* 7 (February, 1969), 71–9.

18. Greenwood, "Social Science and Social Work," p. 25.

19. Amitai Etzioni, " 'Shortcuts' to Social Change?" *Public Interest,* 8 (Summer, 1968), 40–51.

20. George Levinger, "Continuance in Casework and Other Helping Relationships: A Review of Current Research," *Social Work,* 5 (July, 1960), 40–51.

21. Harry Stack Sullivan, *The Psychiatric Interview* (New York, Norton, 1954), pp. 46–47.

22. Leonard Krasner, "Studies of the Conditioning of Verbal Behavior," *Psychological Bulletin,* 55 (May, 1958), 148–70.

23. James Bieri, Alvin L. Atkins, Scott Briar, Robin Lobeck Leaman, Henry Miller and Tony Tripodi, *Clinical and Social Judgement: The Discrimination of Behavioral Information* (New York, London, and Sydney, Wiley, 1966).

CHAPTER NINE

GOALS, OBJECTIVES, AND OUTCOME

1. The writings of Otto Rank are many; for the essence of his therapeutic perspective, however, see Otto Rank, *Will Therapy and Truth and Reality* (New York, Knopf, 1947).

2. Perry London, *The Modes and Morals of Psychotherapy* (New York, Holt, Rinehart and Winston, 1964).

3. David Beres, "Ego Deviation and the Concept of Schizophrenia," in *The Psychoanalytic Study of the Child* (New York, International Universities Press, 1956), II, 164–235.

4. Hans H. Strupp, *Psychotherapists in Action: Explorations of the Therapists' Contribution to the Treatment Process* (New York, Grune and Stratton, 1960).

5. The reader is referred to the following three volumes for a full discussion of the problems involved in psychotherapy research: American Psychological Association, *Research in Psychotherapy,* Vols. I, II, III (Washington D.C., American Psychological Association, 1959, 1962, and 1968).

6. Sigmund Freud, "Analysis Terminable and Interminable," *Collected Papers* (New York, Basic Books, 1959), V, 353–54.

CHAPTER TEN
STRATEGIES AND TACTICS OF INTERVENTION

1. Arnold P. Goldstein and Sanford J. Dean, *The Investigation of Psychotherapy* (New York, Wiley, 1966); Arnold P. Goldstein, Kenneth Heller, and Lee B. Sechrest, *Psychotherapy and the Psychology of Behavior Change* (New York, Wiley, 1966); Leonard Krasner and Leonard P. Ullman, eds., *Research in Behavior Modification: New Developments and Implications* (New York, Holt, Rinehart and Winston, 1965); Leonard P. Ullman and Leonard Krasner, eds., *Case Studies in Behavior Modification* (New York, Holt, Rinehart and Winston, 1965); and Philip Worchel and Donn Byrne, eds., *Personality Change,* (New York, Wiley, 1964).

2. Alfred Kadushin, "The Knowledge Base of Social Work, in Alfred J. Kahn, ed., *Issues in American Social Work* (New York, Columbia University Press, 1959).

3. This discussion draws heavily on Donald H. Ford and Hugh B. Urban, *Systems of Psychotherapy* (New York, Wiley, 1963), pp. 86–88.

4. Ad Hoc Committee on Advocacy, "The Social Worker as Advocate: Champion of Social Victims," *Social Work,* 14 (April, 1969), 16–22; Scott Briar, "The Casework Predicament," *Social Work,* 13 (January, 1968), 5–11; and Henry Miller, "Value Dilemmas in Social Casework," *ibid.,* pp. 27–33.

5. Gordon Hamilton, *Theory and Practice of Social Case Work* (2d ed.; New York, Columbia University Press, 1951), p. 41.

6. Paul Halmos, *The Faith of the Counsellors* (New York, Shocken Books, 1966), p. 115.

7. *Ibid.,* p. 198.

8. *Ibid.,* p. 199.

9. Richard Cloward and Irwin Epstein, "Private Social Welfare's Disengagement from the Poor: The Case of Family Adjustment Agencies," in Mayer N. Zald, ed., *Social Welfare Institutions: A Sociological Reader* (New York, Wiley, 1965), pp. 623–43.

10. Benjamin Bloom, *Stability and Change in Human Characteristics* (New York, Wiley, 1966); and Bettye M. Caldwell, "The Effects of Infant Care," in Martin L. Hoffman and Lois W. Hoffman, eds., *Review of Child Development Research* (New York, Russell Sage Foundation, 1964), I, 9–88.

CHAPTER ELEVEN

CASEWORK WITH THE FAMILY

1. Porter R. Lee, "The Fabric of the Family," *Proceedings of The National Conference of Social Work* (Chicago, Rogers and Hall, 1920), pp. 319–25; and Mary Richmond, *What is Social Case Work?* (New York, Russell Sage Foundation, 1922).

2. Nathan Ackerman, Frances L. Beatman, and Sanford N. Sherman, eds., *Expanding Theory and Practice in Family Therapy* (New York, Family Service Association of America, 1967); Nathan Ackerman, Frances L. Beatman, and Sanford N. Sherman, eds., *Exploring the Base for Family Therapy* (New York, Family Service Association of America, 1961); and Jay Haley, "Whither Family Therapy?" *Family Process,* 1 (March, 1962), 69–100.

3. Florence Hollis, *Women in Marital Conflict: A Casework Study* (New York, Family Service Association of America, 1949).

4. Emily Mudd, *The Practice of Marriage Counselling* (New York, Association Press, 1951).

5. Irene Josselyn, "The Family as a Psychological Unit," *Social Casework,* 34 (October, 1953), 336–42.

6. Andrew Billingsley, *Black Families in White America* (Englewood Cliffs, N.J., Prentice-Hall, 1968); Robert O. Blood Jr. and Donald M. Wolfe, *Husbands and Wives: The Dynamics of Married Life* (Glencoe, Ill., Free Press, 1960); Elliot Liebow, *Tally's Corner* (Boston, Little, Brown, 1967); and Donald G. McKinley, *Social Class and Family Life* (Glencoe, Ill., Free Press, 1964).

7. Nathan Ackerman, *The Psychodynamics of Family Life: Diagnosis and Treatment of Family Relationships* (New York, Basic Books, 1958); Theodore Lidz, Alice R. Cornelison, Stephen Fleck and Dorothy Terry, "Marital Schism and Marital Skew," in T. Lidz, S. Fleck, and A. Cornelison, eds., *Schizophrenia and the Family* (New York, International Universities Press, 1965), pp. 133–46; and R. F. Winch, "The Theory of Complementary Needs in Mate Selection: Final Results of the General Hypothesis," *American Sociological Review,* 20, (September, 1955), 552–55.

8. Gregory Bateson and Jurgen Ruesch, *Communication, the Social Matrix of Psychiatry* (New York, Norton, 1951); Donald Jackson, "Conjoint Family Therapy," *Psychiatry,* 42 (May, 1961), 30–45; Donald Jackson, ed., *Communication, Family and Marriage* (Palo Alto, Science and Behavior Books, 1968); and Virginia Satir, *Conjoint Family Therapy* (Palo Alto, Science and Behavior Books, 1964).

9. L. C. Wynn, I. Ryckoff, J. Day, and S. Hirsch, "Pseudo-Mutuality in the Family Relations of Schizophrenics," *Psychiatry,* 21 (July, 1958), 205–20.

10. Liebow, *Tally's Corner.*

11. Family Service Association of America, *Group Treatment in Family Service Agencies,* Pamphlet, 1964; Edmund C. Levin, "Therapeutic Multiple Family Groups," *International Journal of Group Psychotherapy,* 16 (April, 1966), 203–8; and Jack G. Westman, "A Comparison of Married Couples in the Same and Separate Therapy Groups," *International Journal of Group Psychotherapy,* Vol. 15 (July, 1965), pp. 374–81.

12. For an entertaining but telling illustration, see Leslie Farber, "I'm Sorry Dear," *Commentary,* 38 (November, 1964), 47–54.

13. Ronald A. Feldman and Harry Specht, "The World of Social Group Work," in National Conference on Social Welfare, *Social Work Practice, 1968, Selected Papers* (New York, Columbia University Press, 1968), pp. 77–93; and Paul H. Glasser, *Diagnosis in Social Group Work* (Ann Arbor, University of Michigan, School Social Work, 1964).

14. John Bell, *Family Group Therapy* (Washington D.C., U.S. Department of Health, Education, and Welfare, Public Health Service, 1961).

15. Scott Briar, "The Family as an Organization: An Approach to Family Diagnosis and Treatment."

16. Robert MacGregor et al., *Multiple Impact Therapy with Families* (New York, McGraw-Hill, 1964).

17. Hope J. Leichter et al., *Kinship and Casework* (New York, Russell Sage Foundation, 1967).

18. Marvin B. Sussman and Lee Burchinal, "Kin Family Network: Unheralded Structure in Current Concept Realizations of Family Functioning," *Marriage and Family Living,* 24 (August, 1962), 231–40.

19. Perry London, *The Modes and Morals of Psychotherapy* (New York, Holt, Rinehart and Winston, 1967).

20. Satir, *Conjoint Family Therapy.*

21. Robert MacGregor et al., *Multiple Impact Therapy with Families.*

22. Gordon E. Brown, ed., *The Multi-Problem Dilemma* (Metuchen, N.J., Scarecrow Press, 1968).

CHAPTER TWELVE

CASEWORK WITH SUBSYSTEMS OF THE FAMILY

1. The literature on small groups is enormous. The following references, however, are "classical": Robert F. Bales, "Small Group Therapy and Research," in R. Merton, L. Broom, and L. Cottrell, eds., *Sociology Today: Problems and Prospects* (New York, Basic Books, 1959); Dorwin Cartwright and Alvin Zender, eds., *Group Dynamics: Research and Theory* (Evanston, Row, Peterson, 1958); Paul Hare, Edgar F. Borgatta, and Robert F. Bales, eds., *Small Groups: Studies in Social Interaction* (New York, Knopf, 1955); M. S. Olmstead, *The Small Group* (New York, Random House, 1959); William Schwartz, "Small Group Science and Group Work Practice," *Social Work,* 8 (October, 1963), 39–46; W. J. H. Sprott,

Human Groups (London, Penguin Books, 1958); J. W. Thibaut and H. H. Kelly, *The Social Psychology of Groups* (New York, Wiley, 1959); Gertrude Wilson, "Social Group Work Theory and Practice," *Social Welfare Forum* (New York, Columbia University Press, 1956), pp. 143–59.

2. S. E. Asch, "Effects of Group Pressure Upon the Modification and Distortion of Judgments," in G. E. Swanson, T. M. Newcomb, and E. L. Hartly, eds., *Readings in Social Psychology* (New York, Holt, 1952), pp. 2–11.

3. Stanley Milgrim, "Behavioral Study of Obedience," *Journal of Abnormal and Social Psychology,* 67 (October, 1963), 371–78.

4. Otto Pollak, "Design of a Model of Healthy Family Relationships as a Basis for Evaluative Research," *Social Service Review,* 31 (December, 1957), 369–75.

5. Otto Pollak, "A Family Diagnosis Model," *Social Service Review,* 34 (March, 1960), 25.

6. *Ibid.,* p. 25.

7. Lionel J. Nieman and James W. Hughes, "The Problem of the Concept of Role," in Herman D. Stein and Richard Cloward, eds., *Social Perspectives on Behavior* (Glencoe, Ill., Free Press, 1958), pp. 177–85.

8. Otto Pollak, *Integrating Sociological and Psychoanalytic Concepts* (New York, Russell Sage Foundation, 1956), p. 142.

9. Theodore B. Sarbin, "Role Theory," in Gardner Lindzey, ed., *Handbook of Social Psychology* (Cambridge, Mass., Addison-Wesely, 1954), p. 255.

10. Theodore M. Newcomb, *Social Psychology* (New York, Dryden Press, 1956), pp. 328–29.

11. Carol H. Meyer, *Complementary and Marital Conflict,* unpublished dissertation, New York School of Social Work, 1957, p. 65.

12. S. R. Slavson, *Child Psychotherapy* (New York, Columbia University Press, 1952), p. 69.

13. Nathan Ackerman, *The Role of the Family in Diagnostic Process,* unpublished, pp. 5–6.

14. *Ibid.,* p. 6.

15. Leonard S. Cottrell Jr., "The Analysis of Situational Fields in Social Psychology," *American Social Review,* 7 (June, 1942), 377.

16. Talcott Parsons, "Role Conflict and the Genesis of Deviance," in Herman D. Stein and Richard A. Cloward, eds., *Social Perspectives on Behavior* (Glencoe, Ill., Free Press, 1958), p. 248.

17. Sarbin, "Role Theory," p. 227.

18. Ruth Benedict, "Continuities and Discontinuities in Cultural Conditioning," in Herman D. Stein and Richard A. Cloward, eds., *Social Perspectives on Behavior,* pp. 240–41.

19. John P. Spiegel, M.D., "The Resolution of Role Conflict Within the Family,"

Psychiatry: Journal for the Study of Interpersonal Processes, 20 (February, 1957), 1–16.

20. Nathan Ackerman, "The Diagnosis of Neurotic Marital Interaction," *Social Casework,* 35 (April, 1954), pp. 139–47; and Ackerman, *The Role of the Family in Diagnostic Process.*

21. See the following: G. Bateson, D. Jackson, J. Haley, and J. Weakland, "Toward a Theory of Schizophrenia," *Behavioral Science,* 1 (October, 1956), 251–64; Gregory Bateson and Jurgen Ruesch, *Communication, the Social Matrix of Psychiatry* (New York, Norton, 1951); Jay Haley and Lynn Hoffman, *Techniques of Family Therapy* (New York, Basic Books, 1968); Donald Jackson, "Conjoint Family Therapy," *Psychiatry,* 42 (May, 1961), 30–45; Virginia Satir, *Conjoint Family Therapy* (Palo Alto, Science and Behavior Books, 1964); Geral Zuk and Ivan Boszormenyi-Nagy, eds., *Family Therapy and Disturbed Families* (Palo Alto, Science and Behavior Books, 1967).

22. Satir, *Conjoint Family Therapy,* pp. 112–33.

23. Sigmund Freud, "The Sexual Enlightenment of Children," in *The Collected Papers of Sigmund Freud,* edited by Philip Rieff (New York, Collier Books, 1963).

24. Otto Rank, *Will Therapy and Truth and Reality* (New York, Knopf, 1947).

25. Heinz Ansbacher and Rowena Ansbacher, eds., *The Individual Psychology of Alfred Adler: A Systematic Presentation in Selections from his Writings* (New York, Basic Books, 1959), pp. 376–83.

26. William D. Altus, "Birth Order and Mean Score on a Ten Item Aptitude Test," *Psychological Reports,* 16 (July, 1965), 872.

27. For a sampling of the literature in this area, see: John Bell, "Contrasting Approaches in Marital Counseling," *Family Process,* 6 (March, 1967), 16–26; Edward J. Carroll, C. Glenn Cambor, Jay V. Leopold, Miles D. Miller, and Walter J. Reis, "Psychotherapy of Marital Couples, *Family Process,* 2 (March, 1963), 25–33; Bernard Greene, ed., *The Psychotherapies of Marital Disharmony* (New York, Free Press, 1965); Donald Jackson, ed., *Communications, Family, and Marriage* (Palo Alto, Science and Behavior Books, 1968); C. Sager, "The Development of Marriage Therapy: An Historical Review," *American Journal of Orthopsychiatry,* 36 (November, 1966), 458–68.

28. Robert O. Blood Jr. and Donald Wolfe, *Husbands and Wives: The Dynamics of Married Living* (Glencoe, Ill., Free Press, 1960), pp. 266–67.

29. Jean Charnley, *The Art of Child Placement* (Minneapolis, University of Minnesota Press, 1955); Gordon Hamilton, *Psychotherapy in Child Guidance* (New York, Columbia University Press, 1953).

CHAPTER THIRTEEN

CURRENT DEVELOPMENTS AND TRENDS

1. Isaac M. Marks, *Fears and Phobias* (New York, Academic Press, 1959); and Joseph Wolpe, *Psychotherapy by Reciprocal Inhibition* (Palo Alto, Stanford University Press, 1958).

2. Gordon L. Paul, *Insight Versus Desensitization in Psychotherapy* (Palo Alto, Stanford University Press, 1969).

3. Marks, *Fears and Phobias.*

4. For descriptions of relaxation techniques, see Paul, *Insight Versus Desensitization in Psychotherapy;* and Wolpe, *Psychotherapy by Reciprocal Inhibition.*

5. D. E. Bostow and J. B. Bailey, "Modification of Severe Disruptive and Aggressive Behavior Using Brief Timeout and Reinforcement Procedures," *Journal of Applied Behavior Analysis,* 2 (Spring, 1969), 31–7.

6. For excellent, brief introductions to social learning principles, see Leonard Ullman and Leonard Krasner, eds., *Case Studies in Behavior Modification* (New York, Holt, Rinehart and Winston, 1965), pp. 1–63; and Edwin Thomas, ed., *The Socio-Behavioral Approach and Applications to Social Work* (New York, Council on Social Work Education, 1967). For a more sophisticated presentation, see Albert Bandura, *Principles of Behavior Modification* (New York, Holt, Rinehart and Winston, 1969).

7. Carl D. Williams, "The Elimination of Tantrum Behavior by Extinction Procedures," *Journal of Abnormal and Social Psychology,* 59 (September, 1959), 269; and "The Elimination of Tantrum Behavior of a Child in an Elementary Classroom," *Behavior Research and Therapy,* 6 (February, 1968), 117–20.

8. Werner K. Honig, *Operant Behavior: Areas of Research and Application* (New York, Appleton-Century-Crofts, 1966).

9. Eleanor R. Brawley, Florence R. Harris, K. Eileen Allen, Robert S. Fleming, and Robert F. Peterson, "Behavior Modification of an Autistic Child," *Behavioral Science,* 14 (March, 1969), 87–97; G. Jensen, M. Womack, "Operant Conditioning Techniques Applied in the Treatment of an Autistic Child," *American Journal of Orthopsychiatry,* 37 (January, 1967), 30–4; M. M. Wolf, T. Risley, and H. Mees, "Application of Operant Conditioning Procedures to the Behavior Problems of an Autistic Child," *Behavior Research and Therapy,* 1 (May, 1964), 305–12; and T. Risley, "The Effects and Side Effects of Punishing the Autistic Behaviors of a Deviant Child," *Journal of Applied Behavior Analysis,* 1 (Spring, 1968), 21–34.

10. V. O. Typer and G. D. Brown, "The Use of Swift, Brief Isolation as a Group Control Device for Institutionalized Delinquents," *Behavior Research and Therapy,* 5 (February, 1967), 1–9; and Ralph Schwitzgebel, *Streetcorner Research: An Experimental Approach to the Juvenile Delinquent* (Cambridge, Harvard University Press, 1964); Ralph Schwitzgebel and D. A. Kopl, "Inducing Behavior Change in Adolescent Delinquents," *Behavior Research and Therapy,* 1 (May, 1964), 297–304.

11. Jacob Azerrad and Richard Stafford, "Restoration of Eating Behaviour in Anorexia Nervosa through Operant Conditioning and Environmental Manipulation," *Behavior Research and Therapy,* 7 (May, 1969), 165–72.

12. B. George Blake, "A Follow-up of Alcoholics Treated by Behaviour Therapy," *Behavior Research and Therapy,* 5 (May, 1965), 89–84.

13. N. Azrin, R. J. Jones, and Barbara Flye, "A Synchronization Effect and Its Application to Stuttering by a Portable Apparatus," *Journal of Applied Behavior*

Analysis, 1 (Winter, 1968), 283–95; and H. C. Rickard and M. B. Mundy, "Direct Manipulation of Stuttering Behavior; An Experimental-Clinical Approach," in Leonard P. Ullman and Leonard Krasner, eds., *Case Studies in Behavior Modification* (New York, Holt, Rinehart and Winston, 1965), pp. 268–74.

14. Paul Clement and Courtney Milne, "Group Play Therapy and Tangible Reinforcers Used to Modify the Behaviour of 8-Year Old Boys," *Behavior Research and Therapy,* 5 (May, 1967), 301–12; Arnold A. Lazarus, "Group Therapy of Phobic Disorders by Systematic Desensitization," *Journal of Abnormal and Social Psychology,* 63 (November, 1961), 504–10; and Brunhilde Ritter, "The Group Desensitization of Children's Snake Phobias Using Vicarious and Contact Desensitization Procedures," *Behavior Research and Therapy,* 6 (February, 1968), 1–6.

15. T. Ayllon and N. H. Azrin, *The Token Economy: A Motivational System for Therapy and Rehabilitation* (New York, Appleton-Century-Crofts, 1968); J. S. Birnbrauer, M. Wolf, J. D. Kidder, and Celia Tague, "Classroom Behavior of Retarded Pupils with Token Reinforcement," *Journal of Experimental Child Psychology,* 2 (June, 1965), 219–35; Kenneth E. Lloyd and Warren Garlington, "Weekly Variations in Performance on a Token Economy Psychiatric Ward," *Behavior Research and Therapy,* 6 (November, 1968), 407–10; K. Daniel O'Leary, "The Effects of Self-Instruction on Immoral Behavior," *Journal of Experimental Child Psychology,* 6 (June, 1968), 297–301; K. Daniel O'Leary, Wesley C. Becker, Michael B. Evans, and Richard A. Saudargas, "A Token Reinforcement Program in a Public School: A Replication and Systematic Analysis," *Journal of Applied Behavior Analysis,* 2 (Spring, 1969), 3–14; and M. M. Wolf, D. K. Giles, and R. V. Hall, "Experiments with Token Reinforcement in a Remedial Classroom," *Behavior Research and Therapy,* 6 (February, 1968), 51–64.

16. G. C. Davison, "The Training of Undergraduates as Social Reinforcers for Autistic Children," in Leonard P. Ullman and Leonard Krasner, eds., *Case Studies in Behavior Modification* (New York, Holt, Rinehart and Winston, 1965), pp. 146–52; Roland G. Tharp and Ralph J. Wetzel, *Behavior Modification in the Natural Environment* (New York, Academic Press, 1969); and R. Wetzel, "Use of Behavioral Techniques in a Case of Compulsive Stealing," *Journal of Consulting Psychology,* 30 (October, 1966), 367–74.

17. R. P. Hawkins, R. F. Peterson, E. Schweid, and S. W. Bijou, "Behavior Therapy in the Home: Amelioration of Problem Parent-Child Relations with the Parent in a Therapeutic Role," *Journal of Experimental Child Psychology,* 4 (September, 1966), 99–107; Cornelius J. Holland, "Elimination by the Parents of Fire-Setting Behaviour in a Seven Year Old Boy," *Behavior Research and Therapy,* 7 (February, 1969), 135–38; Gerald R. Patterson, S. McNeal, N. Hawkins, and R. Phelps, "Reprogramming the Social Environment," *Journal of Child Psychology and Psychiatry,* 8 (December, 1967), 181–95; Sheldon Rose, "A Behavioral Approach to the Group Treatment of Parents," *Social Work,* 14 (July, 1969), 21–29; and R. G. Wakler, G. H. Winkel, R. F. Peterson, and D. C. Morrison, "Mothers as Behavior Therapists for Their Own Children," *Journal of Behavior Research and Therapy,* 3 (August, 1965), 113–24.

18. Charles Ferster, "Classification of Behavioral Pathology," in L. Krasner and L. Ullman, eds., *Research in Behavior Modification* (New York, Holt, Rinehart

and Winston, 1965), pp. 6–26; Marvin R. Goldfried and David M. Pomeranz, "Role of Assessment in Behavior Modification," *Psychological Reports,* 23 (August, 1968), 75–87; and Frederick H. Kanfer and George Saslow, "Behavioral Diagnosis," in Cyril M. Franks, ed., *Behavior Therapy: Appraisal and Status* (New York, McGraw-Hill, 1969), pp. 417–44.

19. N. H. Azrin and J. Powell, "Behavioral Engineering: The Use of Response Priming to Improve Prescribed Self-Medication," *Journal of Applied Behavior Analysis,* 2 (Spring, 1969), 39–42; Sandra Bem, "Verbal Self-Control, The Establishment of Effective Self-Instruction," *Journal of Experimental Psychology,* 74 (August, 1967), 485–91; T. C. Lovitt and Karen Curtiss, "Academic Responses Rate as a Function of Teacher and Self-Imposed Contingencies," *Journal of Applied Behavior Analysis,* 2 (Spring, 1969), 49–53; and B. Migler and J. Wolpe, "Automated Self-Desensitization: A Case Report," *Behavior Research and Therapy,* 5 (May, 1967), 133–35.

20. Bandura, *Principles of Behavior Modification;* Joseph Wolpe, *The Practice of Behavior Therapy* (New York, Pergamon Press, 1969); and Aubrey J. Yates, *Principles and Practice of Behavior Therapy* (New York, Wiley, 1970).

21. The principal journals are: *Behavior Research and Therapy; Journal of Applied Behavior Analysis; Journal of Experimental Child Psychology;* and *Journal of Experimental Research in Personality.*

22. Louis Breger and James L. McGaugh, "Critique and Reformulation of 'Learning-Theory' Approaches to Psychotherapy and Neurosis," *Psychological Bulletin,* 63 (May, 1965), 338–58; Marjorie H. Klein, Allen T. Dittmann, Morris B. Parloff, and Merton Gill, "Behavior Therapy: Observations and Reflections," *Consulting and Clinical Psychology,* 33 (June, 1969), 259–66; and S. Rachman and H. J. Eysenck, "Reply to a 'Critique and Reformulation of Behavior Therapy,' " *Psychological Bulletin,* 65 (March, 1966), 165–69.

23. Max Bruck, "Behavior Modification Theory and Practice: A Critical Review," *Social Work,* 13 (April, 1968), 43–55; and Robert D. Carter and Richard B. Stuart, "Behavior Modification Theory and Practice: A Reply," *Social Work,* 15 (January, 1970), 37–50.

24. Albert Bandura, "Value Issues and Objectives," *Principles of Behavior Modification* (New York, Holt, Rinehart and Winston, 1969), pp. 71–117; and Israel Goldiamond, "Justified and Unjustified Alarm over Behavioral Control," in Ohmer Milton, ed., *Behavior Disorder* (New York, Lippincott, 1965), pp. 237–62.

25. Paul Halmos, *The Faith of the Counsellors* (New York, Schocken, 1966).

26. Robert L. Burgess and Don Bushell Jr., eds., *Behavioral Sociology: The Experimental Analysis of Social Process* (New York, Columbia University Press, 1969); John H. Kunkel, *Society and Economic Growth: A Behavioral Perspective of Social Change* (New York, Oxford University Press, 1970).

27. Harry Specht, "Casework Practice and Social Policy Formulation," *Social Work,* 13 (January, 1968), 45–52.

28. Ad Hoc Committee on Advocacy, "The Social Worker as Advocate: Champion of Social Victims," *Social Work,* 14 (April, 1969), 16–22; George A. Brager, "Institutional Change: Perimeters of the Possible," *Social Work,* 12 (January,

1967), 59–69; George A. Brager, "Advocacy and Political Behavior," *Social Work* 13 (April, 1968), 5–15; Scott Briar, "The Casework Predicament," *Social Work,* 13 (January, 1968), 5–11; Scott Briar, "The Current Crisis in Social Work," in National Conference on Social Welfare, *Social Work Practice 1967* (New York, Columbia University Press, 1967); Charles Grosser, "Community Development Programs Serving the Urban Poor," *Social Work,* 10 (July, 1965), 15–21; Henry Miller, "Value Dilemmas in Social Casework," *Social Work,* 13 (January, 1968), 27–33; Martin Rein, "Social Work in Search of a Radical Profession," *Social Work,* 15 (April, 1970), 13–28; Gerald M. Shattuck and John M. Martin, "New Professional Work Roles and Their Integration into a Social Agency Structure," *Social Work,* 14 (July, 1969), 13–20; Paul Terrell, "The Social Worker as Radical: Roles of Advocacy," *New Perspectives: The Berkeley Journal of Social Welfare,* 1 (Spring, 1967), 83–88; and Daniel Thursz, "Social Action as a Professional Responsibility," *Social Work,* 11 (July, 1966), 12–21.

29. Joel Handler, "Controlling Official Behavior in Welfare Administration," in Jacobus tenBroek, ed., *The Law of the Poor* (San Francisco, Chandler, 1966), pp. 46–61.

30. Irving Piliavin, "Restructuring the Provision of Social Services," *Social Work,* 13 (January, 1968), 34–41.

31. Ad Hoc Committee on Advocacy, "The Social Worker as Advocate: Champion of Social Victims"; Scott Briar, "The Social Worker's Responsibility for the Civil Rights of Clients," *New Perspectives: The Berkeley Journal of Social Welfare,* 1 (Spring, 1967), 89–92.

32. Scott Briar and Alan S. Kalmanoff, "Welfare Hearings in California," University of California at Berkeley, School of Social Welfare, unpublished mimeograph, 1968.

33. Alan S. Kalmanoff, *Advocacy: A New Social Work Methodology,* unpublished Master's thesis, University of California at Berkeley, School of Social Welfare, June, 1969.

INDEX

Freudian psychology (*Continued*)
determination, 43, 63-64; emphasis on past, 56, 62; orientation to change, 62-63; deemphasis of social factors, 63; content of communications, 124; and the family, 206, 215-16; mother-child pair, 220-21; differentiated from Otto Rank and the functional school, *see* Functional school; *see also* Diagnostic school of thought; Psychotherapy

Friend, Maurice R., 248*n*

Friendly visitor, 4, 119-20, 122; modern version of, 238; *see also* Social broker services

Frings, John, 101*n*

Frink, H. W., 11

Functional school, 18, 20, 29-30, 69-70, 86, 122; differentiated from Freudian theory, 68-69; development of theoritical framework for casework, 102; importance of worker-client relationship, 122; goals of casework within, 160-61; *see also* Rank, Otto

Galveston project, *see* MacGregor, Robert

Garlington, Warren, 264*n*

Garrett, Annette, 65, 122, 124, 255*n*

Giles, D. K., 264*n*

Glabe, Donald B., 256*n*

Glasser, Paul H., 194, 260*n*

Glenn, Mary W., 243*n*

Goals of casework, 43, 166-67

Goffman, Erving, 253*n*

Goldfried, Marvin R., 265*n*

Goldiamond, Israel, 265*n*

Goldstein, Arnold P., 258*n*

Goode, William J., 247*n*

Greene, Bernard, 262*n*

Greenspoon, J., 255*n*

Greenwook, Ernest, 140, 256*n*, 257*n*

Grosser, Charles, 266*n*

Group work, 194

Haase, William, 255*n*

Haley, Jay, 138-39, 256*n*, 259*n*, 262*n*

Hall, R. V., 264*n*

Halmos, Paul, 178-79, 235, 258*n*, 265*n*

Hamilton, Gordon, 15, 23, 65, 95*n*, 245*n*, 246*n*, 248*n*, 256*n*, 258*n*, 262*n*; quoted, 12, 178; *see also* Diagnostic school of thought

Handler, Joel, 266*n*

Hare, Paul, 260*n*

Harrington, Michael, 20, 246*n*

Hartman, H., 71, 249*n*

Hawkins, N., 264*n*

Hawkins, R., 257*n*, 264*n*

Haworth, Glenn Oscar, 114, 254*n*

Haworth, Joanne, 253*n*

Haworth, Mary, 255*n*

Healy, William, 11, 12; *Individual Delinquent,* 6

Heller, Kenneth, 258*n*

Henry, Jules, 192

Hetherington, E. M., 248*n*

Hoffman, Lynn, 262*n*

Holland, Cornelius J., 264*n*

Hollis, Florence, 15, 23, 122, 245*n*, 246*n*, 247*n*, 249*n*, 253*n*, 254*n*; quoted, 6, 97; *Casework: A Psychosocial Therapy,* 74, 93*n*, 250*n*, 256*n*; necessity of motivation of client, 97-98; duration of treatment, 96*n*; assumption of anxiety in clients, 110; views on family unit, 189, 259*n*; *see also* Diagnostic school of thought

Home Service Bureau, 9-10

Honig, Werner K., 263*n*

Hughes, James W., 209, 261*n*

Induced change: types of, 174-76

Inkeles, Alex, 72, 250*n*

Insight development, 23-25

Intervention, levels of, 186; *see also* Treatment

Involuntary client, 96-97, 111-12; historical perspective on, 5; acceptance as legitimate targets for social work, 20; and self-determination issue, 20; communication with, 130, 137; treatment of, 137

Jackson, Don (family therapy), 259*n*, 262*n*; *see also* Satir, Virginia